Contents

INTERPRETING MAPS

Designed to enhance your knowledge and enjoyment of maps, these pages explain map scales and projections, describe how to locate information quickly and show you how to weave together the sections of this atlas to gain a more dynamic world view.

QUICK REFERENCE GUIDE

The world at your fingertips: a concise, current alphabetical listing of the world's continents, countries, states, provinces and territories, with the size, population and capital of each. Page numbers and reference keys for each entry are visible at a glance.

GLOBAL RELATIONSHIPS

Beginning with general world physical and political maps, subsequent chapters highlight a variety of the earth's natural features, dealing first with its structure and then with its air, water and land components. Next, maps, charts and graphs unveil the complex relationships between people and their environments. Coverage includes: demographic trends, population distribution and growth, and global energy production; assessing the consequences of pollution: acid rain, deforestation, ozone depletion and global warming; also revealing comparisons of GNP per capita and literacy and life expectancy around the globe.

MAPS OF THE WORLD

This new collection of regional maps artfully balances political and physical detail while proprietary map projections present the most distortion-free views of the continents yet seen. Special thematic maps are included in each continental section. Numbers following each entry indicate map scale (M= million).

Europe and Northern Asia

Asia

Australia and Pacific

Africa, Polar Regions

North America

South America

POPULATIONS AND INDEX

68/B3 **Flixecourt**
69/D4 **Flize, Fran**
69/D4 **Floing, Fra**
69/H4 **Flonheim,**
69/F5 **Florange, I**
69/D3 **Floreffe, B**

City population figures are given for all major cities, including capitals. A Master Index lists places and features appearing in this atlas, complete with page numbers, latitude and longitude.

Using This Atlas

How to Locate Information Quickly

For familiar locations such as continents, countries and major political divisions, the Quick Reference Guide helps you quickly pinpoint the map you need. For less familiar places, begin with the Master Index.

Albania
Alberta, Canada
Algeria
American Samoa
Andorra
Angola
Anguilla

Quick Reference Guide

This concise guide lists continents, countries, states, provinces and territories in alphabetical order, complete with the size, population and capital of each. Page numbers and alpha-numeric reference keys are visible at a glance.

A

Aberdeen, Scot. ....
Abidjan, Côte d'Ivoire ....
Abilene, Texas ....
Abu Dhabi,* Un. Arab Emirates
Abuja,* Nigeria ....
Acapulco, Mex. ....
Accra,* Ghana ....
Aconcagua (mt.) ....
Adana, Turkey ....
Dahna' (desert)

Master Index

When you're looking for a specific place or physical feature, your quickest route is the Master Index. This 2,000-entry alphabetical index lists both the page number and latitude-longitude coordinates for major places and features found on the Regional Maps.

This New Comparative World Atlas has been thoughtfully designed to be easy and enjoyable to use, both as a general reference and as a valuable addition to the classroom. A short time spent familiarizing yourself with its organization will help you to benefit fully from its use.

MAP PROJECTIONS

This chapter explores some of the most widely used examples of how map-makers project the curved earth's surface onto a flat plane. Included is Hammond's new Optimal Conformal Projection which keeps scale distortion over selected areas to the minimum degree possible.

GLOBAL RELATIONSHIPS

Double spread World Physical and World Political maps are accompanied by Land Elevation/Ocean Depth Profiles and Comparative Land Areas and Population graphics. World thematic maps, charts and diagrams highlight important social, cultural, economic and geographic factors affecting today's world. Here, readers can explore complex relationships among such topics as population growth, environmental problems, climate and agriculture or compare worldwide standards of living, resources and manufacturing.

CONTINENT COMPARISONS

Eight thematic maps are shown for each continent (except Antarctica) enabling the map reader to visualize a variety of topics for the same region or to compare similar topics for different regions.

REGIONAL MAPS

This atlas section is grouped by continent starting with facing-page physical and political maps. Following two pages of thematic topics, in-depth regional maps offer abundant detail

WORLD THEMATIC TOPIC

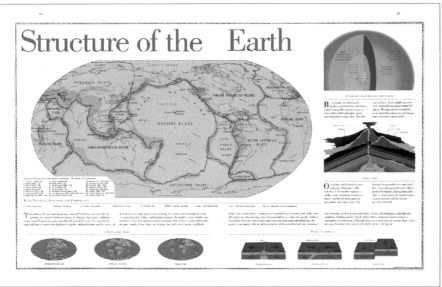

CONTINENT PHYSICAL AND POLITICAL MAPS

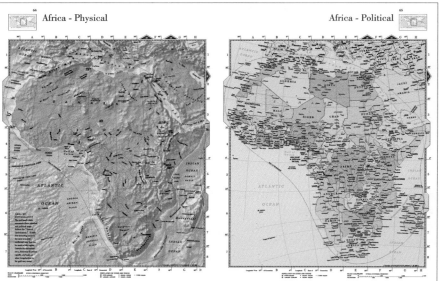

CONTINENT THEMATIC MAPS

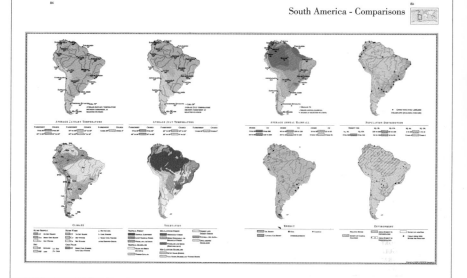

THE NEW
Comparative
WORLD ATLAS

HAMMOND INCORPORATED, MAPLEWOOD, NEW JERSEY

New Comparative World Atlas

ENTIRE CONTENTS
© COPYRIGHT 1999 BY
HAMMOND INCORPORATED
All rights reserved. No part of this book may
be reproduced or utilized in any form or by any
means, electronic or mechanical, including
photocopying, recording or by any information
storage and retrieval system, without permission
in writing from the Publisher.
Printed in The United States of America

LIBRARY OF CONGRESS
CATALOGING-IN-PUBLICATION DATA

Hammond Incorporated.
  The new comparative world atlas.
    p. cm.
  Includes index.
  ISBN 0-8437-7101-1
  ISBN 0-8437-7100-3 (pbk.)
  1. Atlases.   I. Title.
  G1021. H38   1996 <G&M>
  912--DC20   96-27383
                                       CIP
                                      MAPS

REGIONAL MAP

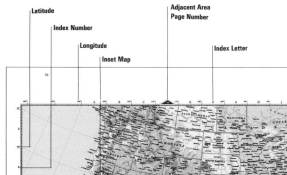
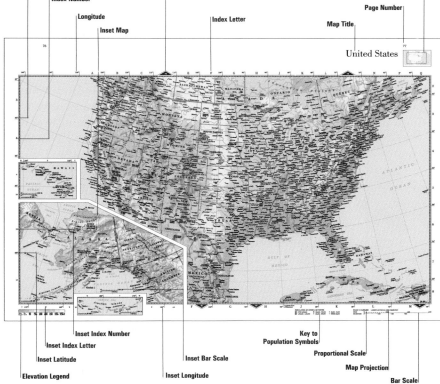

Latitude

Index Number

Longitude

Inset Map

Adjacent Area
Page Number

Index Letter

Map Title

Locator Map

Page Number

United States

76

77

Inset Index Number

Inset Index Letter

Inset Latitude

Elevation Legend

Inset Bar Scale

Inset Longitude

Key to
Population Symbols

Proportional Scale

Map Projection

Bar Scale

SYMBOLS USED ON REGIONAL MAPS

▬▬▬▬ First Order (National) Boundary		Intermittent Lake	⪢ Pass
▬▬▬ First Order Water Boundary		Dry Lake	⚓ Ruins
▬ ▬ First Order Disputed Boundary		Salt Pan	● Falls
▬▬▬ Second Order (Internal) Boundary		Desert/Sand Area	✳ Rapids
▬▬▬ Third Order (Internal) Boundary		Swamp	● Dam
·········· Undefined Boundary		Lava Flow	▲ Point Elevation
▬▬▬ International Date Line		Glacier	♣ Park
▬▬▬ Shoreline, River	Stockholm	First Order (National) Capital	■ Point of Interest
▬ ▬ Intermittent River	Lausanne	Second Order (Internal) Capital	∪ Well
▬▬▬ Canal/Aqueduct			
▬▬▬ Highways/Roads			
▬▬▬ Railroads			
	Lake, Reservoir		

Below Sea Sea Lev. Level	200 700	500 1,600	1,000 3,300	1,500 5,000	2,000 6,500	4,000 13,000	6,000 m. 19,700 ft.

The colors in this bar represent elevation ranges of land areas above or below sea level. Boundaries between colors are labeled both in feet and meters. Selective shading highlights those regions with significant relief variations.

PRINCIPAL MAP ABBREVIATIONS

ARCH.	ARCHIPELAGO	HAR.	HARBOR	PK.	PEAK
AUT.	AUTONOMOUS	I., IS.	ISLAND(S)	PLAT.	PLATEAU
B.	BAY	INT'L	INTERNATIONAL	PN	PARK NATIONAL
C.	CAPE	L.	LAKE	PRSV.	PRESERVE
CAN.	CANAL	LAG.	LAGOON	PT.	POINT
CAP.	CAPITAL	MT.	MOUNT	R.	RIVER
CHAN.	CHANNEL	MTN.	MOUNTAIN	RA.	RANGE
CR.	CREEK	MTS.	MOUNTAINS	REP.	REPUBLIC
DES.	DESERT	NAT'L	NATIONAL	RES.	RESERVOIR,
FD.	FIORD, FJORD	NO.	NORTHERN		RESERVATION
FED.	FEDERAL	NP	NATIONAL PARK	SA.	SIERRA
FK.	FORK	OBL.	OBLAST	SD.	SOUND
FT.	FORT	OCC.	OCCUPIED	SO.	SOUTHERN
G.	GULF	OKR.	OKRUG	STR.	STRAIT
GD.	GRAND	PASSG.	PASSAGE	TERR.	TERRITORY
GT.	GREAT	PEN.	PENINSULA	VOL.	VOLCANO

including boundaries, cities, transportation networks, rivers and major mountain peaks. Map backgrounds are shown in a pleasing combination of elevation coloration and relief shading, with boundary bands defining the extent of each nation's internal and external limits.

CITY POPULATIONS

In addition to population symbols locating cities and towns on the regional maps, an alphabetical listing by country provides at a glance the population of all major cities plus the country's capital.

WORLD STATISTICS

These tables list the dimensions of the earth's principal mountains, islands, rivers and lakes, along with other useful geographic information.

MASTER INDEX

This is an A to Z listing of names found on the world, continent and regional maps. Each entry is accompanied by a page location, as well as latitude and longitude coordinates.

MAP SCALES

A map's scale is the relationship of any length on that map to an identical length on the earth's surface. A scale of 1:7,000,000 means that one inch on the map represents 7,000,000 inches (110 miles, 178 kilometers) on the earth's surface. Thus, a 1:7,000,000 scale is larger than a 1:14,000,000 scale just as 1/7 is larger than 1/14.

Along with these proportional scales, each map is accompanied by a linear (bar) scale, useful in making accurate measurements between places on the maps.

In this atlas, the most densely populated regions are shown at a scale of 1:10,500,000. Other major regions are presented at 1:14,000,000 and smaller scales, allowing you to accurately compare areas and distances of similar regions.

Boundary Policies

This atlas observes the boundary policies of the U.S. Department of State. Boundary disputes are customarily handled with a special symbol treatment, but de facto boundaries are favored if they seem to have any degree of permanence, in the belief that boundaries should reflect current geographic and political realities. The portrayal of independent nations in the atlas follows their recognition by the United Nations and/or the United States government.

Hammond also uses

accepted conventional names for certain major foreign places. Usually, space permits the inclusion of the local form in parentheses. To make the maps more readily understandable to English-speaking readers, many foreign physical features are translated into more recognizable English forms.

A Word About Names

Our source for all foreign names and physical names in the United States is the decision lists of the U.S. Board of Geographic Names, which contain hundreds of thousands of place names. If a place is not listed, the Atlas follows the name form appearing on official foreign maps or in official gazetteers of the country concerned. For rendering domestic city, town and village names, this atlas follows the forms and spelling of the U.S. Postal Service.

Map Projections

There is only one way to represent a sphere with absolute precision: on a globe. All attempts to project our planet's surface onto a plane unevenly stretch or tear the sphere as it flattens, inevitably distorting shapes, areas, distances and/or directions.

Map makers show features on the curved surface of the earth by utilizing an evenly-spaced, imaginary grid pattern on the globe. Points and lines on this pattern are then transferred, or projected, to a corresponding flat surface pattern which has been previously selected and constructed from one of a wide variety of mathematical formulas.

In order to understand some of the most widely used map projections, a brief explanation of the earth's grid pattern is necessary.

The earth rotates around its *axis* once a day. The two end points of this axis are the North and South *poles*; the line circling the earth midway between the poles is the *equator*. The arc from the equator to either pole is divided into 90 degrees. The distance, expressed in degrees, from the equator (0 degrees) north or south to any point is its *latitude*, and circles of equal latitude are called *parallels*. On maps, it is customary to

show parallels of evenly-spaced degrees such as every fifth or every tenth degree.

The equator is divided into 360 degrees. Lines circling the globe from pole to pole through the degree points on the equator are called *meridians*. All meridians are equal in length, but by international agreement the meridian passing through the Greenwich Observatory near London has been chosen as the *prime meridian*.

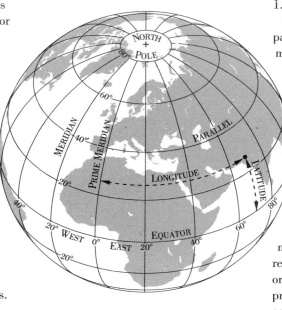

The distance, expressed in degrees, from the prime meridian (0 degrees) east or west to any point is its *longitude*. While meridians are all equal in

length, parallels become shorter as they approach the poles. Whereas one degree of latitude represents approximately 69 miles (112 kilometers) anywhere on the globe, a degree of longitude varies from 69 miles (112 kilometers) at the equator to zero at the poles. Each degree of latitude and longitude is divided into 60 minutes and each minute into 60 seconds. One minute of latitude equals one nautical mile (1.15 land miles or 1.85 kilometers).

On a flat surface, any regular set of parallels and meridians upon which a map can be drawn makes a *map projection*. Since representing a sphere on a flat plane always creates distortion, only the parallels or the meridians or some other set of lines can be *true* (the same length as on a globe at corresponding scale).

The larger the area covered by the map the larger the amount of distortion; thus, distortion is greatest on world maps. Many maps seek to preserve either true area relationships (equal-area projections) or true angles and shapes (conformal projections). Other maps are more concerned with achieving true distance and directional accuracy. Some maps reflect an overall balance by compromise instead of trying to preserve any single true relationship.

WORLD MAP PROJECTIONS

A globe's surface can be transformed to fit within any outline on a flat surface. In fact, such shapes as diamonds, hearts, stars and even stylistic butterflies have enclosed a map of the earth. However, three traditional shapes - rectangles, circles and ovals - are used to portray most maps of the world.

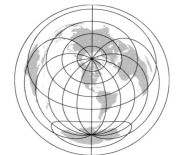

Mercator Projection
A rectangular- shaped map with vertical meridians and horizontal parallels, it is the only map on which a straight line, drawn anywhere on the map, indicates true direction along its entire length. The map has reasonably true shapes and distances within 15 degrees of the equator, but distortion increases dramatically into the higher latitudes.

Miller Cylindrical Projection
Similar in appearance to the Mercator Projection, the Miller Cylindrical lessens distortions in the higher latitudes by closing up the spacing between parallels. Although this destroys the unique navigational property or the Mercator, it does present a more realistic view of land areas in the northern parts of Europe, Asia and North America.

Azimuthal Equidistant Projection
A circular-shaped projection whose oblique view is the only projection in which directions and distances are depicted accurately from the projection's center point to any other place on the globe. Any straight line passing through the center is a great circle route. Distortion of areas and shapes increases away from the center.

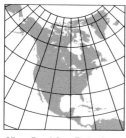

Albers Equal-Area Projection

OTHER MAP PROJECTIONS

Since continents and smaller regions occupy only a part of the entire earth's surface, other projections can be employed to minimize distortion and, where possible, preserve true shapes, areas, distances or directions. But, although smaller in size, the areas being mapped are still parts of a sphere and the flattening process will still result in distortions in the maps.

Conic Projections

These maps are created by mathematically projecting points and lines from a globe onto a cone which caps the globe. The cone can be placed either tangent to the globe at a preselected parallel or it can intersect the globe at two preselected parallels. The use of two standard parallels, one near the top of the map, the other near the bottom of the map, reduces the scale error. In one type of conic projection, Albers, the parallels are spaced evenly to make the projection equal-area. In the Lambert Conformal Conic Projection the parallels are spaced so that any small quadrangle of the grid will have the same shape as on the globe.

Polyconic Projection

Best suited for maps with a long north-south orientation, this projection is mathematically based upon an infinite number of cones tangent to an infinite number of points (parallels) on the globe. All meridians are curved lines except for the central meridian, which shows true distance and direction.

Gnomonic Projection

Viewing the surface of the globe from its center point creates this projection with very bad distortions away from the map's center. However, this projection has a unique quality - all great circles (shortest lines between points on a sphere) are shown as straight lines. Therefore, the path of the shortest distance between any two points on the map is a straight line.

Lambert Azimuthal Equal-Area Projection

Mathematically projected on a plane surface tangent to any point on a globe, this is the most common projection (also known as Zenithal Equal-Area) used for maps of the Eastern and Western hemispheres. It is also a good projection for continents, as it shows correct areas with little distortion of shape.

Hammond's Optimal Conformal Projection

As its name implies, this new conformal projection presents the optimal view of an area by reducing shifts in scale over an entire region to the minimum degree possible. While conformal maps generally preserve all small shapes, large shapes can become very distorted because of varying scales, causing considerable inaccuracy in distance measurements. Consequently, unlike other projections, the Optimal Comformal does not use one standard formula to construct a map. Each map is a unique projection - the optimal projection for that particular area. The result is the most distortion-free conformal map possible.

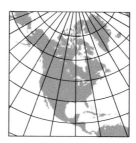

Lambert Conformal Conic Projection

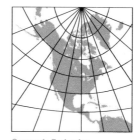

Gnomonic Projection

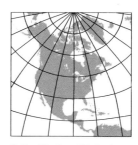

Optimal Conformal Projection

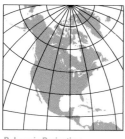

Polyconic Projection

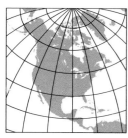

Lambert Azimuthal Equal-Area Projection

Orthographic Projection
This projection looks like a picture of a globe. It is neither conformal nor equal-area. Although the distortion on the peripheries is extreme, we see it correctly, because the eye perceives it not as a map but as a picture of a three-dimensional globe. Obviously, only a hemisphere (half globe) can be shown.

Mollweide Projection
An early example of an oval-shaped (also called pseudocylindrical) projection is this equal-area map of the earth within an ellipse. Shapes are elongated in the lower latitudes. Since its presentation in 1805 it has been an inspiration for similar oval-shaped maps and has even been "interrupted" to minimize distortion of continental or ocean areas.

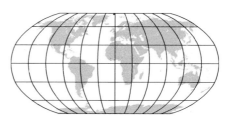

Robinson Projection
This modern, oval-shaped projection uses tabular coordinates rather than mathematical formulas to make the world "look right." Although not true with respect to shapes, sizes, distances or directions, its compromising features show a better balance of size and shape in high latitude lands and very low distortion near the equator.

Quick Reference Guide

This concise alphabetical reference lists continents, countries, states, territories, possessions and other major geographical areas, complete with the size, population and capital or chief town of each. Page numbers and alpha-numeric reference keys (which refer to the grid squares of latitude and longitude on each map) are visible at a glance. The population figures are the latest and most reliable figures obtainable.

Place	Square Miles	Square Kilometers	Population	Capital or Chief Town	Page/Index Ref.
A Afghanistan*	250,000	647,500	21,251,821	Kabul	49/F 6
Africa	11,701,147	30,306,000	705,924,000	....	65
Alabama, U.S.	52,237	135,293	4,273,084	Montgomery	78/C 4
Alaska, U.S.	615,230	1,593,444	607,007	Juneau	76
Albania*	11,100	28,749	3,413,904	Tiranë	44/C 3
Alberta, Canada	255,285	661,185	2,545,553	Edmonton	79/F 4
Algeria*	919,591	2,381,740	28,539,321	Algiers	68/F 2
Andorra*	174	450	65,780	Andorra la Vella	42/E 5
Angola*	481,351	1,246,700	10,069,501	Luanda	70/C 3
Antarctica	5,500,000	14,245,000	....	....	71
Antigua and Barbuda*	170	440	65,176	St. John's	81/J 4
Argentina*	1,068,296	2,766,890	34,292,742	Buenos Aires	88/D 4
Arizona, U.S.	114,006	295,276	4,428,068	Phoenix	76/D 5
Arkansas, U.S.	53,182	137,742	2,509,793	Little Rock	77/H 4
Armenia*	11,506	29,800	3,557,284	Yerevan	45/C 4
Asia	17,159,867	44,444,100	3,407,967,000	....	49
Australia*	2,967,893	7,686,850	18,322,231	Canberra	59
Austria*	32,375	83,851	7,986,664	Vienna	42/G 4
Azerbaijan*	33,436	86,600	7,789,886	Baku	45/D 4
B Bahamas, The*	5,382	13,939	256,616	Nassau	81/F 2
Bahrain*	240	622	575,925	Manama	52/F 3
Bangladesh*	55,598	144,000	128,094,948	Dhaka	53/E 4
Barbados*	166	430	256,395	Bridgetown	81/J 5
Belarus*	80,154	207,600	10,437,418	Minsk	43/G 5
Belgium*	11,780	30,513	10,081,880	Brussels	42/E 3
Belize*	8,865	22,960	214,061	Belmopan	80/D 4
Benin*	43,483	112,620	5,522,677	Porto-Novo	68/F 5
Bhutan*	18,147	47,000	1,780,638	Thimphu	53/E 3
Bolivia*	424,163	1,098,582	7,896,254	La Paz; Sucre	86/F 7
Bosnia & Herzegovina*	19,781	51,233	3,201,823	Sarajevo	44/C 3
Botswana*	231,803	600,370	1,392,414	Gaborone	70/D 5
Brazil*	3,286,470	8,511,965	160,737,489	Brasília	83/D 3
British Columbia, Canada	365,946	947,800	3,282,061	Victoria	79/E 4
Brunei*	2,228	5,770	292,266	Bandar Seri Begawan	56/E 4
Bulgaria*	42,823	110,912	8,775,198	Sofia	44/D 3
Burkina Faso*	105,869	274,200	10,422,828	Ouagadougou	68/E 5
Burundi*	10,745	27,830	6,262,429	Bujumbura	70/E 1
C California, U.S.	158,869	411,470	31,878,234	Sacramento	76/C 4
Cambodia*	69,900	181,040	10,561,373	Phnom Penh	56/C 3
Cameroon*	183,568	475,441	13,521,000	Yaoundé	68/H 7
Canada*	3,851,787	9,976,139	28,434,545	Ottawa	79
Cape Verde*	1,556	4,030	435,983	Praia	12/H 5
Central African Republic*	240,533	622,980	3,209,759	Bangui	69/J 6
Chad*	495,752	1,283,998	5,586,505	N'Djamena	69/J 4
Chile*	292,258	756,950	14,161,216	Santiago	88/B 3
China, People's Rep. of*	3,705,386	9,596,960	1,203,097,268	Beijing	54/G 4
China, Republic of (Taiwan)	13,892	35,980	21,500,583	Taipei	55/M 7
Colombia*	439,733	1,138,910	36,200,251	Bogotá	86/D 3
Colorado, U.S.	104,100	269,618	3,822,676	Denver	76/E 4
Comoros*	838	2,170	549,338	Moroni	65/G 6
Congo, Dem. Rep. of the	905,563	2,345,410	44,060,636	Kinshasa	65/E 5
Congo, Rep. of the*	132,046	342,000	2,504,996	Brazzaville	65/D 4
Connecticut, U.S.	5,544	14,358	3,274,238	Hartford	78/F 2
Costa Rica*	19,730	51,100	3,419,114	San José	80/E 5
Côte d'Ivoire*	124,502	322,460	14,791,257	Yamoussoukro	68/D 5
Croatia*	22,050	56,538	4,665,821	Zagreb	44/C 2
Cuba*	42,803	110,860	10,937,635	Havana	81/F 3
Cyprus*	3,571	9,250	736,636	Nicosia	52/B 1
Czech Republic*	30,387	78,703	10,432,774	Prague	44/B 2
D Delaware, U.S.	2,396	6,206	724,842	Dover	78/E 3
Denmark*	16,629	43,069	5,199,437	Copenhagen	43/C 4
District of Columbia, U.S.	68	177	543,213	Washington	78/E 3
Djibouti*	8,494	22,000	421,320	Djibouti	69/P 5
Dominica*	290	751	82,608	Roseau	81/J 4
Dominican Republic*	18,815	48,730	8,228,151	Santo Domingo	81/H 4
E Ecuador*	109,483	283,561	10,890,950	Quito	86/C 4
Egypt*	386,659	1,001,447	62,359,623	Cairo	69/L 2
El Salvador*	8,124	21,040	5,870,481	San Salvador	80/C 5

* United Nations member (Yugoslavia suspended)

Place	Square Miles	Square Kilometers	Population	Capital or Chief Town	Page/Index Ref.
England, U.K.	50,356	130,423	48,068,400	London	42/D 3
Equatorial Guinea*	10,831	28,052	420,293	Malabo	68/G 7
Eritrea*	46,842	121,320	3,578,709	Asmara	69/N 5
Estonia*	17,413	45,100	1,625,399	Tallinn	43/G 4
Ethiopia*	435,184	1,127,127	55,979,018	Addis Ababa	69/N 5
Europe	4,066,019	10,531,000	732,653,000	....	39
F Fiji*	7,055	18,272	772,891	Suva	62/G 6
Finland*	130,128	337,032	5,085,206	Helsinki	43/G 3
Florida, U.S.	59,928	155,214	14,399,985	Tallahassee	78/D 5
France*	211,208	547,030	58,109,160	Paris	42/E 4
French Guiana	35,135	91,000	145,270	Cayenne	87/H 3
French Polynesia	1,522	3,941	219,999	Papeete	63/L 6
G Gabon*	103,347	267,670	1,155,749	Libreville	68/H 7
Gambia, The*	4,363	11,300	989,273	Banjul	68/B 5
Gaza Strip	139	360	813,322	Gaza	52/B 2
Georgia*	26,911	69,700	5,725,972	T'bilisi	45/C 4
Georgia, U.S.	58,977	152,750	7,353,225	Atlanta	78/D 4
Germany*	137,803	356,910	81,337,541	Berlin	42/F 3
Ghana*	92,100	238,540	17,763,138	Accra	68/E 6
Greece*	50,942	131,940	10,647,511	Athens	44/D 4
Greenland, Denmark	840,000	2,175,600	57,611	Nuuk (Godthåb)	72/N 2
Grenada*	131	340	94,486	St. George's	81/J 5
Guatemala*	42,042	108,889	10,998,602	Guatemala	80/C 4
Guinea*	94,927	245,860	6,549,336	Conakry	68/C 5
Guinea-Bissau	13,946	36,120	1,124,537	Bissau	68/B 5
Guyana*	83,000	214,970	723,774	Georgetown	86/G 3
H Haiti*	10,714	27,750	6,539,983	Port-au-Prince	81/G 4
Hawaii, U.S.	6,459	16,729	1,183,723	Honolulu	76
Honduras*	43,277	112,087	5,459,743	Tegucigalpa	80/D 4
Hong Kong, China	402	1,040	5,542,869	Victoria	55/K 7
Hungary*	35,919	93,030	10,318,838	Budapest	44/C 2
I Iceland*	39,768	103,000	265,998	Reykjavík	39/B 2
Idaho, U.S.	83,574	216,456	1,189,251	Boise	76/C 3
Illinois, U.S.	57,918	150,007	11,846,544	Springfield	78/B 2
India*	1,269,339	3,287,588	936,545,814	New Delhi	53/C 4
Indiana, U.S.	36,420	94,328	5,840,528	Indianapolis	78/C 2
Indonesia*	741,096	1,919,440	203,583,886	Jakarta	56/E 6
Iowa, U.S.	56,275	145,752	2,851,792	Des Moines	77/H 3
Iran*	636,293	1,648,000	64,625,455	Tehran	52/F 2
Iraq*	168,753	437,072	20,643,769	Baghdad	52/D 2
Ireland*	27,136	70,282	3,550,448	Dublin	42/C 3
Ireland, Northern, U.K.	5,459	14,138	1,610,000	Belfast	42/C 3
Israel*	8,019	20,770	5,433,134	Jerusalem	52/B 2
Italy*	116,305	301,230	58,261,971	Rome	39/F 4
J Jamaica*	4,243	10,990	2,574,291	Kingston	81/F 4
Japan*	145,882	377,835	125,506,492	Tokyo	55/Q 4
Jordan*	34,445	89,213	4,100,709	Amman	52/C 2
K Kansas, U.S.	82,282	213,110	2,572,150	Topeka	77/G 4
Kazakhstan*	1,049,150	2,717,300	17,376,615	Aqmola	46/G 5
Kentucky, U.S.	40,411	104,665	3,883,723	Frankfort	77/J 4
Kenya*	224,960	582,646	28,817,227	Nairobi	65/F 4
Kiribati*	277	717	79,386	Tarawa	62/H 5
Korea, North*	46,540	120,539	23,486,550	P'yongyang	55/N 3
Korea, South*	38,023	98,480	45,553,882	Seoul	55/N 4
Kuwait*	6,880	17,820	1,817,397	Kuwait	52/E 3
Kyrgyzstan*	76,641	198,500	4,769,877	Bishkek	46/H 5
L Laos*	91,428	236,800	4,837,237	Vientiane	49/K 8
Latvia*	24,749	64,100	2,762,899	Riga	43/G 4
Lebanon*	4,015	10,399	3,695,921	Beirut	52/B 2
Lesotho*	11,718	30,350	1,992,960	Maseru	70/E 6
Liberia*	43,000	111,370	3,073,245	Monrovia	68/D 6
Libya*	679,358	1,759,537	5,248,401	Tripoli	69/J 2
Liechtenstein*	62	160	30,654	Vaduz	42/F 4
Lithuania*	25,174	65,200	3,876,396	Vilnius	43/F 4
Louisiana, U.S.	49,651	128,595	4,350,579	Baton Rouge	77/H 5
Luxembourg*	999	2,587	404,660	Luxembourg	42/F 4
M Macedonia*	9,781	25,333	2,159,503	Skopje	44/D 3
Madagascar*	226,657	587,041	13,862,325	Antananarivo	70/K 10

Place	Square Miles	Square Kilometers	Population	Capital or Chief Town	Page/Index Ref.
Maine, U.S.	33,741	87,388	1,243,316	Augusta	78/G 1
Malawi*	45,745	118,480	9,808,384	Lilongwe	70/F 3
Malaysia*	127,316	329,750	19,723,587	Kuala Lumpur	56/D 4
Maldives*	116	300	261,310	Male	49/G 9
Mali*	478,764	1,240,000	9,375,132	Bamako	68/E 4
Malta*	124	320	369,609	Valletta	44/B 4
Manitoba, Canada	250,946	649,951	1,091,942	Winnipeg	79/H 4
Marshall Islands*	70	181	56,157	Majuro	62/G 3
Maryland, U.S.	12,297	31,849	5,071,604	Annapolis	78/E 3
Massachusetts, U.S.	9,241	23,934	6,092,352	Boston	78/F 2
Mauritania*	397,953	1,030,700	2,263,202	Nouakchott	68/C 4
Mauritius *	718	1,860	1,127,068	Port Louis	13/M 7
Mexico *	761,601	1,972,546	93,985,848	Mexico City	80/A 3
Michigan, U.S.	96,705	250,506	9,594,350	Lansing	78/C 1
Micronesia, Federated States of*	271	702	122,950	Palikir	62/D 4
Minnesota, U.S.	86,943	225,182	4,657,758	St. Paul	77/G 2
Mississippi, U.S.	48,286	125,060	2,716,115	Jackson	78/B 4
Missouri, U.S.	69,709	180,546	5,358,692	Jefferson City	77/H 4
Moldova*	13,012	33,700	4,489,657	Chişinău	44/E 2
Monaco*	0.7	1.9	31,515	....	42/F 5
Mongolia*	606,163	1,569,962	2,493,615	Ulaanbaatar	54/G 2
Montana, U.S.	147,046	380,849	879,372	Helena	76/D 2
Morocco *	172,414	446,550	29,168,848	Rabat	68/C 1
Mozambique *	309,494	801,590	18,115,250	Maputo	70/G 4
Myanmar (Burma)*	261,969	678,500	45,103,809	Yangon	49/J 7
Namibia*	318,694	825,418	1,651,545	Windhoek	70/C 5
Nauru	8	21	10,149	Yaren (district)	62/F 5
Nebraska, U.S.	77,358	200,358	1,652,093	Lincoln	76/F 3
Nepal*	54,363	140,800	21,560,869	Kathmandu	53/D 3
Netherlands*	14,413	37,330	15,452,903	The Hague; Amsterdam	42/F 3
Nevada, U.S.	110,567	286,367	1,603,163	Carson City	76/C 4
New Brunswick, Canada	28,355	73,440	723,900	Fredericton	79/L 5
Newfoundland, Canada	156,649	405,721	568,474	St. John's	79/L 4
New Hampshire, U.S.	9,283	24,044	1,162,481	Concord	78/F 2
New Jersey, U.S.	8,215	21,277	7,987,933	Trenton	78/F 2
New Mexico, U.S.	121,598	314,930	1,713,407	Santa Fe	76/E 5
New York, U.S.	53,989	139,833	18,184,774	Albany	78/E 2
New Zealand*	103,736	268,676	3,660,364	Wellington	59/H 6
Nicaragua*	49,998	129,494	4,206,353	Managua	80/D 5
Niger*	489,189	1,267,000	9,280,208	Niamey	68/G 4
Nigeria*	356,668	923,770	101,232,251	Abuja	68/G 6
North America	9,355,975	24,232,060	443,438,000	....	73
North Carolina, U.S.	52,672	136,421	7,322,870	Raleigh	78/D 3
North Dakota, U.S.	70,704	183,123	643,539	Bismarck	76/F 2
Northern Ireland, U.K.	5,459	14,138	1,610,000	Belfast	42/C 3
North Korea*	46,540	120,539	23,486,550	P'yŏngyang	55/N 3
Northwest Territories, Canada	1,322,905	3,426,328	57,649	Yellowknife	79/F 3
Norway*	125,181	324,220	4,330,951	Oslo	43/C 3
Nova Scotia, Canada	21,425	55,491	899,942	Halifax	79/L 5
Ohio, U.S.	44,828	116,103	11,172,782	Columbus	78/D 2
Oklahoma, U.S.	69,903	181,048	3,300,902	Oklahoma City	77/G 4
Oman*	82,031	212,460	2,125,089	Muscat	52/G 4
Ontario, Canada	412,580	1,068,582	10,084,885	Toronto	79/H 4
Oregon, U.S.	97,132	251,571	3,203,735	Salem	76/B 3
Pakistan*	310,403	803,944	131,541,920	Islamabad	49/F 7
Palau*	177	458	16,661	Koror	62/C 4
Panama*	30,193	78,200	2,680,903	Panamá	80/E 6
Papua New Guinea*	178,259	461,690	4,294,750	Port Moresby	62/D 5
Paraguay*	157,047	406,752	5,358,198	Asunción	83/C 5
Pennsylvania, U.S.	46,058	119,291	12,056,112	Harrisburg	78/E 2
Peru*	496,223	1,285,220	24,087,372	Lima	86/C 5
Philippines*	115,830	300,000	73,265,584	Manila	57/H 3
Poland*	120,725	312,678	38,792,442	Warsaw	39/F 3
Portugal*	35,552	92,080	10,562,388	Lisbon	42/C 6
Prince Edward Island, Canada	2,184	5,657	129,765	Charlottetown	79/L 5
Puerto Rico, U.S.	3,508	9,085	3,812,569	San Juan	81/H 4
Qatar*	4,247	11,000	533,916	Doha	52/F 3
Québec, Canada	594,857	1,540,680	6,895,963	Québec	79/K 4
Réunion, France	969	2,510	666,067	St-Denis	13/M 7
Rhode Island, U.S.	1,231	3,189	990,225	Providence	78/F 2
Romania*	91,699	237,500	23,198,330	Bucharest	44/D 2
Russia*	6,592,735	17,075,200	149,909,089	Moscow	46/H 3
Rwanda*	10,169	26,337	8,605,307	Kigali	70/E 1

Place	Square Miles	Square Kilometers	Population	Capital or Chief Town	Page/Index Ref.
Saint Kitts and Nevis*	104	269	40,992	Basseterre	81/J 4
Saint Lucia*	239	620	156,050	Castries	81/J 5
Saint Vincent & the Grenadines*	131	340	117,344	Kingstown	81/J 5
Samoa*	1,104	2,860	209,360	Apia	63/H 6
San Marino*	23.4	60.6	24,313	San Marino	42/G 5
São Tomé and Príncipe*	371	960	140,423	São Tomé	68/F 7
Saskatchewan, Canada	251,865	652,330	988,928	Regina	79/G 4
Saudi Arabia*	756,981	1,960,582	18,729,576	Riyadh	52/D 4
Scotland, U.K.	30,414	78,772	5,111,200	Edinburgh	42/C 2
Senegal*	75,749	196,190	9,007,080	Dakar	68/B 5
Seychelles*	176	455	72,709	Victoria	13/M 6
Sierra Leone*	27,699	71,740	4,753,120	Freetown	68/C 6
Singapore*	244	632.6	2,890,468	Singapore	56/C 5
Slovakia*	18,859	48,845	5,432,383	Bratislava	44/C 2
Slovenia*	7,836	20,296	2,051,522	Ljubljana	44/B 2
Solomon Islands*	10,985	28,450	399,206	Honiara	62/E 6
Somalia*	246,200	637,658	7,347,554	Mogadishu	69/Q 6
South Africa*	471,008	1,219,912	45,095,459	Cape Town; Pretoria	70/D 6
South America	6,879,916	17,819,000	314,335,000	....	83
South Carolina, U.S.	31,189	80,779	3,698,746	Columbia	78/D 4
South Dakota, U.S.	77,121	199,744	732,405	Pierre	76/F 3
South Korea	38,023	98,480	45,553,882	Seoul	55/N 4
Spain*	194,884	504,750	39,404,348	Madrid	42/D 5
Sri Lanka*	25,332	65,610	18,342,660	Colombo	53/D 7
Sudan*	967,494	2,505,809	30,120,420	Khartoum	69/L 5
Suriname*	63,039	163,270	429,544	Paramaribo	87/G 3
Swaziland*	6,703	17,360	966,977	Mbabane	70/F 6
Sweden*	173,731	449,964	8,821,759	Stockholm	43/D 3
Switzerland	15,943	41,292	7,084,984	Bern	42/F 4
Syria*	71,498	185,180	15,451,917	Damascus	52/C 1
Taiwan	13,892	35,980	21,500,583	Taipei	55/M 7
Tajikistan*	55,251	143,100	6,155,474	Dushanbe	46/H 6
Tanzania*	364,699	945,090	28,701,077	Dar es Salaam	70/F 2
Tennessee, U.S.	42,146	109,158	5,319,654	Nashville	78/C 3
Texas, U.S.	267,277	692,248	19,128,261	Austin	76/F 5
Thailand*	198,455	513,998	60,271,300	Bangkok	56/C 2
Togo*	21,927	56,790	4,410,370	Lomé	68/F 6
Tonga	289	748	105,600	Nuku'alofa	63/H 7
Trinidad and Tobago*	1,980	5,128	1,271,159	Port-of-Spain	81/J 5
Tunisia*	63,170	163,610	8,879,845	Tunis	68/G 1
Turkey*	301,382	780,580	63,405,526	Ankara	44/F 4
Turkmenistan*	188,455	488,100	4,075,316	Ashkhabad	46/F 6
Tuvalu	10	26	9,991	Funafuti	62/G 5
Uganda*	91,135	236,040	19,573,262	Kampala	69/M 7
Ukraine*	233,089	603,700	51,867,828	Kiev	44/E 2
United Arab Emirates*	29,182	75,581	2,924,594	Abu Dhabi	52/F 4
United Kingdom*	94,525	244,820	58,295,119	London	42/D 2
United States*	3,618,765	9,372,610	266,661,112	Washington, D.C.	76
Uruguay*	68,039	176,220	3,222,716	Montevideo	88/E 3
Utah, U.S.	84,904	219,902	2,000,494	Salt Lake City	76/D 4
Uzbekistan*	172,741	447,400	23,089,261	Tashkent	46/G 5
Vanuatu*	5,699	14,760	173,648	Port-Vila	62/F 6
Vatican City	0.17	0.44	830	....	42/G 5
Venezuela*	352,143	912,050	21,004,773	Caracas	82/E 2
Vermont, U.S.	9,614	24,900	588,654	Montpelier	78/F 2
Vietnam*	127,243	329,560	74,393,324	Hanoi	49/K 8
Virginia, U.S.	42,326	109,625	6,675,451	Richmond	78/E 3
Virgin Islands, British	59	153	16,749	Road Town	81/J 4
Virgin Islands, U.S.	136	352	97,229	Charlotte Amalie	81/H 4
Wales, U.K.	8,017	20,764	2,886,400	Cardiff	42/D 3
Washington, U.S.	70,637	182,949	5,532,939	Olympia	76/B 3
West Bank	2,263	5,860	1,319,991	....	52/C 2
Western Sahara	102,703	266,000	217,211	....	68/B 3
West Virginia, U.S.	24,231	62,758	1,825,754	Charleston	78/D 3
Wisconsin, U.S.	65,499	169,643	5,159,795	Madison	78/B 1
World	(land) 57,505,734	148,940,000	5,819,131,463		12
Wyoming, U.S.	97,818	253,349	481,400	Cheyenne	76/E 3
Yemen*	203,849	527,970	14,728,474	Sanaa	52/E 6
Yugoslavia*	39,517	102,350	11,101,833	Belgrade	44/D 3
Yukon Territory, Canada	186,660	483,450	27,797	Whitehorse	79/D 3
Zambia*	290,583	752,610	9,445,723	Lusaka	70/E 3
Zimbabwe*	150,803	390,580	11,139,961	Harare	70/E 4

World - Physical

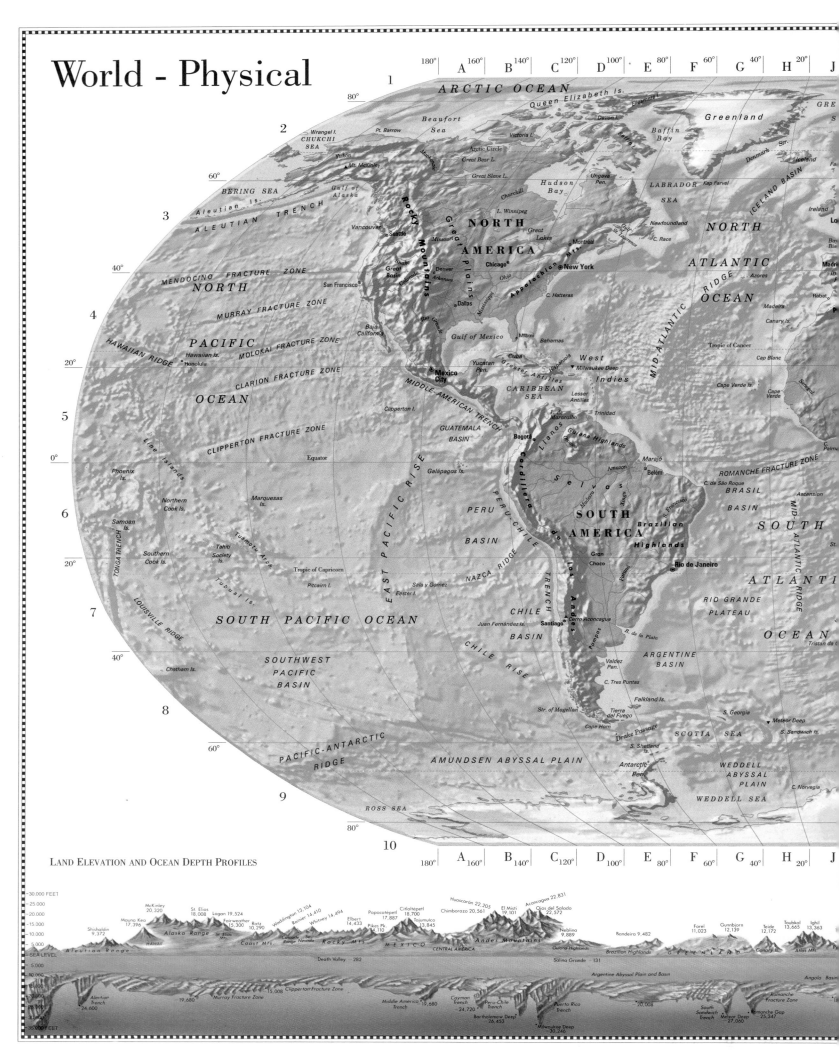

ARCTIC OCEAN

Queen Elizabeth Is.

Greenland

Beaufort Sea

Pt. Barrow

CHUKCHI SEA

Wrangel I.

Victoria I.

Devon I.

Ellesmere I.

Baffin Bay

Mackenzie

Arctic Circle

Great Bear L.

Yukon

Mt. McKinley

BERING SEA

Gulf of Alaska

Great Slave L.

Hudson Bay

Ungava Pen.

LABRADOR SEA

Kap Farvel

ICELAND BASIN

Iceland

Denmark Str.

Ireland

Aleutian Is.

ALEUTIAN TRENCH

Rocky Mountains

Churchill

L. Winnipeg

NORTH AMERICA

Great Lakes

Montreal

C. Race

Newfoundland

St. Lawrence

NORTH

ATLANTIC

Vancouver

Seattle

Great Plains

Missouri

Chicago

Ohio

Appalachian Mts.

New York

MENDOCINO FRACTURE ZONE

NORTH

San Francisco

Great Basin

Snake

Denver

Colorado

Arkansas

Mississippi

C. Hatteras

Madrid

Azores

MID-ATLANTIC

RIDGE

OCEAN

MURRAY FRACTURE ZONE

PACIFIC

Baja California

Dallas

Rio Grande

Gulf of Mexico

Miami

Bahamas

Tropic of Cancer

Madeira

Canary Is.

Cap Blanc

HAWAIIAN RIDGE

MOLOKAI FRACTURE ZONE

Hawaiian Is.

Honolulu

CLARION FRACTURE ZONE

Mexico City

Yucatan Pen.

Cuba

Greater Antilles

Hispaniola

Milwaukee Deep

West Indies

Cape Verde Is.

Cape Verde

OCEAN

CARIBBEAN SEA

Lesser Antilles

Trinidad

MIDDLE-AMERICAN TRENCH

Clipperton I.

GUATEMALA BASIN

L. de Maracaibo

Llanos

Guiana Highlands

ROMANCHE FRACTURE ZONE

CLIPPERTON FRACTURE ZONE

Equator

Galápagos Is.

Bogotá

Cordillera

Amazon

Marajó

Belém

C. de São Roque

BRASIL

BASIN

Ascension

Line Islands

Phoenix Is.

PERU BASIN

Selvas

SOUTH AMERICA

Brazilian Highlands

SOUTH

Northern Cook Is.

Marquesas Is.

Samoan Is.

Tahiti

Society Is.

Tuamotu Arch.

PERU-CHILE

de los Andes

Gran Chaco

Pampas

MID-ATLANTIC RIDGE

ATLANTIC

Southern Cook Is.

Tubuai Is.

Tropic of Capricorn

Pitcairn I.

Sala y Gomez

Easter I.

NAZCA RIDGE

EAST PACIFIC RISE

Rio de Janeiro

RIO GRANDE PLATEAU

TONGA TRENCH

LOUISVILLE RIDGE

SOUTH PACIFIC OCEAN

CHILE BASIN

Juan Fernández Is.

Santiago

Cerro Aconcagua

R. de la Plata

OCEAN

Tristan da C.

CHILE RISE

ARGENTINE BASIN

Chatham Is.

SOUTHWEST PACIFIC BASIN

Valdez Pen.

C. Tres Puntas

Falkland Is.

PACIFIC-ANTARCTIC

Str. of Magellan

Tierra del Fuego

Cape Horn

Drake Passage

S. Georgia

Meteor Deep

S. Sandwich Is.

RIDGE

SCOTIA SEA

S. Shetland

Antarctic Pen.

WEDDELL ABYSSAL PLAIN

AMUNDSEN ABYSSAL PLAIN

C. Norvegia

ROSS SEA

WEDDELL SEA

LAND ELEVATION AND OCEAN DEPTH PROFILES

30,000 FEET
25,000
20,000
15,000
10,000
5,000
SEA LEVEL
5,000
10,000
15,000
20,000
25,000
30,000
35,000 FEET

McKinley 20,320

St. Elias 18,008

Logan 19,524

Huascarán 22,205

Aconcagua 22,831

Mauna Kea 17,396

Fairweather 15,300

Ratz 10,290

Waddington 13,104

Rainier 14,410

Whitney 14,494

Popocatépetl 17,887

Citlaltépetl 18,700

Tajumulco 13,845

Chimborazo 20,561

El Misti 19,101

Ojos del Salado 22,572

Forel 11,023

Gunnbjorn 12,139

Toubkal 13,665

Ighil 13,363

Shishaldin 9,372

Alaska Range

St. Elias Mts.

Concord Sa Range Nevada

Elbert 14,433

Pikes Pk. 14,110

Neblina 9,889

Bandeira 9,482

Teide 12,172

Aleutian Range

HAWAII

Coast Mts.

Rocky Mts.

MEXICO

CENTRAL AMERICA

Andes Mountains

Guiana Highlands

Brazilian Highlands

GREENLAND

Canary Is.

Atlas Mts.

Death Valley -282

Salina Grande -131

Argentine Abyssal Plain and Basin

Angola Basin

Aleutian Trench -24,600

Murray Fracture Zone 19,680

Clipperton Fracture Zone

Middle America Trench -19,680

Cayman Trench -24,720

Peru-Chile Trench

Puerto Rico Trench

Bartholomew Deep -26,453

Milwaukee Deep -30,246

South Sandwich Trench -20,008

Meteor Deep 27,060

Romanche Fracture Zone 25,347

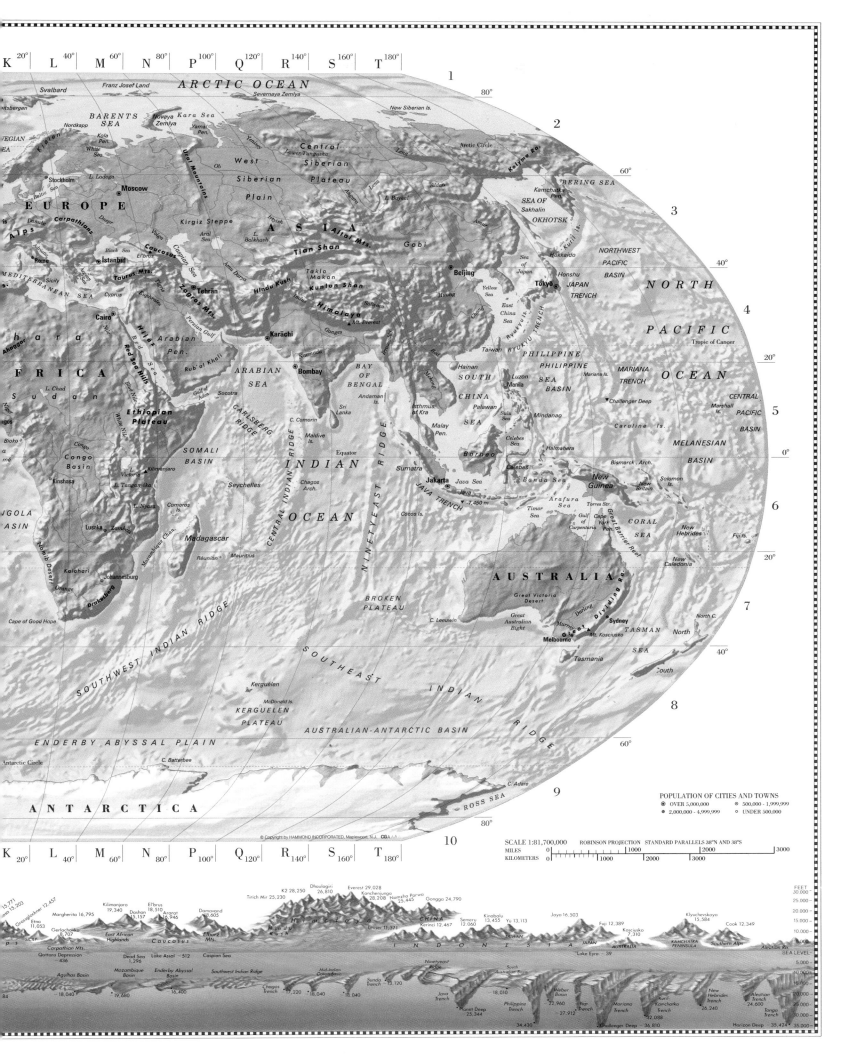

World - Political

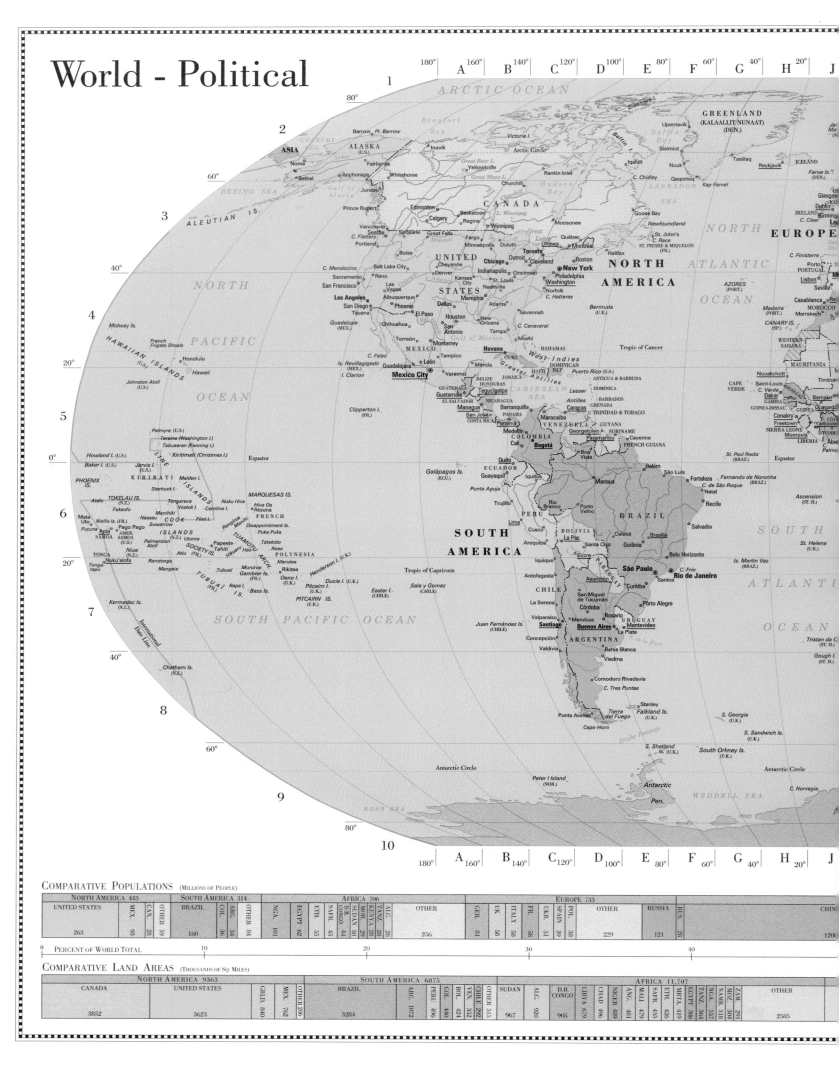

COMPARATIVE POPULATIONS (MILLIONS OF PEOPLE)

NORTH AMERICA 443				SOUTH AMERICA 314				AFRICA 706											EUROPE 733									RUSSIA		CHINA
UNITED STATES	MEX.	CAN.	OTHER	BRAZIL	COL.	ARG.	OTHER	NGA.	EGYPT	ETH.	SAFR.	D.R. CONGO	MOR.	SUDAN	KENYA	TANZ.	ALG.	OTHER	GER.	UK	ITALY	FR.	UKR.	SPAIN	POL.	OTHER	RUSSIA	RUS.	CHINA
263	93	28	59	160	36	34	84	101	62	55	45	44	30	29	28	28	28	256	81	58	58	58	51	39	38	229	121	28	1208

PERCENT OF WORLD TOTAL: 0 10 20 30 40

COMPARATIVE LAND AREAS (THOUSANDS OF SQ. MILES)

NORTH AMERICA 9363					SOUTH AMERICA 6875							AFRICA 11,707																	OTHER
CANADA	UNITED STATES	GRLD.	MEX.	OTHER	BRAZIL	ARG.	PERU	BOL.	VEN.	CHILE	OTHER	SUDAN	ALG.	D.R. CONGO	LIBYA	CHAD	NIGER	ANG.	MALI	SAFR.	ETH.	META.	TANZ.	N.CA.	NAMB.	MOZ.	ZAM.		
3852	3623	840	762	226	3284	1072	496	424	352	292	313	967	920	905	679	496	489	481	479	455	426	419	364	357	318	304	291		2585

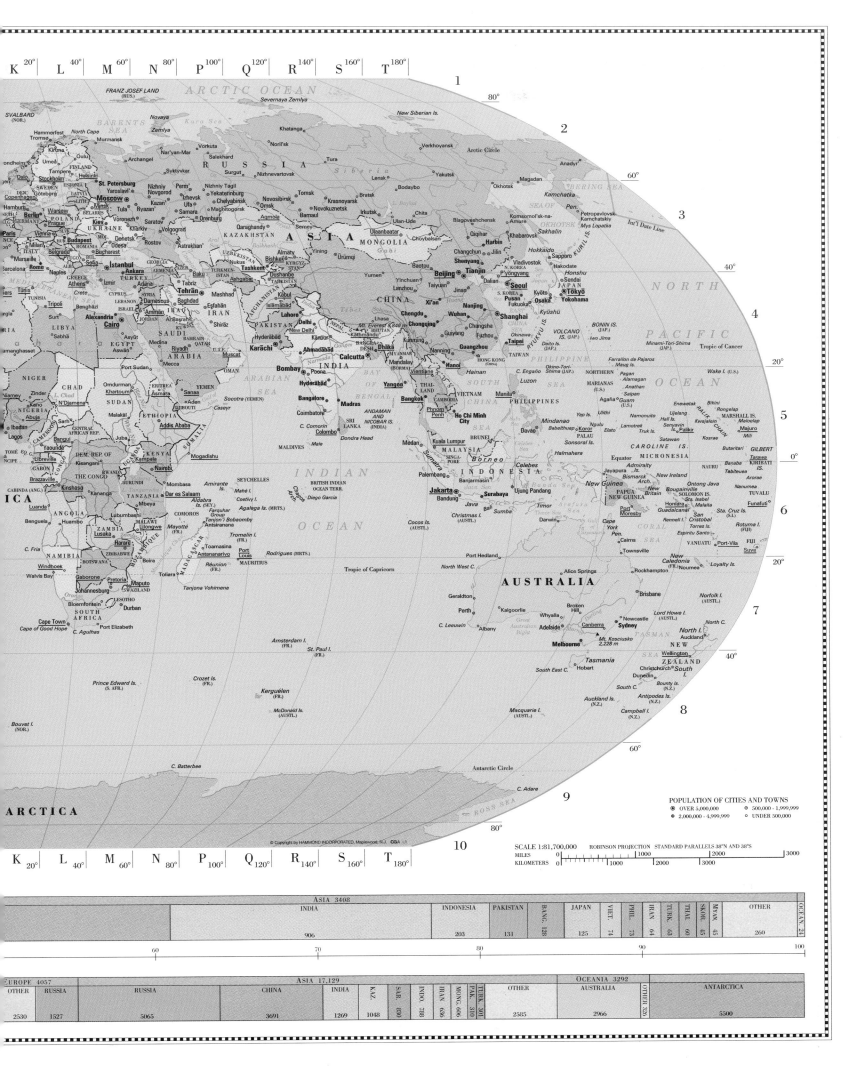

Structure of the

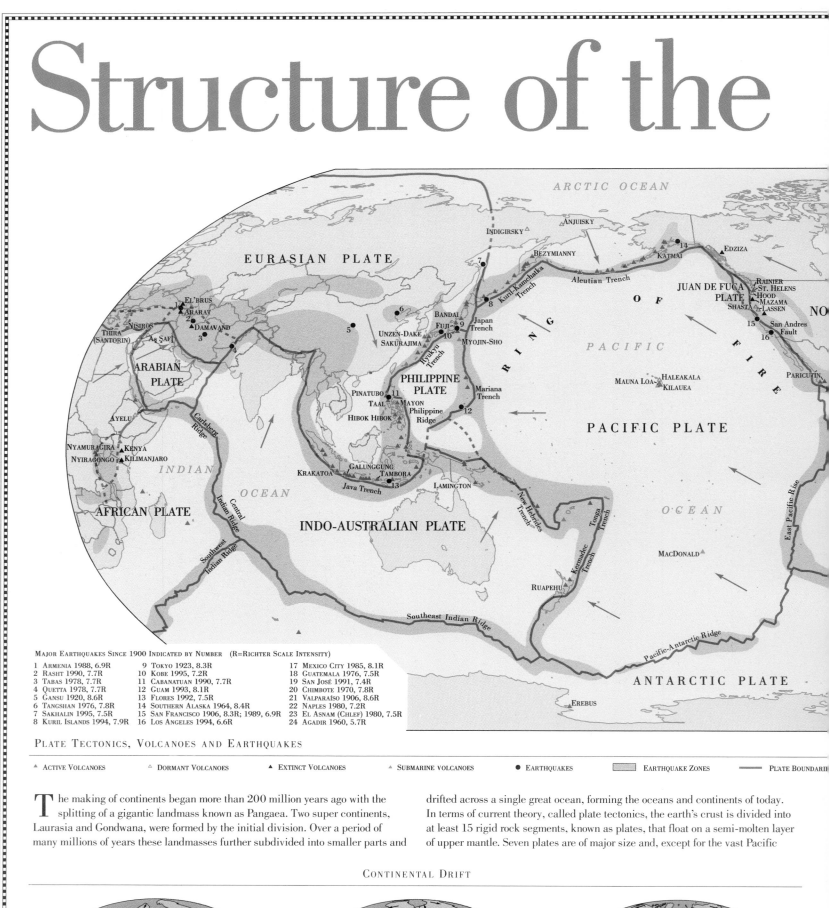

EURASIAN PLATE

ARCTIC OCEAN

ANJUISKY

INDIGIRSKY

BEZYMIANNY

KATMAI 14

EDZIZA

Aleutian Trench

Kuril-Kamchatka Trench

JUAN DE FUCA PLATE

RING

O F

RAINIER
ST. HELENS
HOOD
MAZAMA
LASSEN
SHASTA

NO

Japan Trench

8

Kuril-Kamchatka Trench

EL'BRUS
ARARAT
2
DAMAVAND
3

5

6

BANDAI
FUJI 9
10

9

Japan Trench

PACIFIC

15

San Andres
Fault

16

NISIROS
THIRA
(SANTORINI)
As Safi

4

UNZEN-DAKE
SAKURAJIMA

MYOJIN-SHO

Ryukyu Trench

PARICUTIN

MAUNA LOA
HALEAKALA
KILAUEA

ARABIAN PLATE

PHILIPPINE PLATE

Mariana Trench

PACIFIC PLATE

AYELU

Carlsberg Ridge

PINATUBO 11
TAAL
HIBOK HIBOK

MAYON
Philippine Ridge

12

NYAMURAGIRA
NYIRAGONGO

KENYA
KILIMANJARO

INDIAN

Central Indian Ridge

KRAKATOA

GALUNGGUNG
TAMBORA
13

LAMINGTON

New Hebrides Trench

OCEAN

AFRICAN PLATE

OCEAN

Java Trench

INDO-AUSTRALIAN PLATE

Southwest Indian Ridge

MACDONALD

East Pacific Rise

Tonga Trench

Kermadec Trench

RUAPEHU

Southeast Indian Ridge

Pacific-Antarctic Ridge

ANTARCTIC PLATE

EREBUS

MAJOR EARTHQUAKES SINCE 1900 INDICATED BY NUMBER   (R=RICHTER SCALE INTENSITY)

1 ARMENIA 1988, 6.9R	9 TOKYO 1923, 8.3R	17 MEXICO CITY 1985, 8.1R
2 RASHT 1990, 7.7R	10 KOBE 1995, 7.2R	18 GUATEMALA 1976, 7.5R
3 TABAS 1978, 7.7R	11 CABANATUAN 1990, 7.7R	19 SAN JOSÉ 1991, 7.4R
4 QUETTA 1978, 7.7R	12 GUAM 1993, 8.1R	20 CHIMBOTE 1970, 7.8R
5 GANSU 1920, 8.6R	13 FLORES 1992, 7.5R	21 VALPARAÍSO 1906, 8.6R
6 TANGSHAN 1976, 7.8R	14 SOUTHERN ALASKA 1964, 8.4R	22 NAPLES 1980, 7.2R
7 SAKHALIN 1995, 7.5R	15 SAN FRANCISCO 1906, 8.3R; 1989, 6.9R	23 EL ASNAM (CHLEF) 1980, 7.5R
8 KURIL ISLANDS 1994, 7.9R	16 LOS ANGELES 1994, 6.6R	24 AGADIR 1960, 5.7R

PLATE TECTONICS, VOLCANOES AND EARTHQUAKES

△ ACTIVE VOLCANOES   △ DORMANT VOLCANOES   ▲ EXTINCT VOLCANOES   ▲ SUBMARINE VOLCANOES   ● EARTHQUAKES   ▨ EARTHQUAKE ZONES   —— PLATE BOUNDARIE

T he making of continents began more than 200 million years ago with the splitting of a gigantic landmass known as Pangaea. Two super continents, Laurasia and Gondwana, were formed by the initial division. Over a period of many millions of years these landmasses further subdivided into smaller parts and drifted across a single great ocean, forming the oceans and continents of today. In terms of current theory, called plate tectonics, the earth's crust is divided into at least 15 rigid rock segments, known as plates, that float on a semi-molten layer of upper mantle. Seven plates are of major size and, except for the vast Pacific

CONTINENTAL DRIFT

LAURASIA
(N. AMER.)   (ASIA)

Equator

(AFRICA)
GONDWANA   (INDIA)
(S. AMER.)
(ANTARCTICA)

180 MILLION YEARS AGO

N. AMER.   ASIA
EUROPE

Equator

Atlantic Ocean

AFRICA
S. AMER.   INDIA

AUSTRALIA

ANTARCTICA

70 MILLION YEARS AGO

NORTH AMERICA   EUROPE   ASIA

Equator

AFRICA

SOUTH AMERICA

AUSTRALIA

ANTARCTICA

PRESENT TIME

Earth

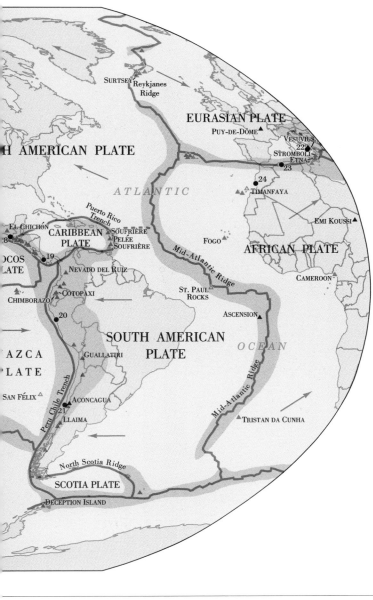

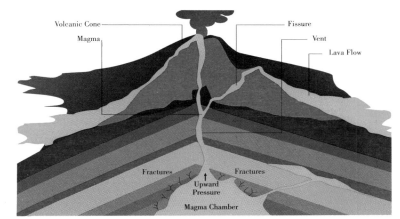

INTERIOR AND CRUST OF THE EARTH

B y studying records of earth-quakes, scientists have developed a fairly reasonable picture (cross section) of the earth's principal layers, including their composition. The inner core is a very dense, highly-pressur-ized, extremely hot (about 9,000° F.) sphere. Moving outward toward the crust, densities, pressures and temper-atures decrease significantly.

VOLCANOES

O ne of the earth's most dynamic and colorful builders is the volcano. In the mantle, magma—molten rock containing compressed gases—probes for weak spots in the earth's crust and bursts forth through the ground in an eruption of fiery lava, ash, gas and steam. After a period of eruption, lasting from a few days to many years, the magma ceases to push upward and the volcano becomes dormant.

Plate, carry a continental landmass with surrounding ocean floor and island areas. The plates are slow-moving, driven by powerful forces within the mantle. At their boundaries they are either slowly separating with new material added from the mantle, converging, with one plate being forced down (subducted) and consumed under another, or sliding past each other. Almost all earthquake, volcanic and mountain-building activity closely follows these boundaries and is related to movements between them. Although these movements may be no more than inches per year, the destructive power unleashed can be cataclysmic.

PLATE TECTONICS

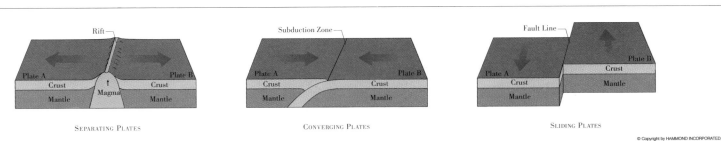

SEPARATING PLATES   CONVERGING PLATES   SLIDING PLATES

Atmosphere &

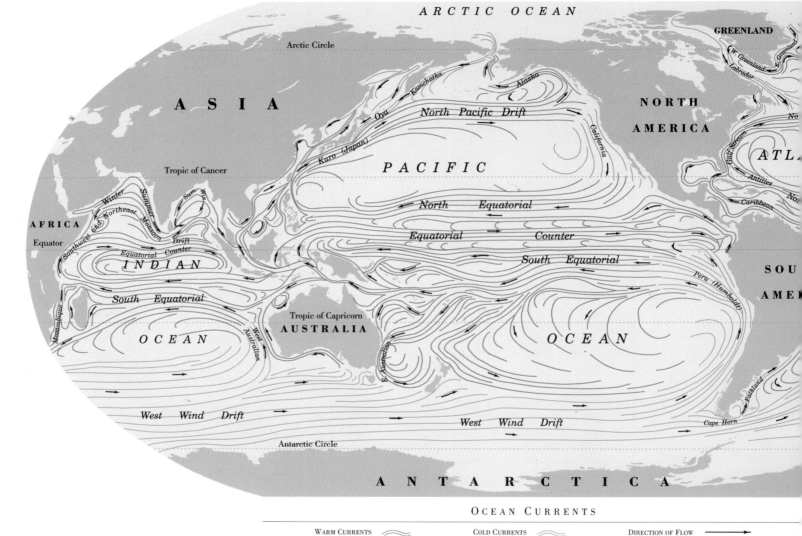

OCEAN CURRENTS

WARM CURRENTS 〜   COLD CURRENTS 〜   DIRECTION OF FLOW ⟶

Hurricane

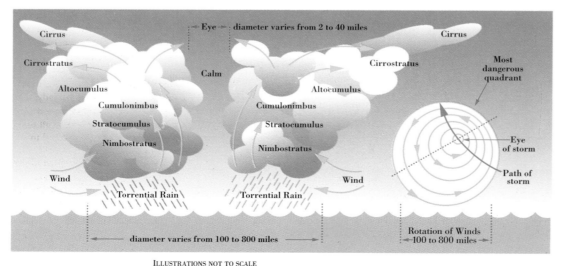

Cirrus

Cirrostratus

Altocumulus

Cumulonimbus

Stratocumulus

Nimbostratus

Wind

Torrential Rain

← Eye → diameter varies from 2 to 40 miles

Calm

Cirrus

Cirrostratus

Most dangerous quadrant

Altocumulus

Cumulonimbus

Stratocumulus

Nimbostratus

Wind

Torrential Rain

Eye of storm

Path of storm

diameter varies from 100 to 800 miles

Rotation of Winds ←100 to 800 miles→

ILLUSTRATIONS NOT TO SCALE

Hurricanes are great whirling storms accompanied by violent destructive winds, torrential rains and high waves and tides. They originate over the oceans, and usually move from lower to higher latitudes with increasing speed, size and intensity. Movement over land quickly reduces their force. Hurricane winds cause severe property damage, but drowning is the greatest cause of hurricane deaths. Floods can be the hurricane's most serious threat.

Oceans

(Atlantic Ocean map with currents: Atlantic Drift, Bennett, Portugal, Canary, EUROPE, AFRICA, North Equatorial, Equat. Counter, Guinea, South Equatorial, Brazil, Benguela, Algulhas, OCEAN, West Wind Drift)

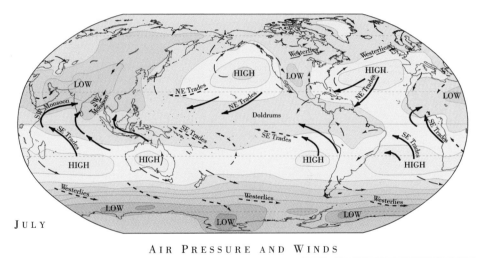

JANUARY

JULY

AIR PRESSURE AND WINDS

PRESSURE IN MILLIBARS				WINDS
OVER 1038	1020 TO 1026	1002 TO 1008	984 TO 990	LESS OFTEN
1032 TO 1038	1014 TO 1020	996 TO 1002	UNDER 984	MORE OFTEN
1026 TO 1032	1008 TO 1014	990 TO 996		CONSTANT

Warm Front

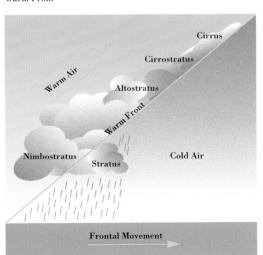

(Warm front diagram: Cirrus, Cirrostratus, Warm Air, Altostratus, Warm Front, Nimbostratus, Stratus, Cold Air, Frontal Movement)

Cold Front

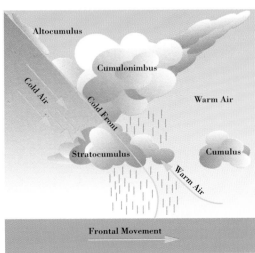

(Cold front diagram: Altocumulus, Cumulonimbus, Cold Air, Cold Front, Warm Air, Stratocumulus, Cumulus, Warm Air, Frontal Movement)

A front is the boundary surface between two air masses which have different characteristics, primarily different temperatures. Depending upon the amount of moisture in the warm air, warm fronts usually produce steady, moderate precipitation over a broad area ahead of the front on the ground. Cold fronts tend to move faster than warm fronts. They are generally confined to a narrower frontal zone but may contain dense thunderheads and severe storms.

Climate

SELECTED CLIMATE REGIONS

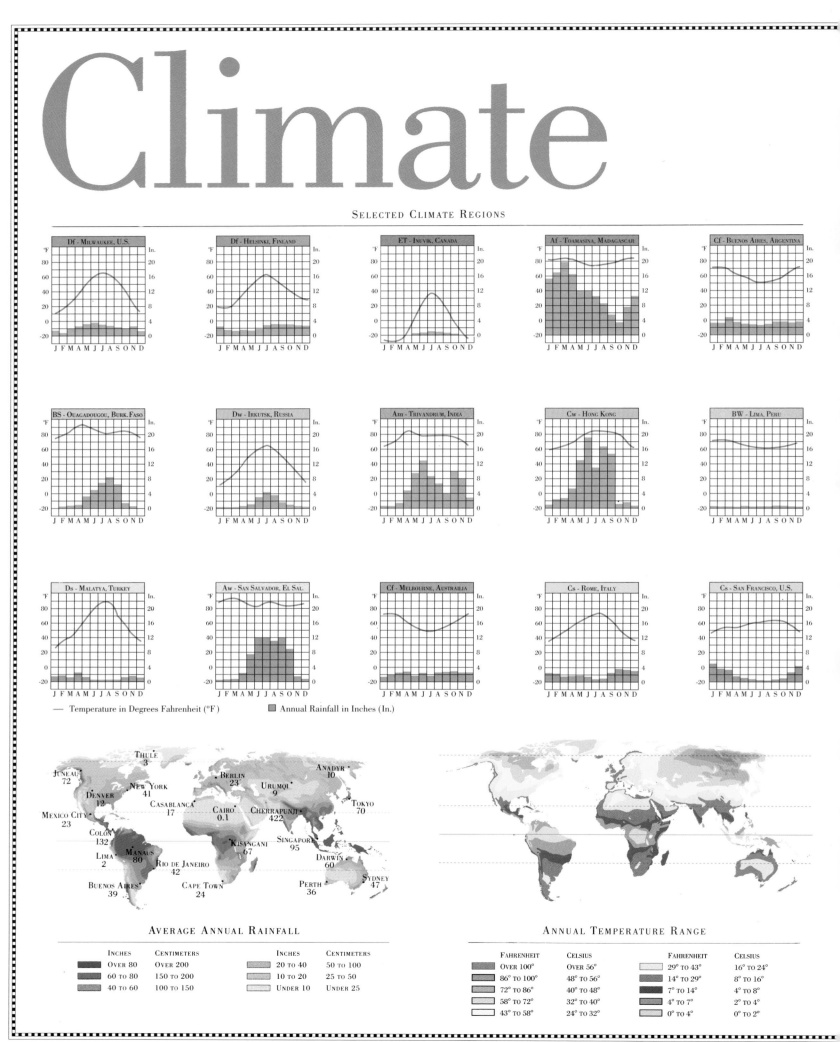

Df - Milwaukee, U.S.

Df - Helsinki, Finland

ET - Inuvik, Canada

Af - Toamasina, Madagascar

Cf - Buenos Aires, Argentina

BS - Ouagadougou, Burk. Faso

Dw - Irkutsk, Russia

Am - Trivandrum, India

Cw - Hong Kong

BW - Lima, Peru

Ds - Malatya, Turkey

Aw - San Salvador, El Sal.

Cf - Melbourne, Australia

Cs - Rome, Italy

Cs - San Francisco, U.S.

— Temperature in Degrees Fahrenheit (°F)   ▨ Annual Rainfall in Inches (In.)

THULE 3
JUNEAU 72
BERLIN 23
ANADYR 10
NEW YORK 41
URUMQI 9
DENVER 12
CASABLANCA 17
CAIRO 0.1
CHERRAPUNJI 422
TOKYO 70
MEXICO CITY 23
COLON 132
KISANGANI 67
SINGAPORE 95
LIMA 2
MANAUS 80
DARWIN 60
RIO DE JANEIRO 42
BUENOS AIRES 39
CAPE TOWN 24
PERTH 36
SYDNEY 47

AVERAGE ANNUAL RAINFALL

	INCHES	CENTIMETERS		INCHES	CENTIMETERS
■	OVER 80	OVER 200	▨	20 TO 40	50 TO 100
■	60 TO 80	150 TO 200	▨	10 TO 20	25 TO 50
■	40 TO 60	100 TO 150	□	UNDER 10	UNDER 25

ANNUAL TEMPERATURE RANGE

	FAHRENHEIT	CELSIUS		FAHRENHEIT	CELSIUS
■	OVER 100°	OVER 56°	▨	29° TO 43°	16° TO 24°
■	86° TO 100°	48° TO 56°	■	14° TO 29°	8° TO 16°
■	72° TO 86°	40° TO 48°	■	7° TO 14°	4° TO 8°
■	58° TO 72°	32° TO 40°	▨	4° TO 7°	2° TO 4°
□	43° TO 58°	24° TO 32°	□	0° TO 4°	0° TO 2°

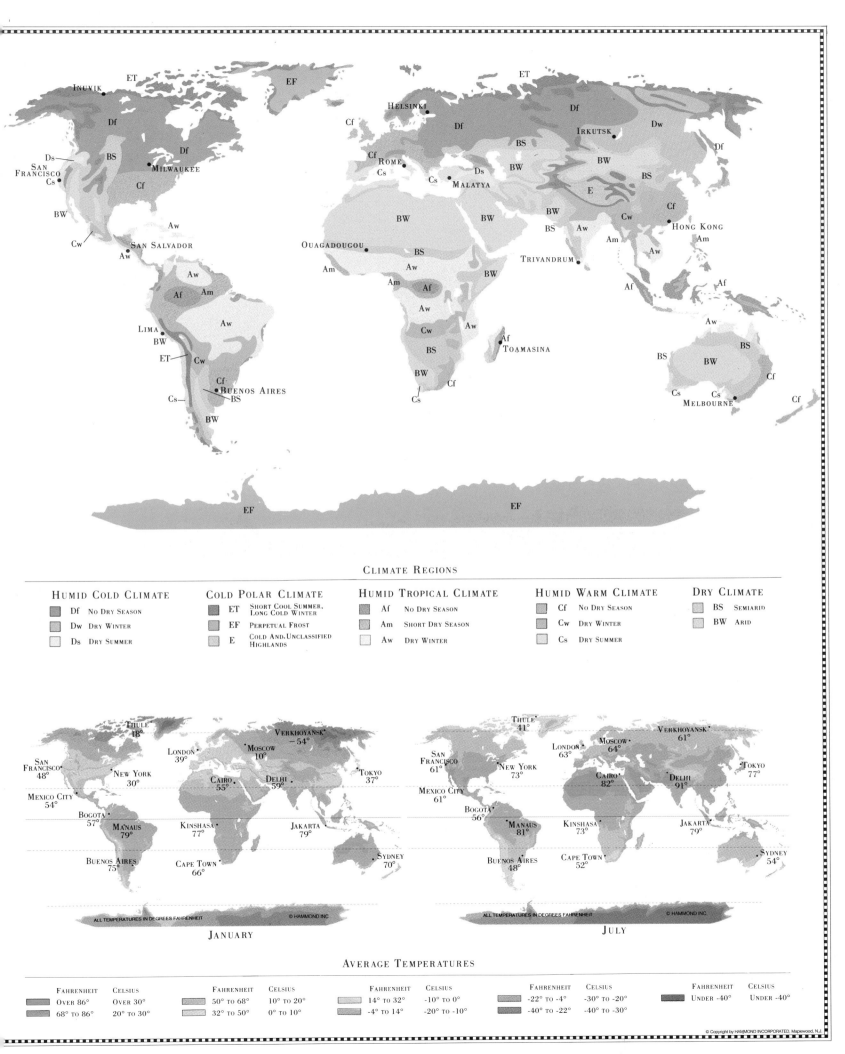

CLIMATE REGIONS

HUMID COLD CLIMATE

Df — No Dry Season
Dw — Dry Winter
Ds — Dry Summer

COLD POLAR CLIMATE

ET — Short Cool Summer, Long Cold Winter
EF — Perpetual Frost
E — Cold And Unclassified Highlands

HUMID TROPICAL CLIMATE

Af — No Dry Season
Am — Short Dry Season
Aw — Dry Winter

HUMID WARM CLIMATE

Cf — No Dry Season
Cw — Dry Winter
Cs — Dry Summer

DRY CLIMATE

BS — Semiarid
BW — Arid

AVERAGE TEMPERATURES

JANUARY

JULY

FAHRENHEIT	CELSIUS	FAHRENHEIT	CELSIUS	FAHRENHEIT	CELSIUS	FAHRENHEIT	CELSIUS	FAHRENHEIT	CELSIUS
OVER 86°	OVER 30°	50° TO 68°	10° TO 20°	14° TO 32°	-10° TO 0°	-22° TO -4°	-30° TO -20°	UNDER -40°	UNDER -40°
68° TO 86°	20° TO 30°	32° TO 50°	0° TO 10°	-4° TO 14°	-20° TO -10°	-40° TO -22°	-40° TO -30°		

ALL TEMPERATURES IN DEGREES FAHRENHEIT.   © HAMMOND INC

© Copyright by HAMMOND INCORPORATED, Maplewood, N.J.

Vegetation & Soils

NATURAL VEGETATION

ARCTIC CIRCLE

TROPIC OF CANCER

EQUATOR

TROPIC OF CAPRICORN

NEEDLELEAF FOREST
Found in higher latitudes with shorter growing seasons, and dominated by pure stands of softwood, evergreen conifers (cone-bearing trees) such as pine, fir and spruce. The light undergrowth consists of small shrubs, mosses, lichens and pine needles.

BROADLEAF FOREST
Found in the middle latitudes, this forest of deciduous (seasonal leaf-shedding) trees includes the hardwoods maple, hickory and oak. The forest floor is relatively barren, except for thick leaf cover during colder months.

MIXED NEEDLELEAF AND BROADLEAF FOREST
A transitional zone between northern softwoods and temperate hardwoods.

WOODLAND AND SHRUB (MEDITERRANEAN)
A mid-latitude area of broadleaf evergreens, dense growths of woody shrubs and open grassy woodland, characterized by pronounced dry summers and wet winters.

SHORT GRASS (STEPPE)
A mid-latitude, semi-arid area usually found on the fringe of desert regions, with continuous short-grass cover up to 8" (20cm.) tall, used chiefly to graze livestock.

TALL GRASS (PRAIRIE)
Mid-latitude, semi-moist areas with continuous tall-grass cover up to 24" (61cm.) in height, used for agricultural purposes. Rainfall is insufficient to support larger plants.

TROPICAL RAIN FOREST (SELVA)
A dense, evergreen forest of tall, varied hardwood trees with a thick broadleaf canopy and a dark, moist interior with minimal undergrowth.

LIGHT TROPICAL FOREST (TROPICAL SEMIDECIDUOUS OR MONSOON FOREST)
As above, with more widely spaced trees, heavier undergrowth, larger concentrations of single species. Dry season prevents most trees from remaining evergreen. Found in monsoon areas.

TROPICAL WOODLAND AND SHRUB (THORN FOREST)
Longer dry season results in low trees with thick bark and smaller leaves. Dense undergrowth of thorny plants, brambles and grasses. Transition belt between denser forests and grasslands.

TROPICAL GRASSLAND AND SHRUB (SAVANNA)
Stiff, sharp-edged grasses, from 2' to 12' (0.6m. to 3.7m.) high, with large areas of bare ground. Scattered shrubs and low trees in some areas.

WOODED SAVANNA
A transitional area where savanna joins a tropical or shrub forest, with low trees and shrubs dotting the grasslands.

DESERT AND DESERT SHRUB
Barren stretches of soft brown, yellow or red sand and rock wastes with isolated patches of short grass and stunted bushes, turning bright green when fed by infrequent precipitation.

RIVER VALLEY AND OASIS
River valleys are lush, fertile lands, with varied vegetation. An oasis is a fertile or verdant spot found in a desert near a natural spring or pool.

HEATH AND MOOR
A heath is open, uncultivated land covered with low, flowering evergreen shrubs such as heather. Moors are often high and poorly drained lands, with patches of heath and peat bogs.

TUNDRA AND ALPINE
An area of scarce moisture and short, cool summers where trees cannot survive. A permanently frozen subsoil supports low-growing lichens, mosses and stunted shrubs.

UNCLASSIFIED HIGHLANDS
Sequential bands or vertical zones of all vegetation types, which generally follow the warm-to-cold upward patterns found in corresponding areas of vegetation. (Map scale does not permit delineation of these areas.)

PERMANENT ICE COVER
Permanently ice and snow-covered terrain found in polar regions and atop high mountains.

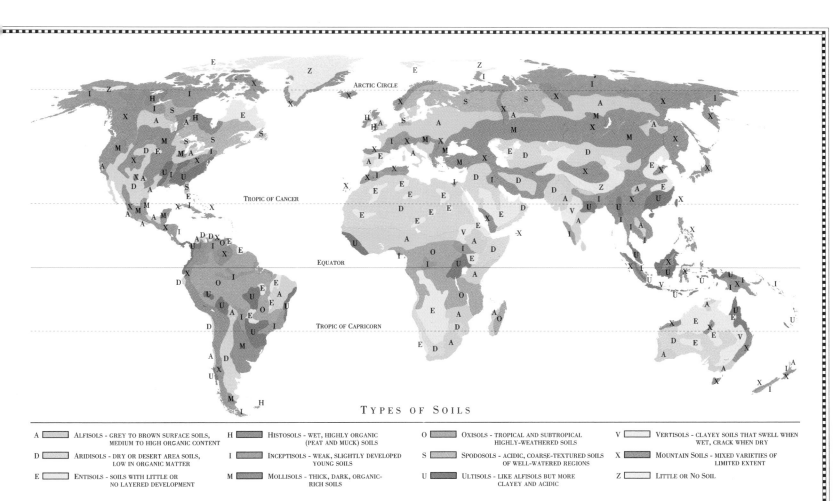

TYPES OF SOILS

A ALFISOLS - GREY TO BROWN SURFACE SOILS, MEDIUM TO HIGH ORGANIC CONTENT	**H** HISTOSOLS - WET, HIGHLY ORGANIC (PEAT AND MUCK) SOILS	**O** OXISOLS - TROPICAL AND SUBTROPICAL HIGHLY-WEATHERED SOILS	**V** VERTISOLS - CLAYEY SOILS THAT SWELL WHEN WET, CRACK WHEN DRY
D ARIDISOLS - DRY OR DESERT AREA SOILS, LOW IN ORGANIC MATTER	**I** INCEPTISOLS - WEAK, SLIGHTLY DEVELOPED YOUNG SOILS	**S** SPODOSOLS - ACIDIC, COARSE-TEXTURED SOILS OF WELL-WATERED REGIONS	**X** MOUNTAIN SOILS - MIXED VARIETIES OF LIMITED EXTENT
E ENTISOLS - SOILS WITH LITTLE OR NO LAYERED DEVELOPMENT	**M** MOLLISOLS - THICK, DARK, ORGANIC-RICH SOILS	**U** ULTISOLS - LIKE ALFISOLS BUT MORE CLAYEY AND ACIDIC	**Z** LITTLE OR NO SOIL

TYPES OF VEGETATION

Needleleaf Forest

These typically coniferous soft-wood forests of Europe, Asia and North America cover about 9 percent of the earth's land.

Broadleaf Forest

Located in the most pleasant hab-itable climatic regions, temperate broadleaf forests have suffered the greatest destruction by people.

Mixed Forest

These hardwood and softwood forests, when added to the broadleaf forest area, are home to over half the world's population.

Prairie

Unique to the Americas, tall grass prairie lands have been success-fully cultivated to become great grain fields of the world

Steppe

Slightly more moist than desert, steppe areas are sometimes cul-tivated but more often used for livestock ranching and herding.

Tropical Rain Forest

Teak, mahogany, balsawood, quinine, cocoa and rubber are some of the major products found in the world's tropical rain forest regions.

Savanna

A place of winter droughts and summer rainfall, these tropical grass and shrub areas are home to a wide variety of big-game animals.

Mediterranean

In addition to southern Europe and northern Africa, this vege-tation also can be found in California, Chile, South Africa and Western Australia.

Desert Shrub

One-fifth of the world's land is desert and desert shrub, too dry for farming and ranching and populated largely by nomads and oases-dwellers.

Tundra

Found along the Arctic fringe of North America and Eurasia, tundra is of little economic sig-nificance except for mineral exploitation.

Environmental Concerns

DESERTIFICATION AND ACID RAIN DAMAGE

- AREAS OF PRODUCTIVE DRYLANDS DESERTIFIED BY EARLY 1980'S
- AREAS OF DAMAGE FROM ACID RAIN AND OTHER AIRBORNE POLLUTANTS

Greenhouse gases in atmosphere: carbon dioxide, methane, nitrous oxide, water vapor, industrial gases, ozone

Sun

solar radiation

reflected back to space

Atmosphere

absorbed by clouds and atmosphere

absorbed by clouds and greenhouse gases

heat radiates back into atmophere

reradiated back to earth

about 50% of sun's radiation reaches ground and is converted to infrared (heat) radiation

Earth

GREENHOUSE EFFECT

MAIN TANKER ROUTES AND MAJOR OIL SPILLS

—— ROUTES OF VERY LARGE CRUDE OIL CARRIERS ● MAJOR OIL SPILLS

GRIZZLY BEAR Much of Pacific temperate rain forest has been clear-cut. Remainder could be gone in 35 years.

WOODLAND CARIBOU

HUMPBACK WHALE

Hydroelectric power projects and development in Quebec are disrupting wildlife habitats.

Commercial fishing harvest in the northwest Atlantic has declined over 30 percent since 1970.

Fragile barrier beaches of the Atlantic coast have been damaged by agricultural runoff sewage and overdevelopment.

Ecological balance in coral reefs of the Gulf and Caribbean area is being upset by a booming tourist industry.

At the present rate of clearing, half of Central America's rain forest will disappear by the year 2000.

One-third of Guinea's tropical forest is expected to disappear in the next decade.

SPOTTED OWL

BLACK-FOOTED FERRET

BALD EAGLE

CONDOR

WHOOPING CRANE

MANATEE

ATLANTIC RIDLEY TURTLE

HOWLER MONKEY

Erosion, the depletion of water resources for irrigation, and overgrazing have turned range and cropland into desert.

GALÁPAGOS TORTOISE

BLACK CAIMAN

JAGUAR

VICUÑA

GOLDEN LION TAMARIN

Every year over 5000 square miles (13,000 sq km) of rain forest is destroyed in Brazil's Amazon Basin.

CHINCHILLA

GIANT ARMADILLO

The Atlantic waters off Patagonia have suffered from over-fishing and oil spills.

Southern Chile's rain forest is threatened by development.

BLUE WHALE

Acid Rain

Acid rain of nitric and sulfuric acids has killed all life in thousands of lakes, and over 15 million acres (6 million hectares) of virgin forest in Europe and North America are dead or dying.

Deforestation

Each year, 50 million acres (20 million hectares) of tropical rainforests are being felled by loggers. Trees remove carbon-dioxide from the atmosphere and are vital to the prevention of soil erosion.

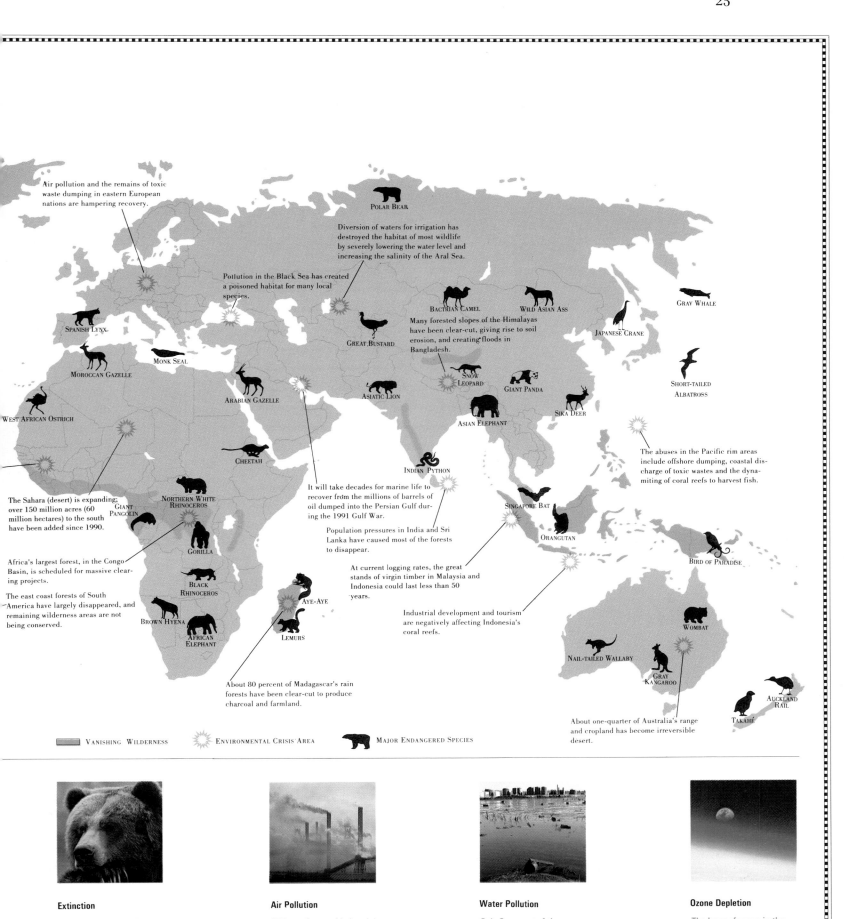

The map contains the following labels:

POLAR BEAR

Air pollution and the remains of toxic waste dumping in eastern European nations are hampering recovery.

Diversion of waters for irrigation has destroyed the habitat of most wildlife by severely lowering the water level and increasing the salinity of the Aral Sea.

Pollution in the Black Sea has created a poisoned habitat for many local species.

BACTRIAN CAMEL   WILD ASIAN ASS   GRAY WHALE

SPANISH LYNX   GREAT BUSTARD   JAPANESE CRANE

Many forested slopes of the Himalayas have been clear-cut, giving rise to soil erosion, and creating floods in Bangladesh.

MONK SEAL   SNOW LEOPARD   GIANT PANDA   SHORT-TAILED ALBATROSS

MOROCCAN GAZELLE   ARABIAN GAZELLE   ASIATIC LION   SIKA DEER

WEST AFRICAN OSTRICH   ASIAN ELEPHANT

CHEETAH   INDIAN PYTHON

The abuses in the Pacific rim areas include offshore dumping, coastal discharge of toxic wastes and the dynamiting of coral reefs to harvest fish.

The Sahara (desert) is expanding; over 150 million acres (60 million hectares) to the south have been added since 1990.

GIANT PANGOLIN   NORTHERN WHITE RHINOCEROS   SINGAPORE BAT

It will take decades for marine life to recover from the millions of barrels of oil dumped into the Persian Gulf during the 1991 Gulf War.

Population pressures in India and Sri Lanka have caused most of the forests to disappear.

ORANGUTAN   BIRD OF PARADISE

Africa's largest forest, in the Congo Basin, is scheduled for massive clearing projects.

GORILLA

At current logging rates, the great stands of virgin timber in Malaysia and Indonesia could last less than 50 years.

The east coast forests of South America have largely disappeared, and remaining wilderness areas are not being conserved.

BLACK RHINOCEROS   AYE-AYE

Industrial development and tourism are negatively affecting Indonesia's coral reefs.

BROWN HYENA   LEMURS   AFRICAN ELEPHANT

WOMBAT

NAIL-TAILED WALLABY   GRAY KANGAROO   AUCKLAND RAIL   TAKAHE

About 80 percent of Madagascar's rain forests have been clear-cut to produce charcoal and farmland.

About one-quarter of Australia's range and cropland has become irreversible desert.

VANISHING WILDERNESS   ENVIRONMENTAL CRISIS AREA   MAJOR ENDANGERED SPECIES

Extinction
Biologists estimate that over 50,000 plant and animal species inhabiting the world's rain forests are disappearing each year due to pollution, unchecked hunting and the destruction of natural habitats.

Air Pollution
Billions of tons of industrial emissions and toxic pollutants are released into the air each year, depleting our ozone layer, killing our forests and lakes with acid rain and threatening our health.

Water Pollution
Only 3 percent of the earth's water is fresh. Pollution from cities, farms and factories has made much of it unfit to drink. In the developing world, most sewage flows untreated into lakes and rivers.

Ozone Depletion
The layer of ozone in the stratosphere shields earth from harmful ultraviolet radiation. But man-made gases are destroying this vital barrier, increasing the risk of skin cancer and eye disease.

Population

GREAT CITIES

WORLD'S LARGEST URBAN AREAS: MILLIONS OF INHABITANTS

TOKYO, Japan 26.5

NEW YORK, U.S. 18.0

SÃO PAULO, Brazil 16.9

OSAKA, Japan 16.9

SEOUL, Korea 15.8

MEXICO CITY, Mexico 15.5

SHANGHAI, China 14.7

BOMBAY, India 14.5

LOS ANGELES, U.S. 14.5

MOSCOW, Russia 13.1

BEIJING, China 12.0

CALCUTTA, India 11.4

LONDON, U.K. 11.1

RIO DE JANEIRO, Brazil 11.0

JAKARTA, Indonesia 11.0

TOWN & COUNTRY

URBAN & RURAL POPULATION COMPONENTS OF SELECTED COUNTRIES

▢ URBAN   ▣ RURAL

Uruguay 87% / 13%

Australia 85% / 15%

Japan 77% / 23%

United States 74% / 26%

Russia 73% / 27%

Hungary 62% / 38%

Iran 54% / 46%

Egypt 44% / 56%

Philippines 37% / 63%

Portugal 30% / 70%

China 26% / 74%

Maldives 20% / 80%

Bangladesh 15% / 85%

Nepal 6% / 94%

AGE DISTRIBUTION

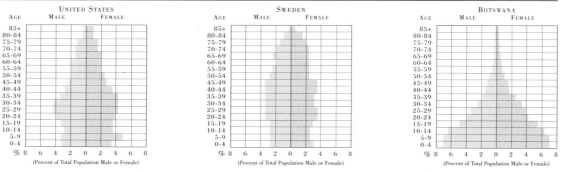

UNITED STATES — AGE / MALE / FEMALE
(Percent of Total Population Male or Female)

SWEDEN — AGE / MALE / FEMALE
(Percent of Total Population Male or Female)

BOTSWANA — AGE / MALE / FEMALE
(Percent of Total Population Male or Female)

Age groups: 85+, 80-84, 75-79, 70-74, 65-69, 60-64, 55-59, 50-54, 45-49, 40-44, 35-39, 30-34, 25-29, 20-24, 15-19, 10-14, 5-9, 0-4

% 8 6 4 2 0 2 4 6 8

LARGEST COUNTRIES: ESTIMATED POPULATIONS IN 2020

MILLIONS OF INHABITANTS   ▢ 1995   ▣ 2020 (ESTIMATE)

Scale: 0   100   200   300   900   1000   1100   1200   1300   1400   1500   1600

China 1203 / 1541

India 936 / 1317

United States 263 / 294

Indonesia 203 / 287

Brazil 160 / 231

Russia 149 / 153

Pakistan 131 / 251

Bangladesh 128 / 209

Japan 125 / 127

Nigeria 101 /273

Mexico 93 / 147

Vietnam 74 / 102

Iran 64 / 143

Ethiopia 55 / 123

ALASKA

MEXICO

▣ 3.5 PERCENT OR MORE

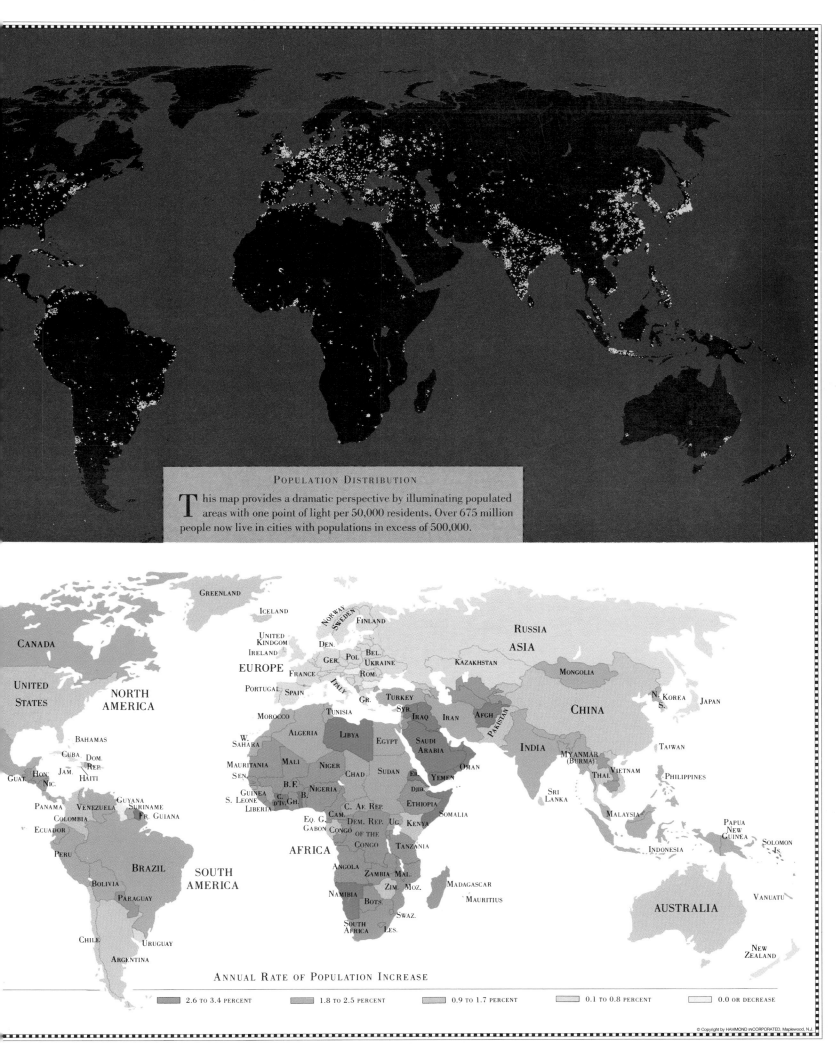

POPULATION DISTRIBUTION

This map provides a dramatic perspective by illuminating populated areas with one point of light per 50,000 residents. Over 675 million people now live in cities with populations in excess of 500,000.

ANNUAL RATE OF POPULATION INCREASE

| 2.6 to 3.4 percent | 1.8 to 2.5 percent | 0.9 to 1.7 percent | 0.1 to 0.8 percent | 0.0 or decrease |

Languages & Religions

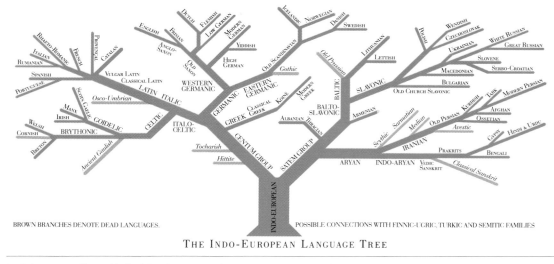

THE INDO-EUROPEAN LANGUAGE TREE

BROWN BRANCHES DENOTE DEAD LANGUAGES.

POSSIBLE CONNECTIONS WITH FINNIC-UGRIC, TURKIC AND SEMITIC FAMILIES

T he most well-established family tree is Indo-European. Spoken by more than 2.5 billion people, it contains dozens of languages. Some linguists theorize that all people - and all languages - are descended from a tiny population that lived in Africa some 200,000 years ago.

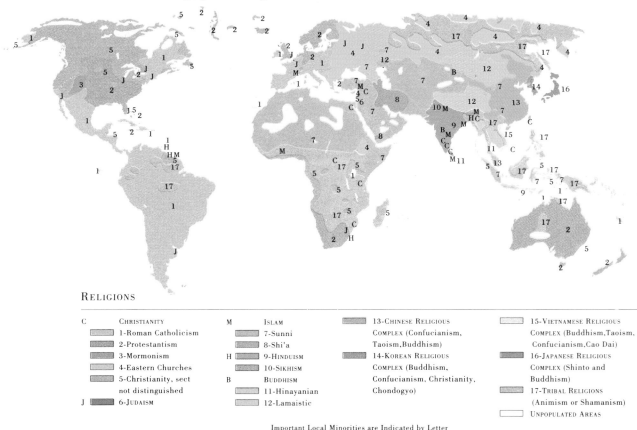

RELIGIONS

C	**CHRISTIANITY**	**M**	**ISLAM**
	1-Roman Catholicism		7-Sunni
	2-Protestantism		8-Shi'a
	3-Mormonism	**H**	9-Hinduism
	4-Eastern Churches		10-Sikhism
	5-Christianity, sect	**B**	Buddhism
	not distinguished		11-Hinayanian
J	6-Judaism		12-Lamaistic

13-Chinese Religious Complex (Confucianism, Taoism, Buddhism)

14-Korean Religious Complex (Buddhism, Confucianism, Christianity, Chondogyo)

15-Vietnamese Religious Complex (Buddhism, Taoism, Confucianism, Cao Dai)

16-Japanese Religious Complex (Shinto and Buddhism)

17-Tribal Religions (Animism or Shamanism)

Unpopulated Areas

Important Local Minorities are Indicated by Letter

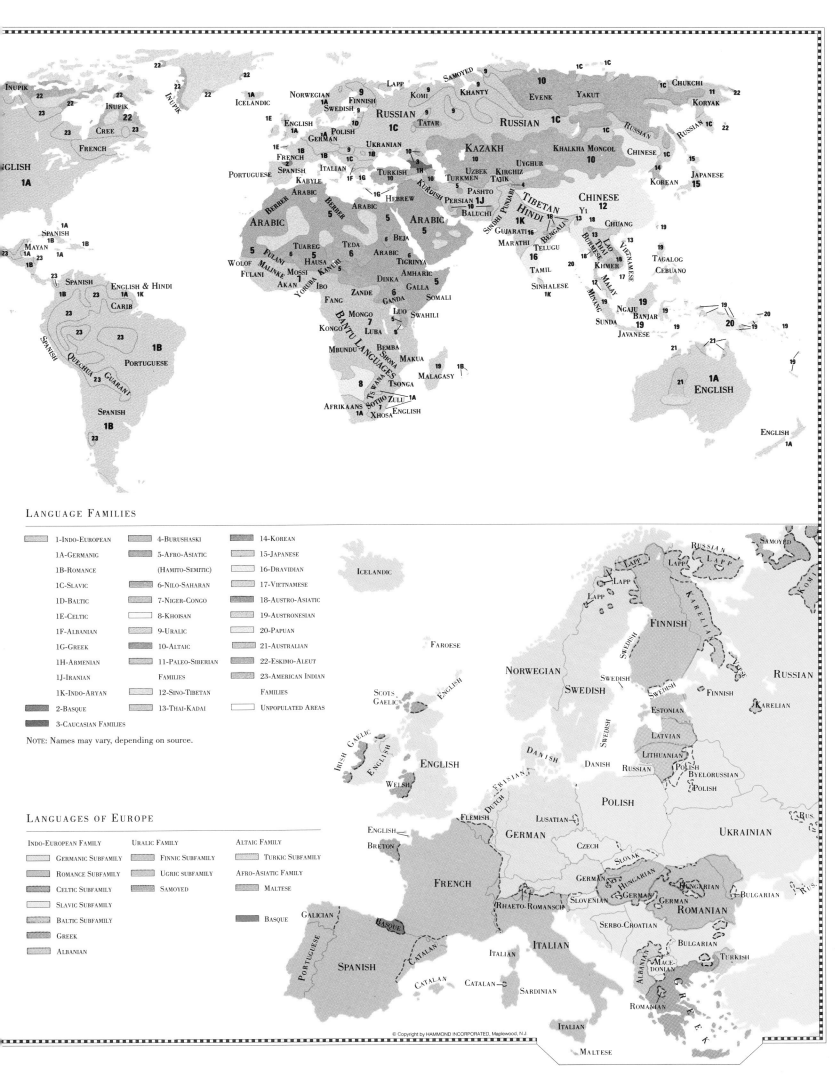

Standards of Living

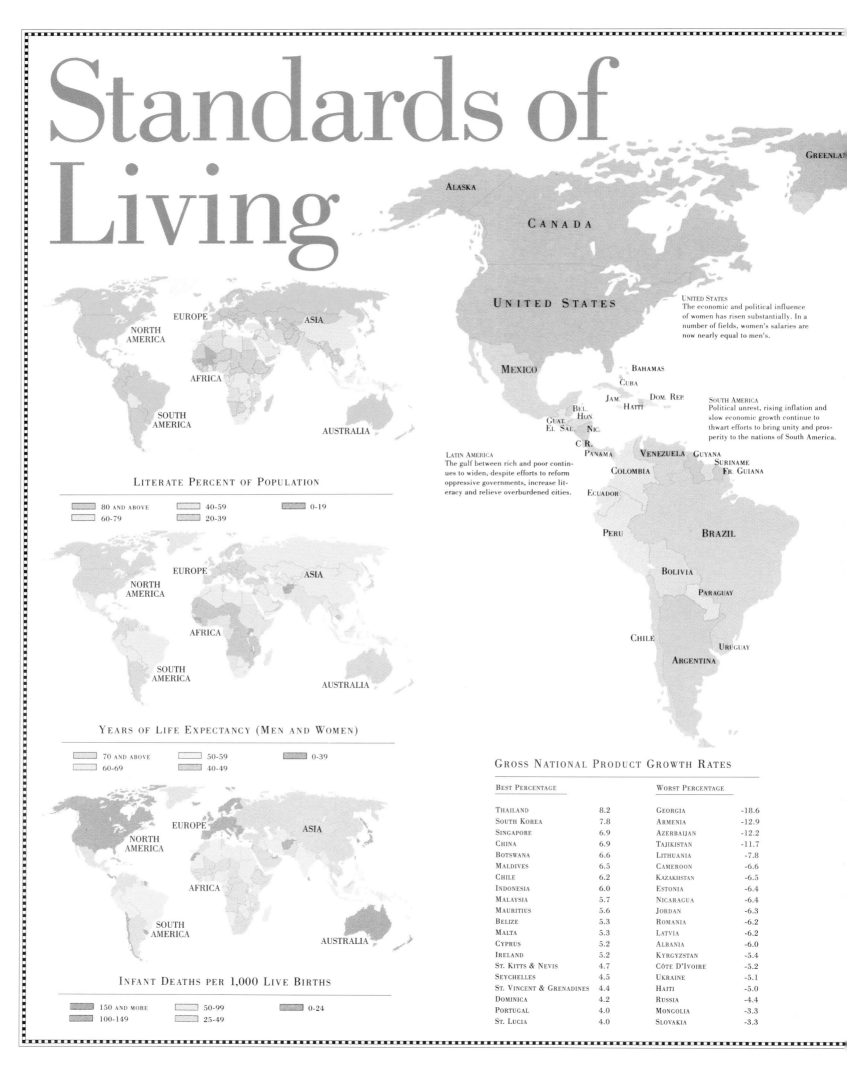

LITERATE PERCENT OF POPULATION

80 AND ABOVE	40-59	0-19
60-79	20-39	

YEARS OF LIFE EXPECTANCY (MEN AND WOMEN)

70 AND ABOVE	50-59	0-39
60-69	40-49	

INFANT DEATHS PER 1,000 LIVE BIRTHS

150 AND MORE	50-99	0-24
100-149	25-49	

UNITED STATES
The economic and political influence of women has risen substantially. In a number of fields, women's salaries are now nearly equal to men's.

SOUTH AMERICA
Political unrest, rising inflation and slow economic growth continue to thwart efforts to bring unity and prosperity to the nations of South America.

LATIN AMERICA
The gulf between rich and poor continues to widen, despite efforts to reform oppressive governments, increase literacy and relieve overburdened cities.

GROSS NATIONAL PRODUCT GROWTH RATES

BEST PERCENTAGE		WORST PERCENTAGE	
THAILAND	8.2	GEORGIA	-18.6
SOUTH KOREA	7.8	ARMENIA	-12.9
SINGAPORE	6.9	AZERBAIJAN	-12.2
CHINA	6.9	TAJIKISTAN	-11.7
BOTSWANA	6.6	LITHUANIA	-7.8
MALDIVES	6.5	CAMEROON	-6.6
CHILE	6.2	KAZAKHSTAN	-6.5
INDONESIA	6.0	ESTONIA	-6.4
MALAYSIA	5.7	NICARAGUA	-6.4
MAURITIUS	5.6	JORDAN	-6.3
BELIZE	5.3	ROMANIA	-6.2
MALTA	5.3	LATVIA	-6.2
CYPRUS	5.2	ALBANIA	-6.0
IRELAND	5.2	KYRGYZSTAN	-5.4
ST. KITTS & NEVIS	4.7	CÔTE D'IVOIRE	-5.2
SEYCHELLES	4.5	UKRAINE	-5.1
ST. VINCENT & GRENADINES	4.4	HAITI	-5.0
DOMINICA	4.2	RUSSIA	-4.4
PORTUGAL	4.0	MONGOLIA	-3.3
ST. LUCIA	4.0	SLOVAKIA	-3.3

EUROPE
The healthy, high-tech economies of many western European nations stand in sharp relief to the obsolete factories, high unemployment and ethnic rivalries of Eastern Europe.

RUSSIA
The struggle to replace Soviet-style socialism with a capitalist economy will create new business opportunities and ultimately bring more food and goods into the stores — at drastically increased prices.

JAPAN
Despite growing affluence, the Japanese endure stressful lifestyles of 50-80 hour work weeks and high prices for most goods, food and housing.

CHINA
The limited relaxation of Communist dogma has encouraged growing industrialization and exports, creating new wealth in parts of China.

MIDDLE EAST
Water has emerged as a significant factor in Middle East politics. Projected water shortages could lead to economic hardship and regional conflicts.

...RICA
...sastrous droughts, discriminatory ...ernment policies and ancient tribal ...alries, particularly in South Africa ...d the Sudan, have resulted in politi-...l instability and economic hardship.

AUSTRALIA
An influx of Japanese tourists and investors is generating new capital and development, escalating coastal real estate prices and regional tensions.

ICELAND, NORWAY, SWEDEN, FINLAND, UNITED KINGDOM, IRELAND, DEN., N., B., GER., POLAND, BEL., UKRAINE, FRANCE, S., C.S., A., HUN., ROM., M., L., Y., A., BUL., ITALY, GR., SPAIN, PORTUGAL, M., TUNISIA, MOROCCO, RUSSIA, KAZAKHSTAN, UZB., G. A. A., TURKM., KYR., TAJ., MONGOLIA, N. KOREA, S. KOREA, JAPAN, TURKEY, C. L. SYR., IRAQ, IRAN, AFGH., CHINA, TAIWAN, ISR. JOR., K., B. Q., U.A.E., SAUDI ARABIA, OMAN, PAKISTAN, NEPAL, BH., BANG., MYANMAR (BURMA), INDIA, LAOS, THAI., VIETNAM, CAM., PHILIPPINES, ALGERIA, LIBYA, EGYPT, YEMEN, W. HARA, MAURITANIA, MALI, NIGER, CHAD, SUDAN, B., INEA, LEONE, B.F., B., NIGERIA, GH., T., LIBERIA, EQ. G., GABON, CAM., C. AF. REP., CONGO, DEM. REP. OF THE CONGO, R. B., UG., KENYA, ETHIOPIA, SOMALIA, SRI LANKA, MALAYSIA, BR., SING., INDONESIA, PAPUA NEW GUINEA, SOLOMON IS., TANZANIA, MAL., COMOROS, VANUATU, ANGOLA, ZAMBIA, MOZAMBIQUE, ZIM., MADAGASCAR, MAURITIUS, NEW CAL., NAMIBIA, BOTS., AUSTRALIA, SOUTH AFRICA, SWAZ., LES., NEW ZEALAND

GROSS NATIONAL PRODUCT PER CAPITA IN DOLLARS

- OVER 8000 PER YEAR
- 5000-8000 PER YEAR
- 2000-5000 PER YEAR
- 1000-2000 PER YEAR
- 500-1000 PER YEAR
- UNDER 500 PER YEAR
- DATA NOT AVAILABLE

TOTAL GROSS NATIONAL PRODUCT
BILLIONS OF DOLLARS

- UNITED STATES 6257
- JAPAN 4321
- GERMANY 2075
- FRANCE 1355
- ITALY 1101
- UNITED KINGDOM 1069
- CHINA 630
- CANADA 569
- BRAZIL 536
- SPAIN 525
- RUSSIA 392
- MEXICO 368
- SOUTH KOREA 366

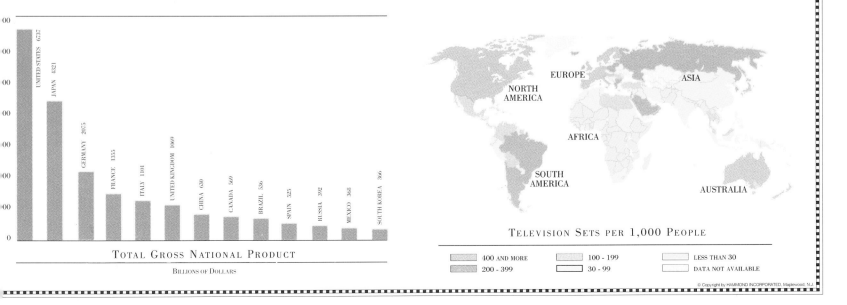

NORTH AMERICA, SOUTH AMERICA, EUROPE, AFRICA, ASIA, AUSTRALIA

TELEVISION SETS PER 1,000 PEOPLE

- 400 AND MORE
- 200 - 399
- 100 - 199
- 30 - 99
- LESS THAN 30
- DATA NOT AVAILABLE

Agriculture & Manufacturing

TOP FIVE WORLD PRODUCERS OF SELECTED AGRICULTURAL COMMODITIES

	1	2	3	4	5
WHEAT	CHINA	UNITED STATES	INDIA	RUSSIA	FRANCE
RICE	CHINA	INDIA	INDONESIA	BANGLADESH	MYANMAR (BURMA)
OATS	RUSSIA	CANADA	UNITED STATES	GERMANY	UKRAINE
CORN (MAIZE)	UNITED STATES	CHINA	BRAZIL	MEXICO	FRANCE
SOYBEANS	UNITED STATES	BRAZIL	CHINA	ARGENTINA	INDIA
POTATOES	CHINA	RUSSIA	POLAND	UNITED STATES	UKRAINE
COFFEE	BRAZIL	COLOMBIA	INDONESIA	MEXICO	ETHIOPIA
TEA	INDIA	CHINA	SRI LANKA	KENYA	TURKEY
TOBACCO	CHINA	UNITED STATES	BRAZIL	INDIA	TURKEY
COTTON	CHINA	UNITED STATES	INDIA	PAKISTAN	UZBEKISTAN
CATTLE (STOCK)	BRAZIL	UNITED STATES	CHINA	ARGENTINA	RUSSIA
SHEEP (STOCK)	AUSTRALIA	CHINA	NEW ZEALAND	RUSSIA	INDIA
HOGS (STOCK)	CHINA	UNITED STATES	BRAZIL	RUSSIA	GERMANY
COW'S MILK	UNITED STATES	RUSSIA	INDIA	GERMANY	FRANCE
HEN'S EGGS	CHINA	UNITED STATES	JAPAN	RUSSIA	INDIA
WOOL	AUSTRALIA	NEW ZEALAND	CHINA	RUSSIA	KAZAKHSTAN
ROUNDWOOD	UNITED STATES	RUSSIA	CHINA	INDIA	BRAZIL
NATURAL RUBBER	THAILAND	INDONESIA	MALAYSIA	INDIA	CHINA
FISH CATCHES	CHINA	JAPAN	PERU	CHILE	RUSSIA

Names in Black Indicate More Than 10% of Total World Production

HERDING
SHIFTING CROPS
LIVESTOCK RANCHING

PERCENT OF TOTAL EMPLOYMENT IN AGRICULTURE, MANUFACTURING AND OTHER INDUSTRIES

AGRICULTURE (INCLUDES FORESTRY AND FISHING)
MANUFACTURING
CONSTRUCTION
TRADE AND COMMERCE
FINANCE, INSURANCE, REAL ESTATE
SERVICES
OTHER (INCLUDES MINING, UTILITIES, TRANSPORTATION)

0   20   40   60   80   100

India
China
Indonesia
Pakistan
Mexico
Brazil
Spain
Argentina
Italy
Japan
France
Canada
Australia
Germany
United States
United Kingdom

Finance, Insurance, Real Estate Data Included With "Other" for India, China, Indonesia and Pakistan

SEATTLE - TACOMA
CHICAGO - GA
SAN FRANCISCO - SAN JOSE
ST. LOUI
DETRO
SOUTHERN CALIFORNIA
HOUS
MEXICO CITY - PUEBLA
SANTIAGO - VALPARAI

AIRCRAFT
MOTOR VEHICLES
SHIPBUILDING

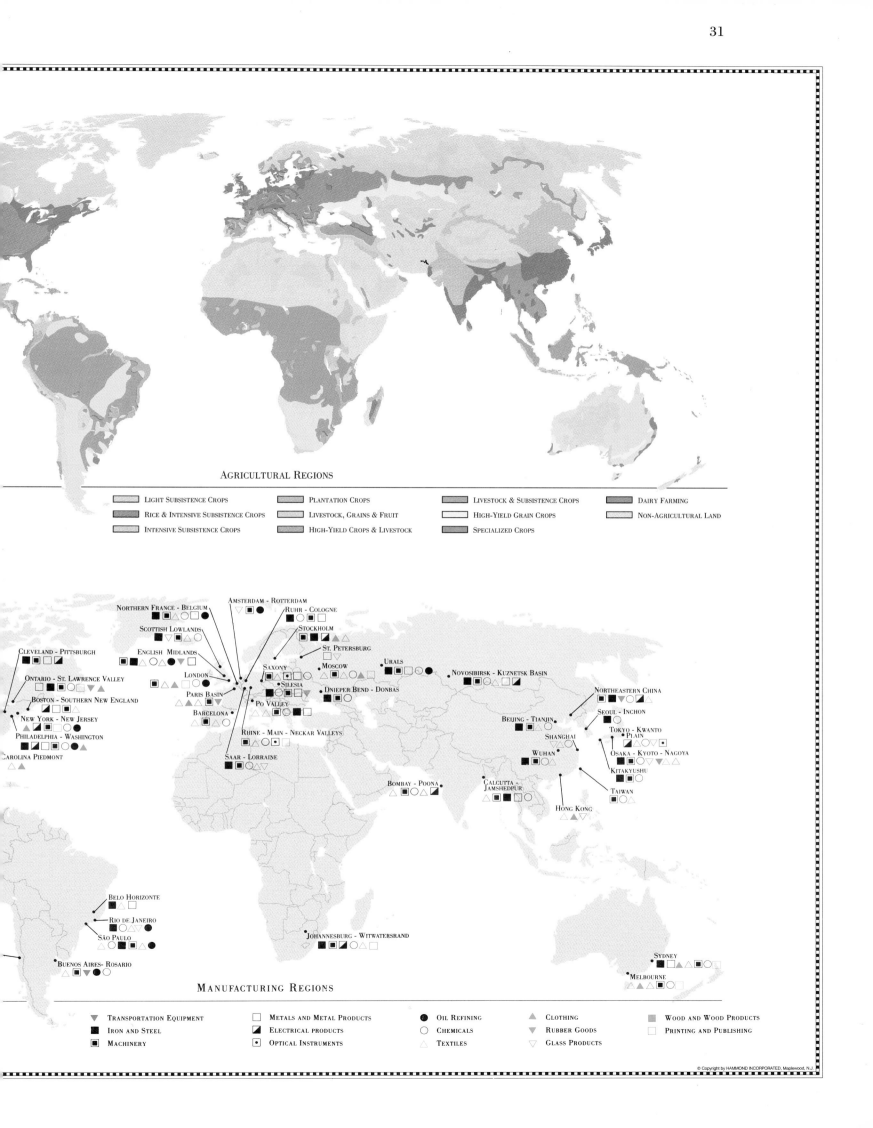

AGRICULTURAL REGIONS

- LIGHT SUBSISTENCE CROPS
- RICE & INTENSIVE SUBSISTENCE CROPS
- INTENSIVE SUBSISTENCE CROPS
- PLANTATION CROPS
- LIVESTOCK, GRAINS & FRUIT
- HIGH-YIELD CROPS & LIVESTOCK
- LIVESTOCK & SUBSISTENCE CROPS
- HIGH-YIELD GRAIN CROPS
- SPECIALIZED CROPS
- DAIRY FARMING
- NON-AGRICULTURAL LAND

MANUFACTURING REGIONS

AMSTERDAM - ROTTERDAM
NORTHERN FRANCE - BELGIUM
RUHR - COLOGNE
SCOTTISH LOWLANDS
STOCKHOLM
CLEVELAND - PITTSBURGH
ST. PETERSBURG
ENGLISH MIDLANDS
SAXONY
URALS
MOSCOW
NOVOSIBIRSK - KUZNETSK BASIN
ONTARIO - ST. LAWRENCE VALLEY
LONDON
SILESIA
BOSTON - SOUTHERN NEW ENGLAND
PARIS BASIN
DNIEPER BEND - DONBAS
NORTHEASTERN CHINA
NEW YORK - NEW JERSEY
PO VALLEY
BEIJING - TIANJIN
SEOUL - INCHON
PHILADELPHIA - WASHINGTON
BARCELONA
SHANGHAI
TOKYO - KWANTO PLAIN
CAROLINA PIEDMONT
RHINE - MAIN - NECKAR VALLEYS
OSAKA - KYOTO - NAGOYA
SAAR - LORRAINE
WUHAN
KITAKYUSHU
BOMBAY - POONA
CALCUTTA - JAMSHEDPUR
TAIWAN
HONG KONG

BELO HORIZONTE
RIO DE JANEIRO
SÃO PAULO
JOHANNESBURG - WITWATERSRAND
SYDNEY
BUENOS AIRES - ROSARIO
MELBOURNE

- ▼ TRANSPORTATION EQUIPMENT
- ■ IRON AND STEEL
- ▣ MACHINERY
- □ METALS AND METAL PRODUCTS
- ◪ ELECTRICAL PRODUCTS
- ⊡ OPTICAL INSTRUMENTS
- ● OIL REFINING
- ○ CHEMICALS
- △ TEXTILES
- ▲ CLOTHING
- ▼ RUBBER GOODS
- ▽ GLASS PRODUCTS
- ▨ WOOD AND WOOD PRODUCTS
- □ PRINTING AND PUBLISHING

© Copyright by HAMMOND INCORPORATED, Maplewood, N.J.

Energy & Resources

TOP FIVE WORLD PRODUCERS OF SELECTED MINERAL COMMODITIES

MINERAL FUELS	1	2	3	4	5
CRUDE OIL	SAUDI ARABIA	RUSSIA	UNITED STATES	IRAN	CHINA
GASOLINE	UNITED STATES	RUSSIA	JAPAN	CHINA	UNITED KINGDOM
NATURAL GAS	RUSSIA	UNITED STATES	CANADA	NETHERLANDS	TURKMENISTAN
COAL (AND LIGNITE)	CHINA	UNITED STATES	RUSSIA	GERMANY	INDIA
URANIUM-BEARING ORES	CANADA	NIGER	KAZAKHSTAN	RUSSIA	UZBEKISTAN

METALS	1	2	3	4	5
CHROMITE	KAZAKHSTAN	SOUTH AFRICA	INDIA	FINLAND	TURKEY
IRON ORE	BRAZIL	AUSTRALIA	CHINA	RUSSIA	UKRAINE
MANGANESE ORE	UKRAINE	CHINA	SOUTH AFRICA	AUSTRALIA	BRAZIL
MINE NICKEL	RUSSIA	CANADA	NEW CALEDONIA	INDONESIA	AUSTRALIA
MINE SILVER	MEXICO	UNITED STATES	PERU	AUSTRALIA	CANADA
BAUXITE	AUSTRALIA	GUINEA	JAMAICA	BRAZIL	RUSSIA
ALUMINUM	UNITED STATES	RUSSIA	CANADA	AUSTRALIA	CHINA
MINE GOLD	SOUTH AFRICA	UNITED STATES	AUSTRALIA	CHINA	CANADA
MINE COPPER	CHILE	UNITED STATES	CANADA	RUSSIA	PERU
MINE LEAD	AUSTRALIA	CHINA	UNITED STATES	PERU	CANADA
MINE TIN	CHINA	INDONESIA	BRAZIL	BOLIVIA	PERU
MINE ZINC	CANADA	AUSTRALIA	CHINA	PERU	UNITED STATES

NONMETALS	1	2	3	4	5
NATURAL DIAMOND	AUSTRALIA	BOTSWANA	RUSSIA	DEM. REP. CONGO	SOUTH AFRICA
POTASH	CANADA	GERMANY	RUSSIA	BELARUS	UNITED STATES
PHOSPHATE ROCK	UNITED STATES	CHINA	MOROCCO	RUSSIA	KAZAKHSTAN
SULFUR (ALL FORMS)	UNITED STATES	CANADA	CHINA	JAPAN	POLAND

Names in Black Indicate More Than 10% of Total World Production

COMMERCIAL ENERGY PRODUCTION/CONSUMPTION

PERCENTAGE OF WORLD TOTAL

- PRODUCTION
- CONSUMPTION

United States 20% / 25%

Russia 12% / 17.2%

China 9% / 8.9%

Saudi Arabia 5.8% / 0.9%

Canada 3.6% / 2.7%

United Kingdom 2.7% / 2.9%

Iran 2.5% / 0.9%

Mexico 2.4% / 1.5%

India 2.3% / 2.8%

Indonesia 2.0% / 0.7%

Germany 2.0% / 4.3%

Australia 2% / 1.2%

Venezuela 1.9% / 0.6%

Norway 1.8% / 0.3%

NATIONS WITH HIGHEST PERCENTAGE OF NUCLEAR POWER PRODUCTION

- NUCLEAR
- THERMAL
- HYDROELECTRIC

Belgium 98% / 1% / 1%

France 75% / 11% / 14%

South Korea 71% / 21% / 8%

Japan 65% / 9% / 26%

Finland 58% / 42%

Sweden 43% / 57%

Spain 41% / 40% / 19%

Switzerland 39% / 61%

Germany 26% / 71% / 3%

Hungary 22% / 78%

Ukraine 21% / 77% / 2%

Bulgaria 17% / 80% / 3%

United Kingdom 11% / 88% / 1%

United States 10% / 86% / 4%

Map legend

- OIL FIELDS
- NATURAL GAS FIELDS
- MAJOR COAL DEPOSITS
- OIL SANDS
- OIL SHALE
- MAJOR URANIUM DEPOSITS
- IMPORTANT PEAT DEPOSITS

IRON AND FERROALLOY METALS

1	COBALT	5	MOLYBDENUM
2	CHROMIUM	6	NICKEL
3	IRON ORE	7	VANADIUM
4	MANGANESE	8	TUNGSTEN

OTHER METALS

1	SILVER	7	PLATINUM
2	BAUXITE	8	ANTIMONY
3	GOLD	9	TIN
4	COPPER	10	TITANIUM
5	MERCURY	11	ZINC
6	LEAD		

NONMETALS

1	ASBESTOS	10	MICA
2	BORAX	11	NITRATES
3	DIAMONDS	12	OPALS
4	EMERALDS	13	PHOSPHATES
5	FLUORSPAR	14	PEARLS
6	GRAPHITE	15	RUBIES
7	IODINE	16	SULFUR
8	JADE	17	SAPPHIRES
9	POTASH		

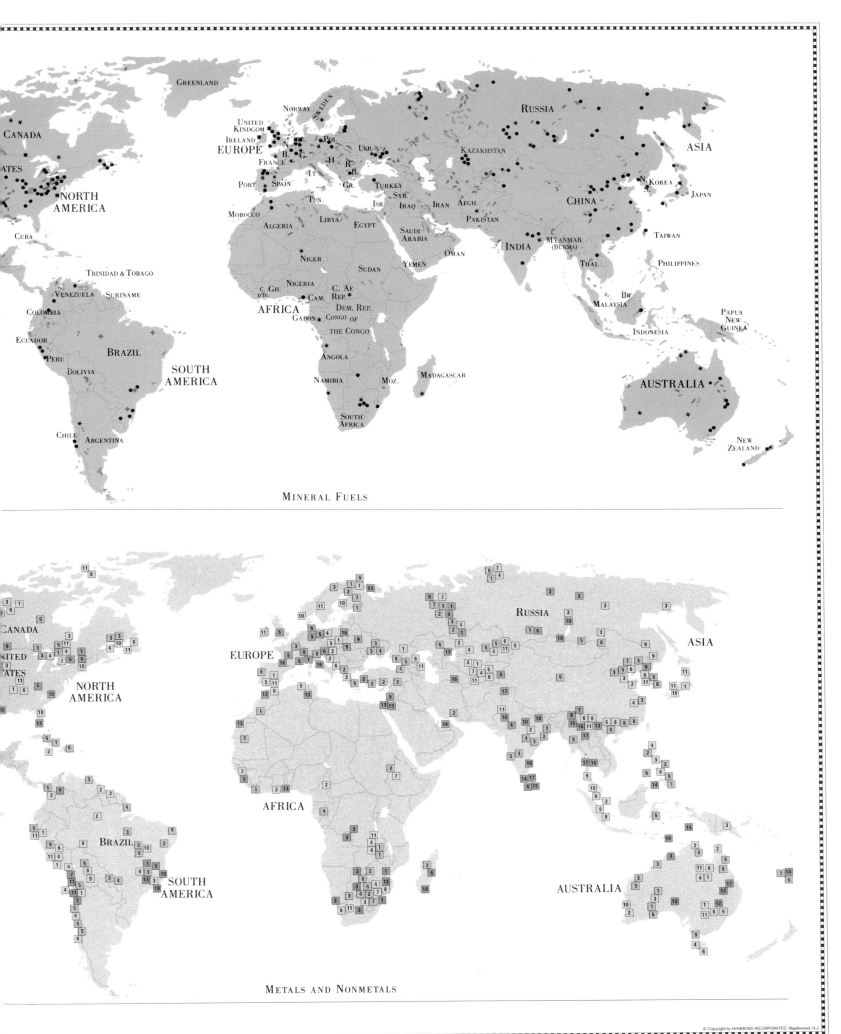

MINERAL FUELS

METALS AND NONMETALS

Transportation & Trade

WORLD EXPORTS BY REGIONS

PERCENT (BY VALUE) OF TOTAL EXPORTS

- To EUROPEAN COMMUNITY
- To UNITED STATES
- To ASIA (EXCLUDING JAPAN)
- To JAPAN
- To EUROPEAN FREE TRADE ASSN.
- To CANADA
- To LATIN AMERICA
- To AFRICA
- To OTHERS

EUROPEAN COMMUNITY
| 25 | 20 | 17 | 8 | 5 | 5 | 20 |

UNITED STATES
| 24 | 20 | 20 | 15 | 12 | 9 |

ASIA (EXCLUDING JAPAN)
| 33 | 25 | 22 | 20 |

JAPAN
| 37 | 29 | 19 | 4 | 11 |

EUROPEAN FREE TRADE ASSN.
| 68 | 9 | 7 | 16 |

CANADA
| 76 | 8 | 6 | 5 | 5 |

LATIN AMERICA
| 43 | 30 | 8 | 7 | 12 |

AFRICA
| 62 | 20 | 6 | 12 |

AUSTRALIA AND NEW ZEALAND
| 35 | 28 | 13 | 11 | 13 |

TRADE BALANCES OF LEADING EXPORT NATIONS

VALUE IN BILLIONS OF DOLLARS

ANNUAL EXPORTS   ANNUAL IMPORTS   (DATA BASED ON AVERAGE, 1992-1994)

| 0 | 50 | 100 | 150 | 150 | 200 | 300 | 400 | 500 | 600 |

United States 468 / 596

Germany 402 / 363

Japan 365 / 249

France 244 / 240

United Kingdom 192 / 215

Italy 179 / 175

Canada 140 / 131

Belgium 117 / 120

China 99 / 100

Taiwan 87 / 78

South Korea 85 / 88

Spain 69 / 95

Sweden 55 / 48

| 0 | 50 | 100 |

Mexico 46 / 64

Australia 45 / 44

Russia 43 / 33

Saudi Arabia 43 / 27

Brazil 39 / 26

Indonesia 36 / 28

Thailand 35 / 44

South Africa 24 / 19

India 22 / 24

Iran 16 / 21

Turkey 15 / 24

Venezuela 15 / 10

Argentina 14 / 17

ANCHORAGE

SEATTLE
DENVER
SAN FRANCISCO
PHOENIX
LOS ANGELES
DALLAS

MEXICO CITY

VANCOUVER
SEATTLE
YOKO-HAMA
SAN FRANCISCO
LOS ANGELES
HOUST

MANILA

SYDNEY

AUCKLAND,
SYDNEY

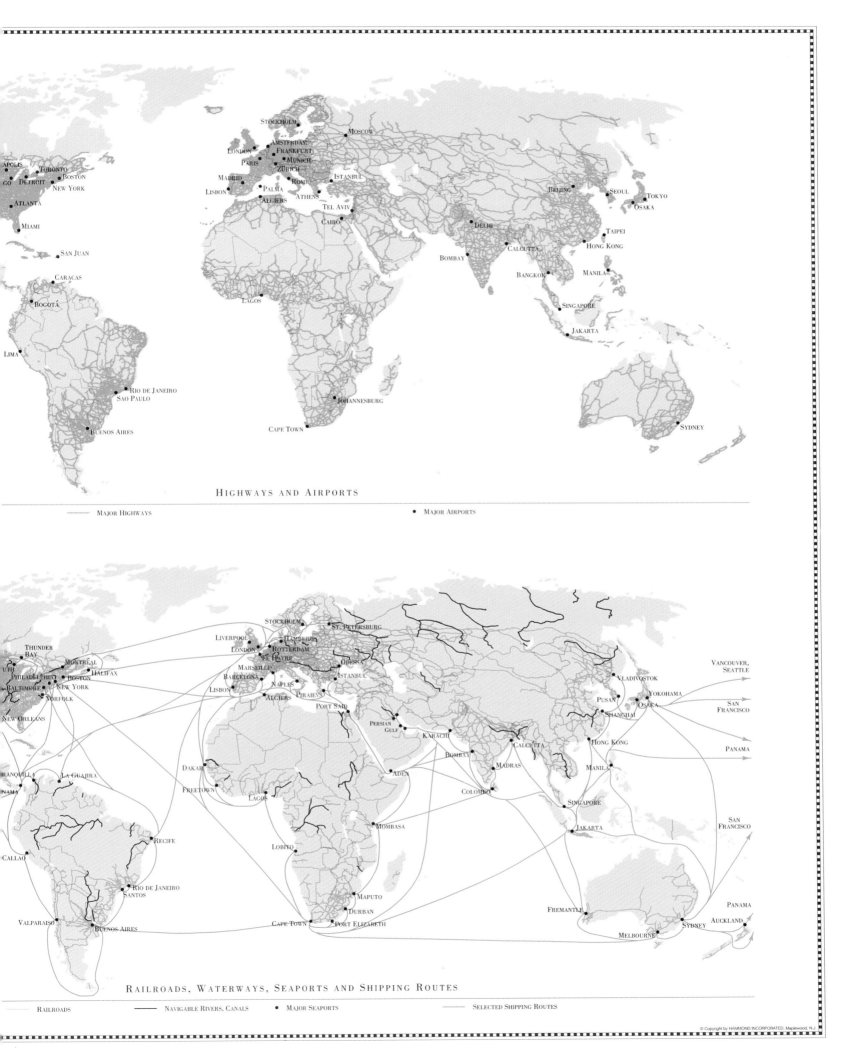

HIGHWAYS AND AIRPORTS

MAJOR HIGHWAYS   ● MAJOR AIRPORTS

RAILROADS, WATERWAYS, SEAPORTS AND SHIPPING ROUTES

RAILROADS   NAVIGABLE RIVERS, CANALS   ● MAJOR SEAPORTS   SELECTED SHIPPING ROUTES

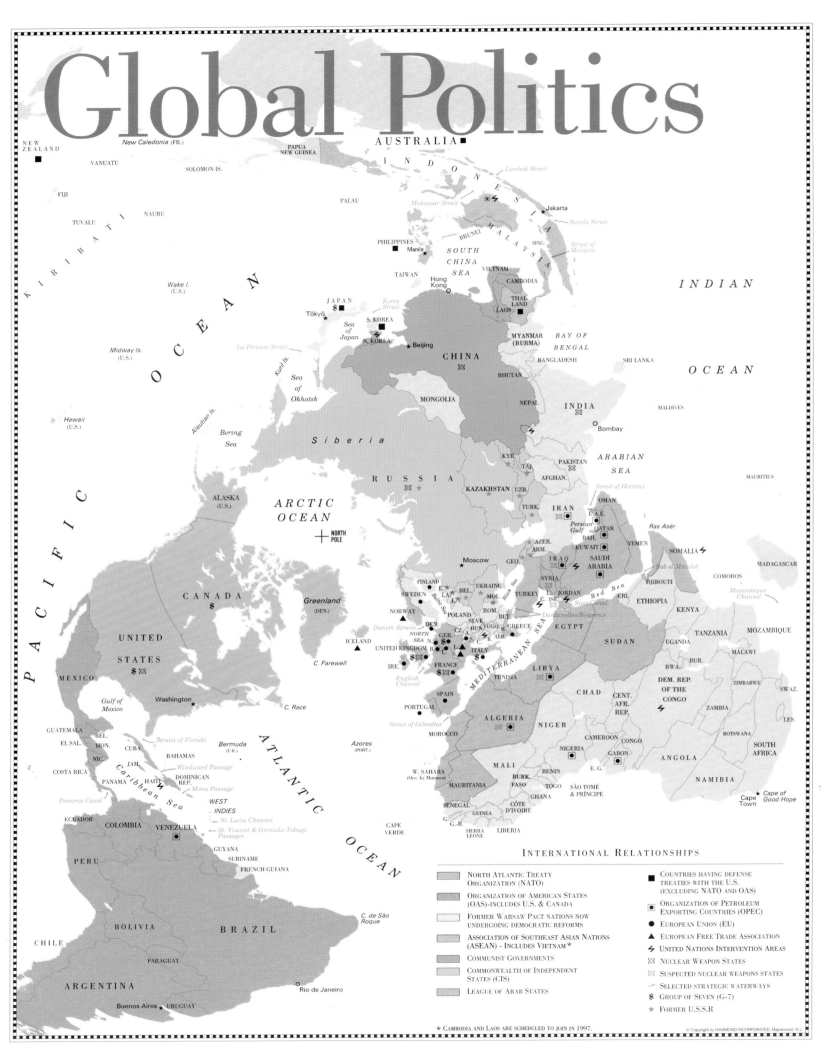

Regional Maps

Globe circa 1955

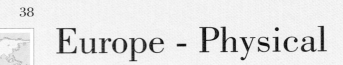

Europe - Physical

SCALE 1:21,000,000   OPTIMAL CONFORMAL PROJECTION

MILES
KILOMETERS

0   300   600   900

POPULATION OF CITIES AND TOWNS

◻ OVER 3,000,000
◻ 1,000,000 - 2,999,999
⊛ 500,000 - 999,999
⊛ 100,000 - 499,999
○ UNDER 100,000

Europe - Political

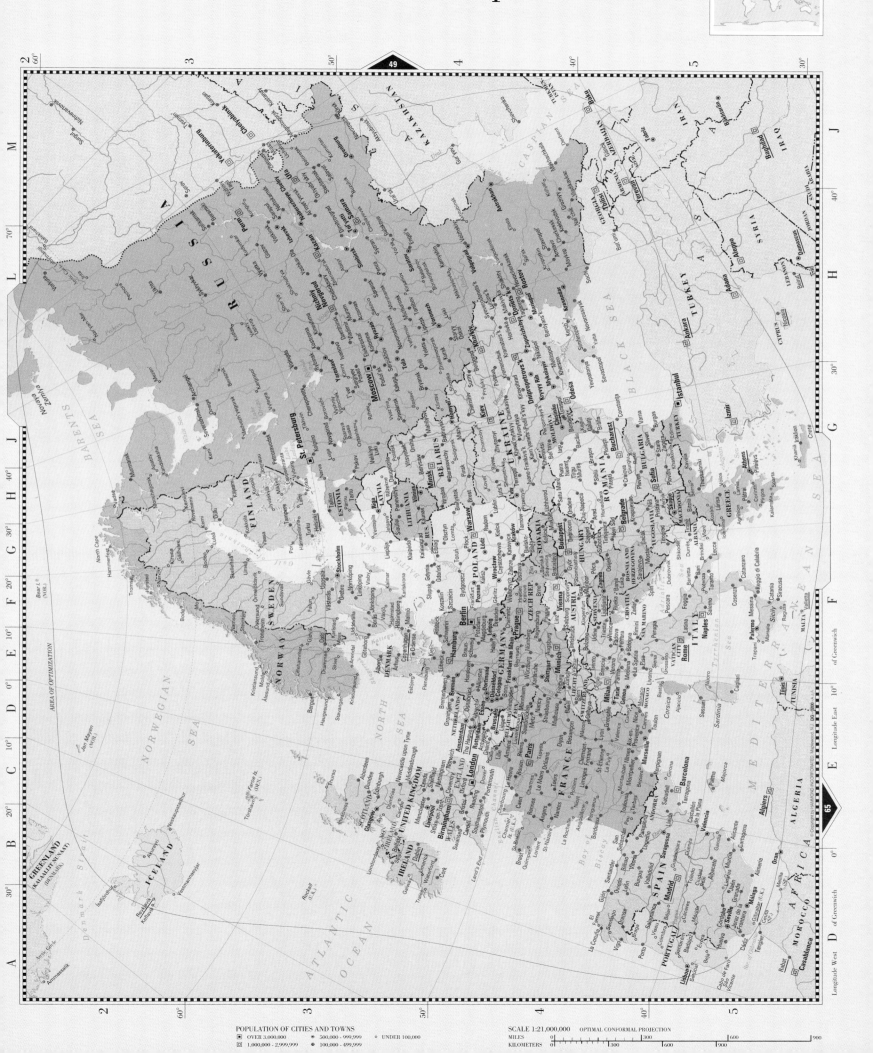

POPULATION OF CITIES AND TOWNS

■ OVER 3,000,000 ● 500,000 - 999,999 ○ UNDER 100,000

▣ 1,000,000 - 2,999,999 ● 100,000 - 499,999

SCALE 1:21,000,000 OPTIMAL CONFORMAL PROJECTION

MILES 0 300 600 900

KILOMETERS 0 300 600

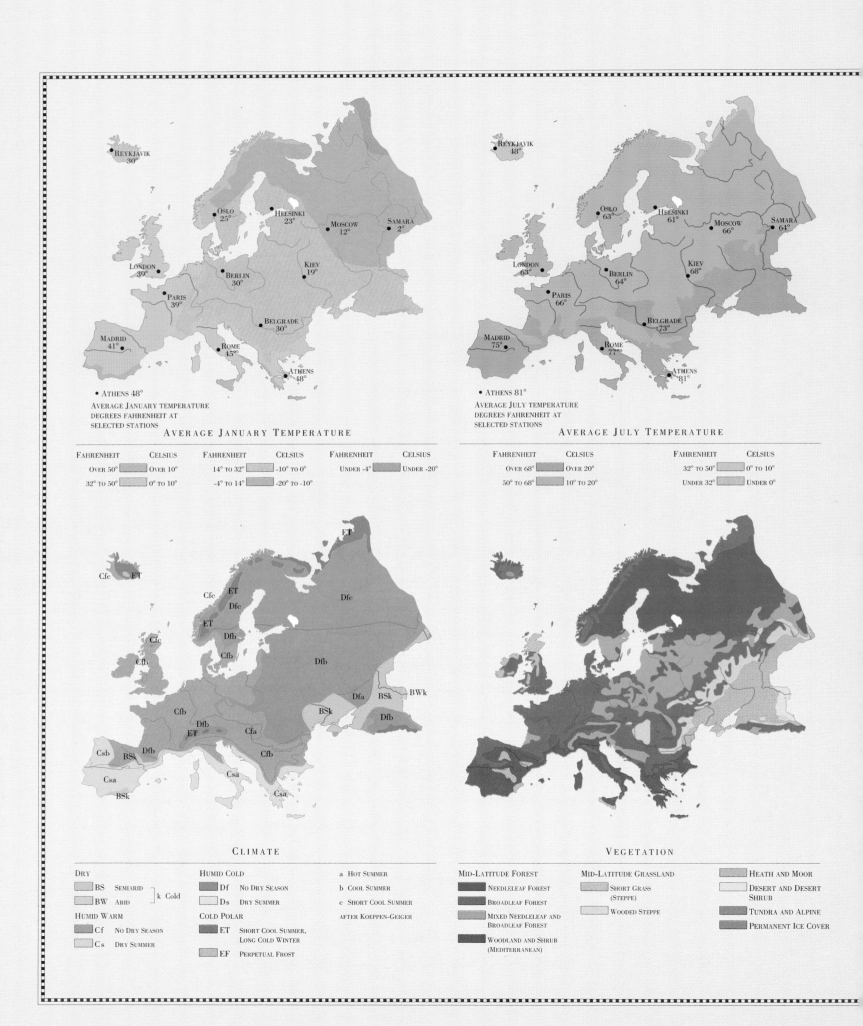

Europe - Comparisons

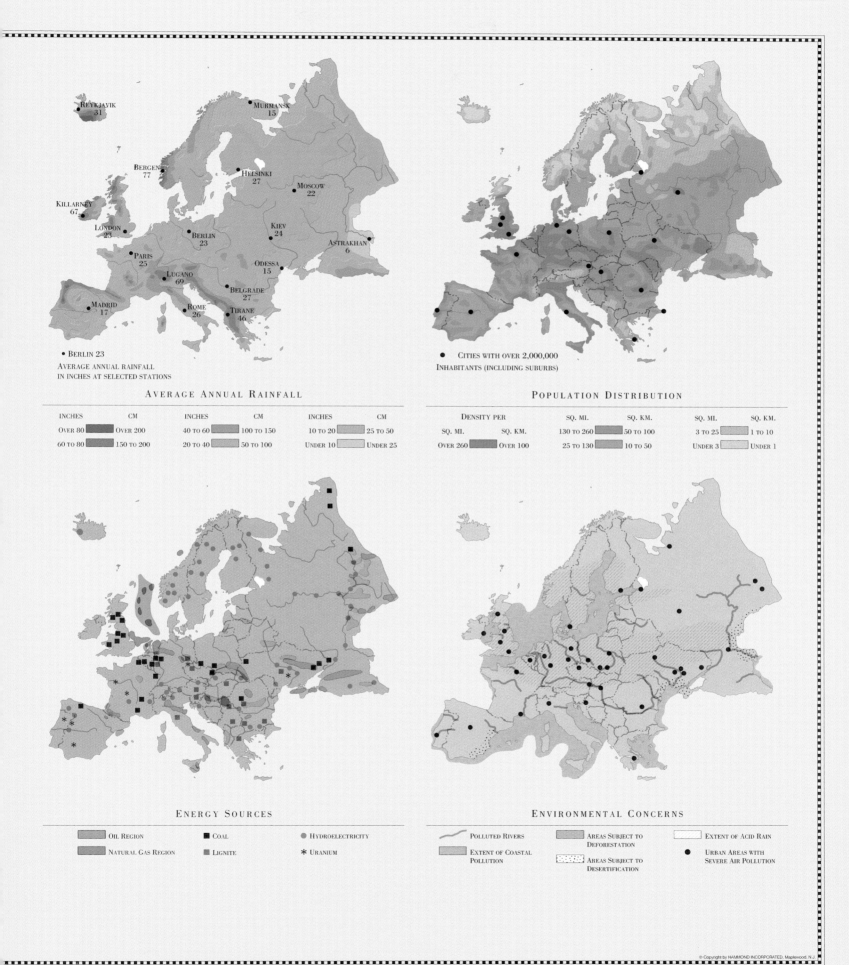

AVERAGE ANNUAL RAINFALL

REYKJAVIK 31
MURMANSK 15
BERGEN 77
HELSINKI 27
MOSCOW 22
KILLARNEY 67
LONDON 23
BERLIN 23
KIEV 24
ASTRAKHAN 6
PARIS 25
ODESSA 15
LUGANO 69
BELGRADE 27
MADRID 17
ROME 26
TIRANE 46

• BERLIN 23
AVERAGE ANNUAL RAINFALL
IN INCHES AT SELECTED STATIONS

INCHES	CM	INCHES	CM	INCHES	CM
OVER 80	OVER 200	40 TO 60	100 TO 150	10 TO 20	25 TO 50
60 TO 80	150 TO 200	20 TO 40	50 TO 100	UNDER 10	UNDER 25

POPULATION DISTRIBUTION

• CITIES WITH OVER 2,000,000
INHABITANTS (INCLUDING SUBURBS)

DENSITY PER		SQ. MI.	SQ. KM.	SQ. MI.	SQ. KM.
SQ. MI.	SQ. KM.	130 TO 260	50 TO 100	3 TO 25	1 TO 10
OVER 260	OVER 100	25 TO 130	10 TO 50	UNDER 3	UNDER 1

ENERGY SOURCES

	OIL REGION		COAL		HYDROELECTRICITY
	NATURAL GAS REGION		LIGNITE	∗	URANIUM

ENVIRONMENTAL CONCERNS

	POLLUTED RIVERS		AREAS SUBJECT TO DEFORESTATION		EXTENT OF ACID RAIN
	EXTENT OF COASTAL POLLUTION		AREAS SUBJECT TO DESERTIFICATION	•	URBAN AREAS WITH SEVERE AIR POLLUTION

Western Europe

POPULATION OF CITIES AND TOWNS

■ OVER 2,000,000	● 500,000 - 999,999
▢ 1,000,000 - 1,999,999	◉ 250,000 - 499,999

● 100,000 - 249,999
○ 30,000 - 99,999

● 10,000 - 29,999
○ UNDER 10,000

Northern Europe

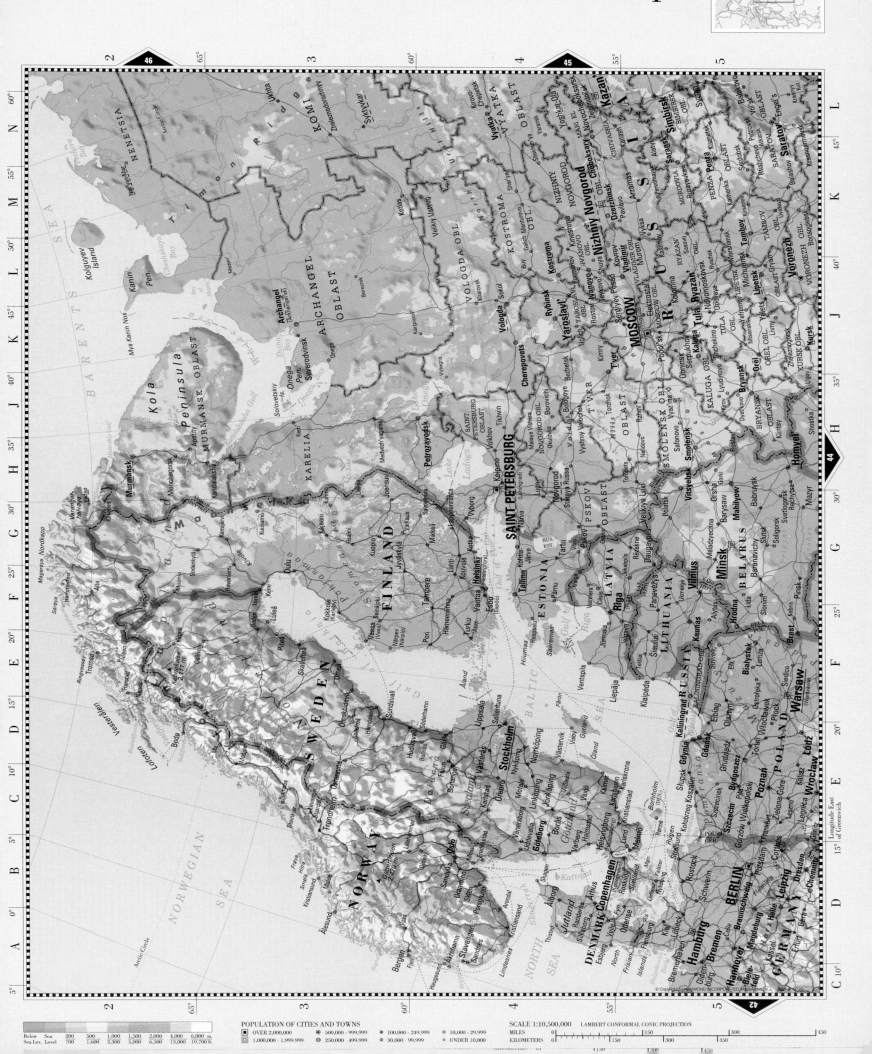

Below Sea	200	500	1,000	1,500	2,000	4,000	6,000 m.
Sea Lev. Level	700	1,600	3,300	5,000	6,500	13,000	19,700 ft.

POPULATION OF CITIES AND TOWNS

■ OVER 2,000,000   ● 500,000 - 999,999   ● 100,000 - 249,999   ◦ 10,000 - 29,999
□ 1,000,000 - 1,999,999   ● 250,000 - 499,999   ● 30,000 - 99,999   ◦ UNDER 10,000

SCALE 1:10,500,000   LAMBERT CONFORMAL CONIC PROJECTION

MILES   0   150   300   450
KILOMETERS   0   150   300   450

© Copyright by HAMMOND INCORPORATED, Maplewood, N.J.

Northern Europe

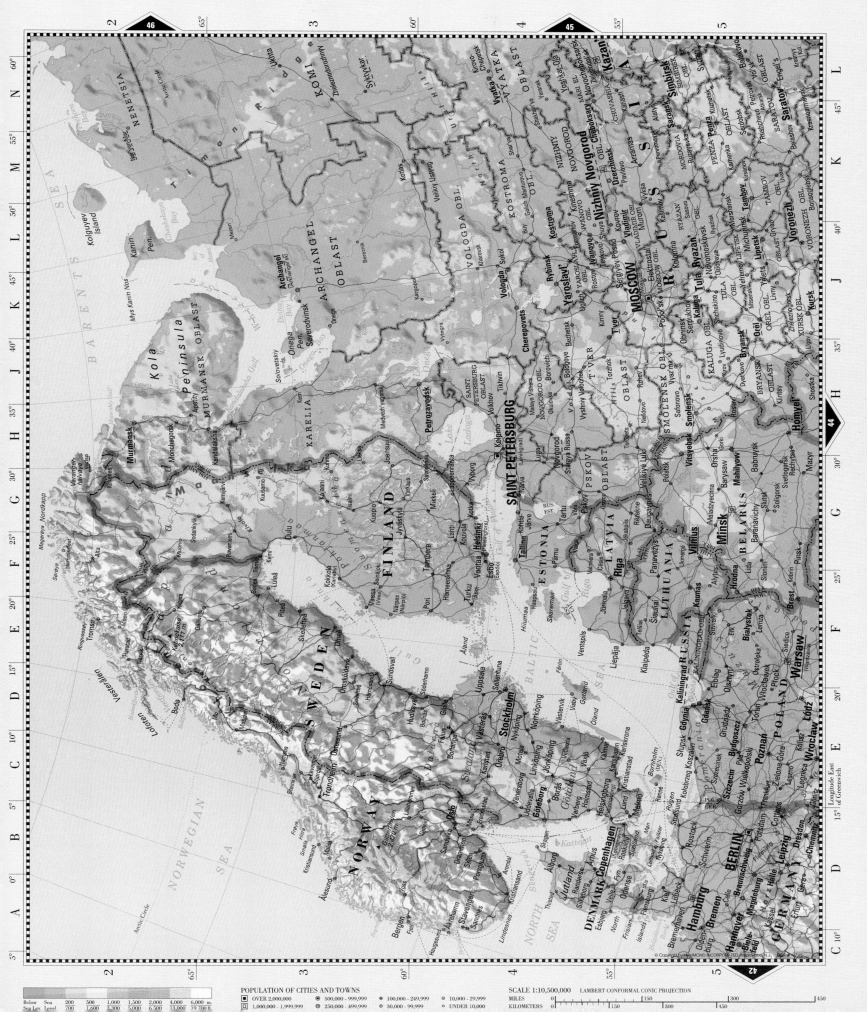

POPULATION OF CITIES AND TOWNS

| ▪ OVER 2,000,000 | ● 500,000 - 999,999 | ⊕ 100,000 - 249,999 | ○ 10,000 - 29,999 |
| ▫ 1,000,000 - 1,999,999 | ⊙ 250,000 - 499,999 | ⊕ 30,000 - 99,999 | · UNDER 10,000 |

SCALE 1:10,500,000   LAMBERT CONFORMAL CONIC PROJECTION

MILES 0   150   300   450

KILOMETERS 0   150   300   450

South Central Europe

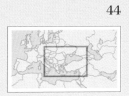

SCALE 1:10,500,000   LAMBERT CONFORMAL CONIC PROJECTION

MILES   0   150   300   450

KILOMETERS   0   150   300   450

POPULATION OF CITIES AND TOWNS

| ■ OVER 2,000,000 | ◉ 500,000 - 999,999 | ● 100,000 - 249,999 | ⊙ 10,000 - 29,999 |
| □ 1,000,000 - 1,999,999 | ◎ 250,000 - 499,999 | ⊚ 30,000 - 99,999 | ○ UNDER 10,000 |

| Below Sea | 200 | 500 | 1,000 | 1,500 | 2,000 | 4,000 | 6,000 m. |
| Sea Lev. Level | 700 | 1,600 | 3,300 | 5,000 | 6,500 | 13,000 | 19,700 ft. |

© Copyright by HAMMOND INCORPORATED, Maplewood, N.J.   GG·�’·A·¹⁄₄

Central Eurasia

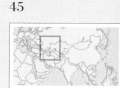

POPULATION OF CITIES AND TOWNS

SCALE 1:10,500,000 LAMBERT CONFORMAL CONIC PROJECTION

| ■ OVER 2,000,000 | ◉ 500,000 - 999,999 | ● 100,000 - 249,999 | ○ 10,000 - 29,999 |
| ▣ 1,000,000 - 1,999,999 | ◉ 250,000 - 499,999 | ○ 30,000 - 99,999 | ○ UNDER 10,000 |

MILES

KILOMETERS

Below Sea 200 500 1,000 1,500 2,000 4,000 6,000 m.
Sea Lev. Level 700 1,600 3,300 5,000 6,500 13,000 19,700 ft.

Russia and Neighboring Countries

Administrative Divisions bear same names
as their respective capitals, except:

Ukraine
1. Krym (Crimea)
2. Zakarpats'ka
3. Volyn

Georgia
4. Abkhazia
5. Ajaria

Azerbaijan
6. Nagorno-Karabakh

Russia
7. Dagestan
8. Ingushetia, Chechnya
9. North Ossetia
10. Kabardino-Balkaria
11. Karachay-Cherkessia
12. Adygea
13. Kalmykia
14. Mordovia
15. Chuvashia
16. Mari El
17. Tatarstan
18. Bashkortostan
19. Udmurtia
20. Permyakia
21. Khakassia
22. Ust'-Orda Buryat
23. Aga Buryat
24. Nizhnegorod

Kazakhstan
25. Soltustik Qazaqstan
26. Ongtustik Qazaqstan

Kyrgyzstan
27. Issyk-Kul' Oblast
28. Chuy

Tajikistan
29. Khatlon
30. Leninobad

Uzbekistan
31. Sidaryo
32. Surkhondaryo
33. Qashqadaryo
34. Khorazm

POPULATION OF CITIES AND TOWNS

■ OVER 2,000,000	● 500,000 - 999,999	⊙ 50,000 - 99,999
▣ 1,000,000 - 1,999,999	◉ 100,000 - 499,999	○ UNDER 50,000

SCALE 1:21,000,000   LAMBERT CONFORMAL CONIC PROJECTION

MILES 0 ___ 300 ___ 600

KILOMETERS 0 ___ 300 ___ 600 ___ 900

Asia-Physical

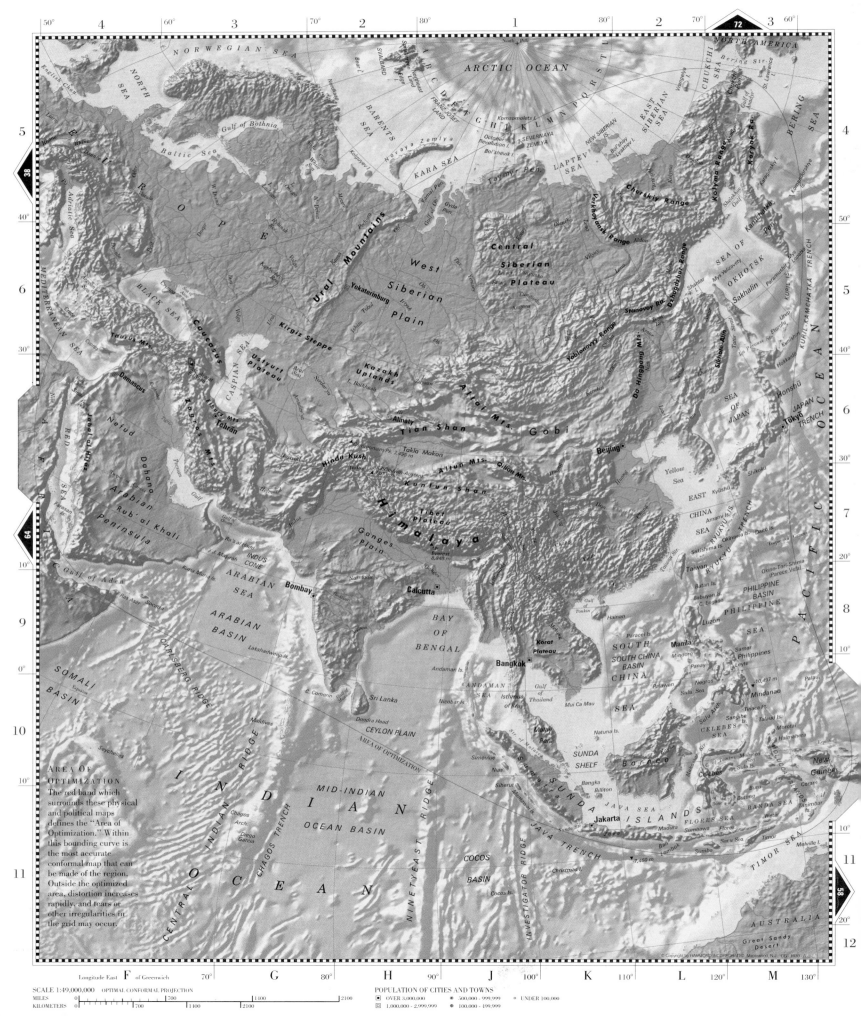

Asia - Political

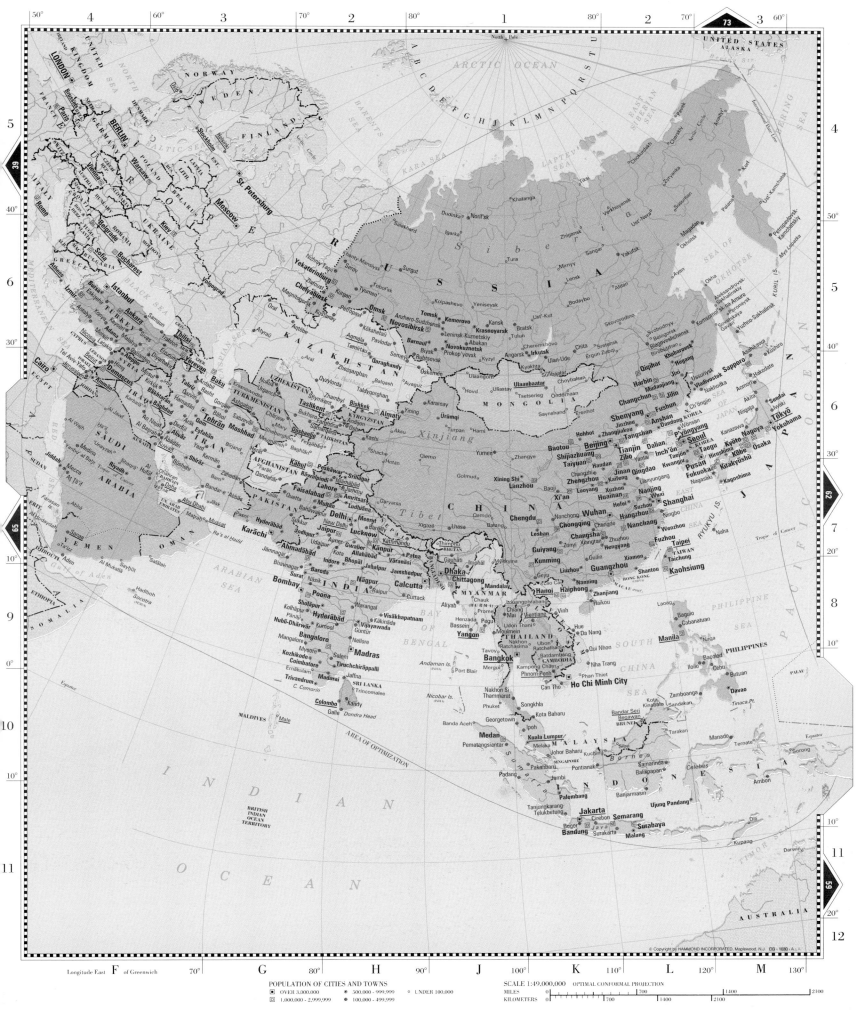

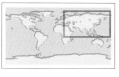

POPULATION OF CITIES AND TOWNS

| ■ OVER 3,000,000 | ● 500,000 - 999,999 | ○ UNDER 100,000 |
| ▣ 1,000,000 - 2,999,999 | ◉ 100,000 - 499,999 | |

SCALE 1:49,000,000 OPTIMAL CONFORMAL PROJECTION

MILES 0   700   1400   2100

KILOMETERS 0   700   1400   2100

Longitude East F of Greenwich

© Copyright by HAMMOND INCORPORATED, Maplewood, N.J. OG · 1030 · A · A

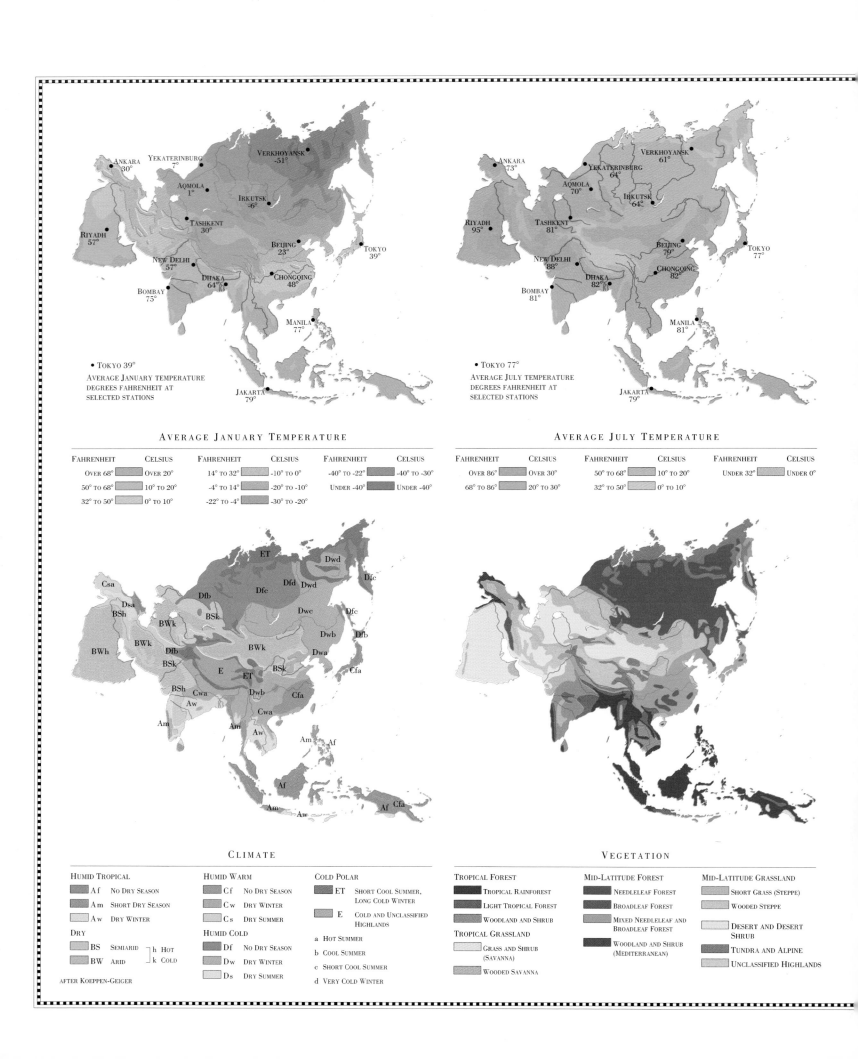

• TOKYO 39°
AVERAGE JANUARY TEMPERATURE
DEGREES FAHRENHEIT AT
SELECTED STATIONS

• TOKYO 77°
AVERAGE JULY TEMPERATURE
DEGREES FAHRENHEIT AT
SELECTED STATIONS

AVERAGE JANUARY TEMPERATURE

FAHRENHEIT	CELSIUS	FAHRENHEIT	CELSIUS	FAHRENHEIT	CELSIUS
OVER 68°	OVER 20°	14° TO 32°	-10° TO 0°	-40° TO -22°	-40° TO -30°
50° TO 68°	10° TO 20°	-4° TO 14°	-20° TO -10°	UNDER -40°	UNDER -40°
32° TO 50°	0° TO 10°	-22° TO -4°	-30° TO -20°		

AVERAGE JULY TEMPERATURE

FAHRENHEIT	CELSIUS	FAHRENHEIT	CELSIUS	FAHRENHEIT	CELSIUS
OVER 86°	OVER 30°	50° TO 68°	10° TO 20°	UNDER 32°	UNDER 0°
68° TO 86°	20° TO 30°	32° TO 50°	0° TO 10°		

CLIMATE

HUMID TROPICAL
Af NO DRY SEASON
Am SHORT DRY SEASON
Aw DRY WINTER

DRY
BS SEMIARID   ┐h HOT
BW ARID   ┘k COLD

AFTER KOEPPEN-GEIGER

HUMID WARM
Cf NO DRY SEASON
Cw DRY WINTER
Cs DRY SUMMER

HUMID COLD
Df NO DRY SEASON
Dw DRY WINTER
Ds DRY SUMMER

COLD POLAR
ET SHORT COOL SUMMER,
    LONG COLD WINTER
E   COLD AND UNCLASSIFIED
    HIGHLANDS

a HOT SUMMER
b COOL SUMMER
c SHORT COOL SUMMER
d VERY COLD WINTER

VEGETATION

TROPICAL FOREST
TROPICAL RAINFOREST
LIGHT TROPICAL FOREST
WOODLAND AND SHRUB

TROPICAL GRASSLAND
GRASS AND SHRUB
(SAVANNA)
WOODED SAVANNA

MID-LATITUDE FOREST
NEEDLELEAF FOREST
BROADLEAF FOREST
MIXED NEEDLELEAF AND
BROADLEAF FOREST
WOODLAND AND SHRUB
(MEDITERRANEAN)

MID-LATITUDE GRASSLAND
SHORT GRASS (STEPPE)
WOODED STEPPE
DESERT AND DESERT
SHRUB
TUNDRA AND ALPINE
UNCLASSIFIED HIGHLANDS

Asia - Comparisons

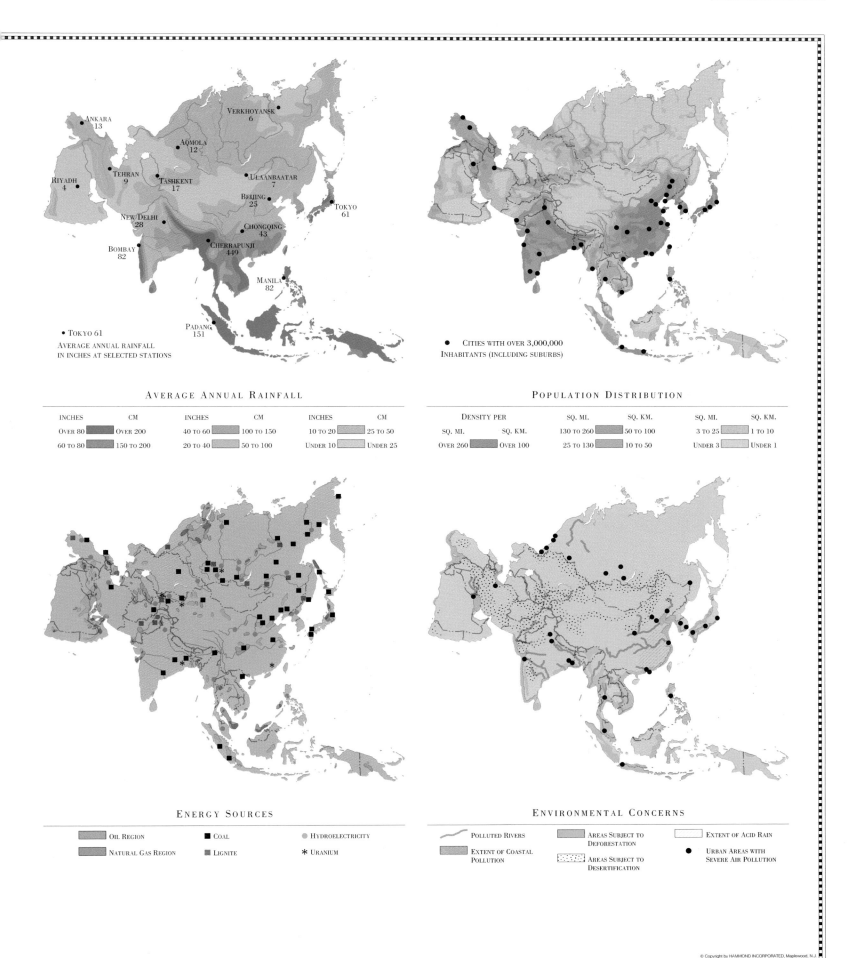

Average Annual Rainfall

• TOKYO 61
AVERAGE ANNUAL RAINFALL
IN INCHES AT SELECTED STATIONS

ANKARA 13
VERKHOYANSK 6
AQMOLA 12
RIYADH 4
TEHRAN 9
TASHKENT 17
ULAANBAATAR 7
BEIJING 25
TOKYO 61
NEW DELHI 28
CHONGQING 43
BOMBAY 82
CHERRAPUNJI 449
MANILA 82
PADANG 151

INCHES	CM	INCHES	CM	INCHES	CM
OVER 80	OVER 200	40 TO 60	100 TO 150	10 TO 20	25 TO 50
60 TO 80	150 TO 200	20 TO 40	50 TO 100	UNDER 10	UNDER 25

Population Distribution

• CITIES WITH OVER 3,000,000
INHABITANTS (INCLUDING SUBURBS)

DENSITY PER		SQ. MI.	SQ. KM.	SQ. MI.	SQ. KM.
SQ. MI.	SQ. KM.	130 TO 260	50 TO 100	3 TO 25	1 TO 10
OVER 260	OVER 100	25 TO 130	10 TO 50	UNDER 3	UNDER 1

Energy Sources

■ OIL REGION	■ COAL	● HYDROELECTRICITY
■ NATURAL GAS REGION	■ LIGNITE	✳ URANIUM

Environmental Concerns

～ POLLUTED RIVERS	AREAS SUBJECT TO DEFORESTATION	EXTENT OF ACID RAIN
EXTENT OF COASTAL POLLUTION	AREAS SUBJECT TO DESERTIFICATION	● URBAN AREAS WITH SEVERE AIR POLLUTION

© Copyright by HAMMOND INCORPORATED, Maplewood, N.J.

Southwestern Asia

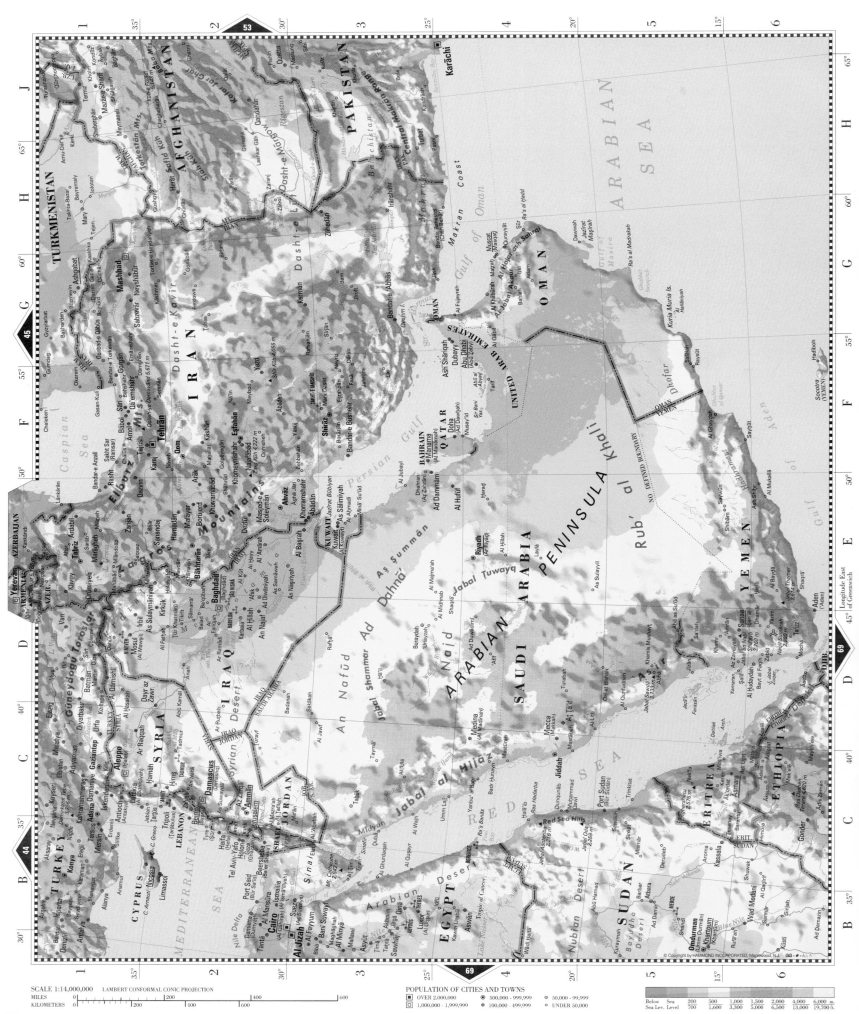

SCALE 1:14,000,000   LAMBERT CONFORMAL CONIC PROJECTION

MILES 0   200   400   600
KILOMETERS 0   200   400   600

POPULATION OF CITIES AND TOWNS

☐ OVER 2,000,000   ● 500,000 - 999,999   ◉ 50,000 - 99,999
☐ 1,000,000 - 1,999,999   ● 100,000 - 499,999   ○ UNDER 50,000

© Copyright by HAMMOND INCORPORATED, Maplewood, N.J.

Below Sea	Sea	200	500	1,000	1,500	2,000	4,000	6,000 m.
Sea Lev. Level		700	1,600	3,300	5,000	6,500	13,000	19,700 ft.

Indian Subcontinent

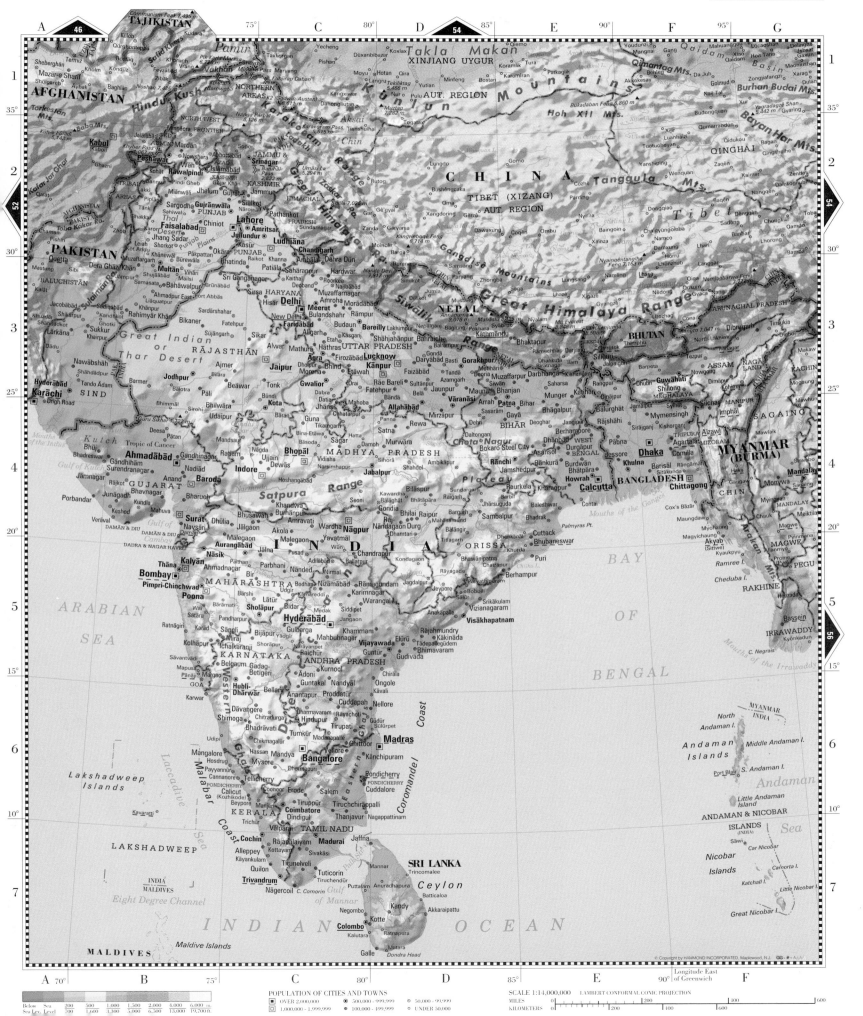

POPULATION OF CITIES AND TOWNS

■ OVER 2,000,000 ● 500,000 - 999,999 ○ 50,000 - 99,999
▣ 1,000,000 - 1,999,999 ● 100,000 - 199,999 ○ UNDER 50,000

SCALE 1:14,000,000 LAMBERT CONFORMAL CONIC PROJECTION

MILES 0 100 200 300 400 600
KILOMETERS 0 200 400 600

© Copyright by HAMMOND INCORPORATED, Maplewood, N.J.

Below Sea 200 500 1,000 1,500 2,000 4,000 6,000 m.
Sea Lev. Level 700 1,600 3,300 5,000 6,500 13,000 19,700 ft.

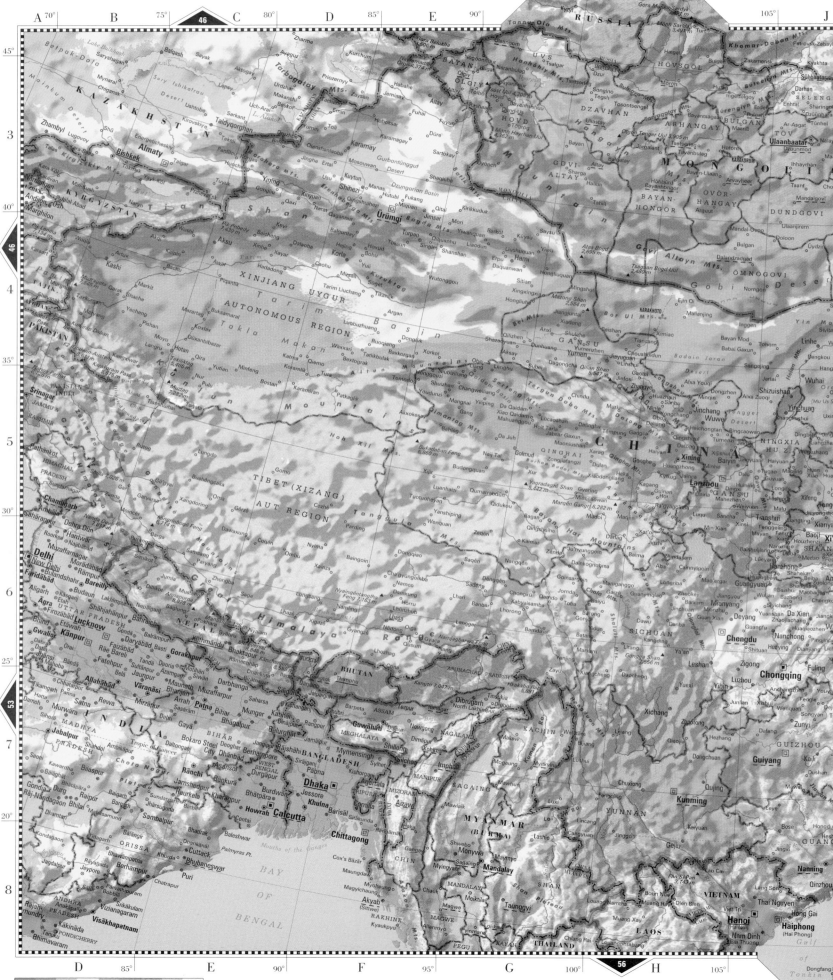

Eastern Asia

POPULATION OF CITIES AND TOWNS

- ☐ OVER 2,000,000
- ☐ 1,000,000 - 1,999,999
- ● 500,000 - 999,999
- ● 100,000 - 499,999
- ◉ 50,000 - 99,999
- ○ UNDER 50,000

SCALE 1:14,000,000   LAMBERT CONFORMAL CONIC PROJECTION

MILES 0   200   400   600

KILOMETERS 0   200   400   600

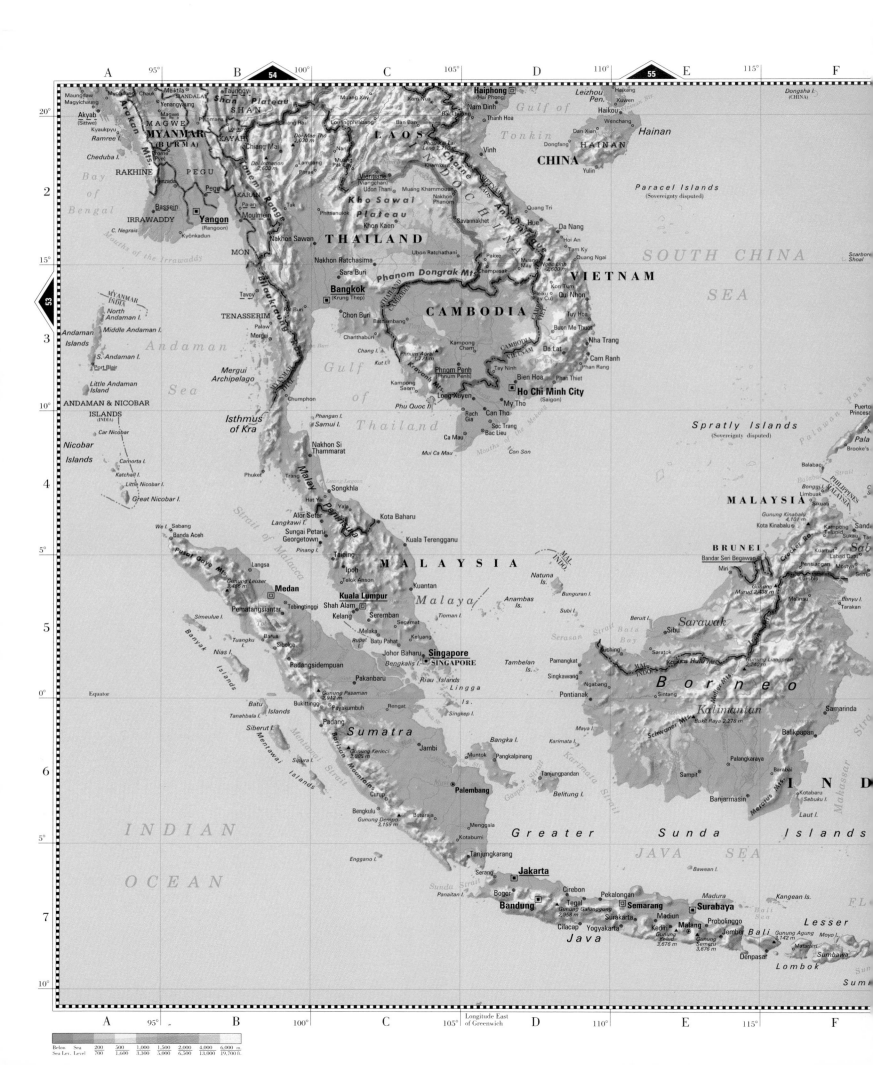

Southeastern Asia

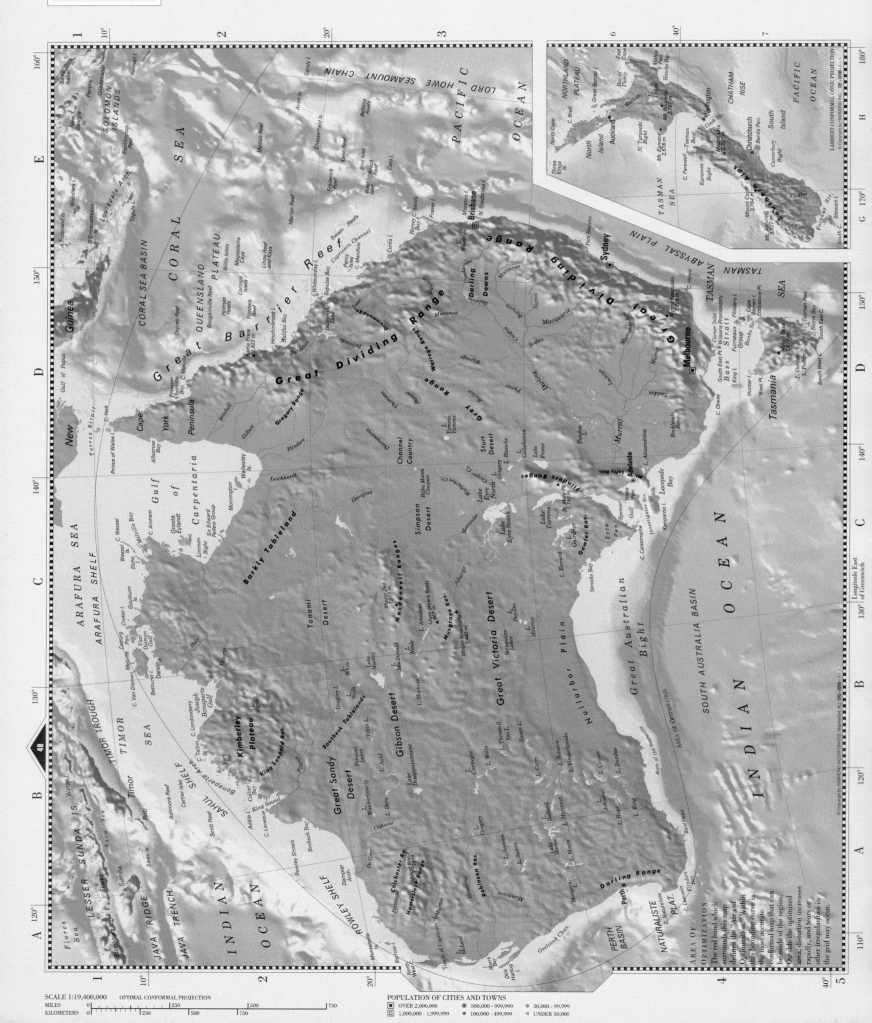

SCALE 1:19,400,000   OPTIMAL CONFORMAL PROJECTION

MILES 0   250   500   750

KILOMETERS 0   250   500   750

POPULATION OF CITIES AND TOWNS

▣ OVER 2,000,000   ● 500,000 - 999,999   ○ 50,000 - 99,999

▢ 1,000,000 - 1,999,999   ● 100,000 - 499,999   ∘ UNDER 50,000

AREA OF OPTIMIZATION
The red band which surrounds this map defines the "Area of Optimization." Within this bounding curve is the most accurate conformal map that can be made of the region. Outside the optimized area, distortion increases rapidly, and tears or other irregularities in the grid may occur.

Australia, New Zealand - Political

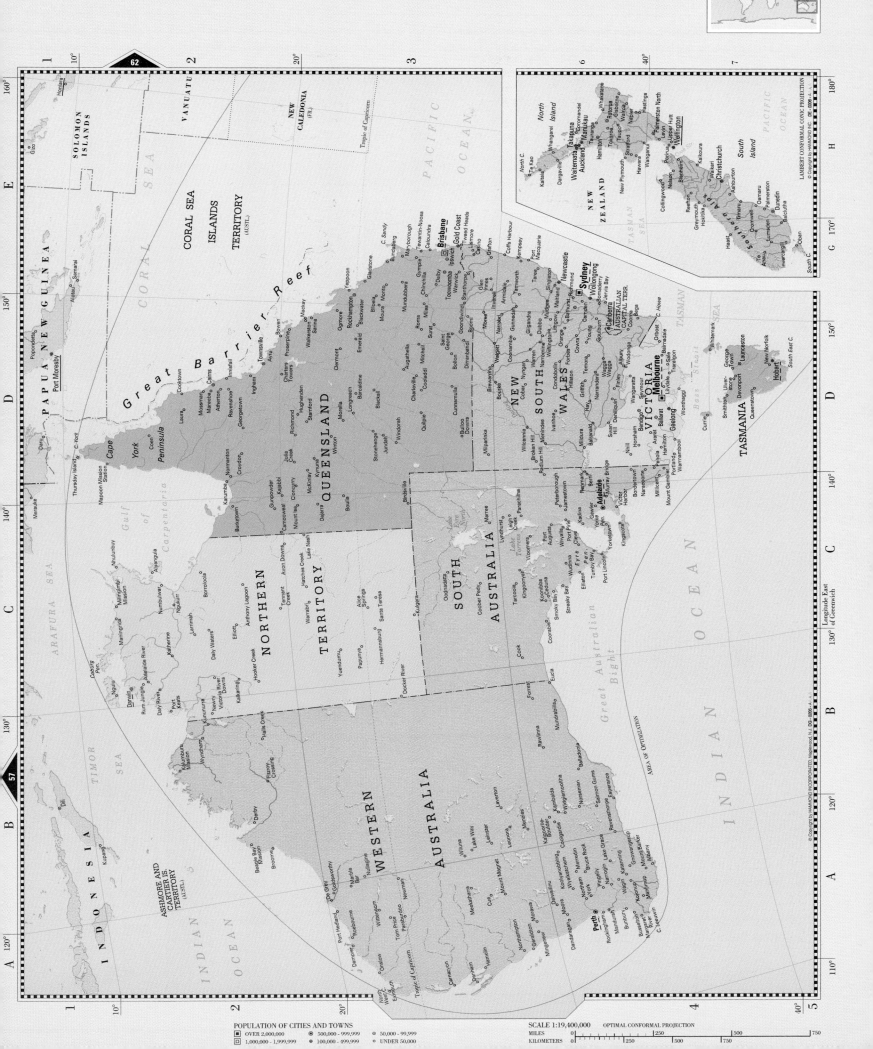

POPULATION OF CITIES AND TOWNS

- ▣ OVER 2,000,000
- ▢ 1,000,000 - 1,999,999
- ● 500,000 - 999,999
- ● 100,000 - 499,999
- ⊙ 50,000 - 99,999
- ○ UNDER 50,000

SCALE 1:19,400,000   OPTIMAL CONFORMAL PROJECTION

MILES 0 ... 250 ... 500 ... 750
KILOMETERS 0 ... 250 ... 500

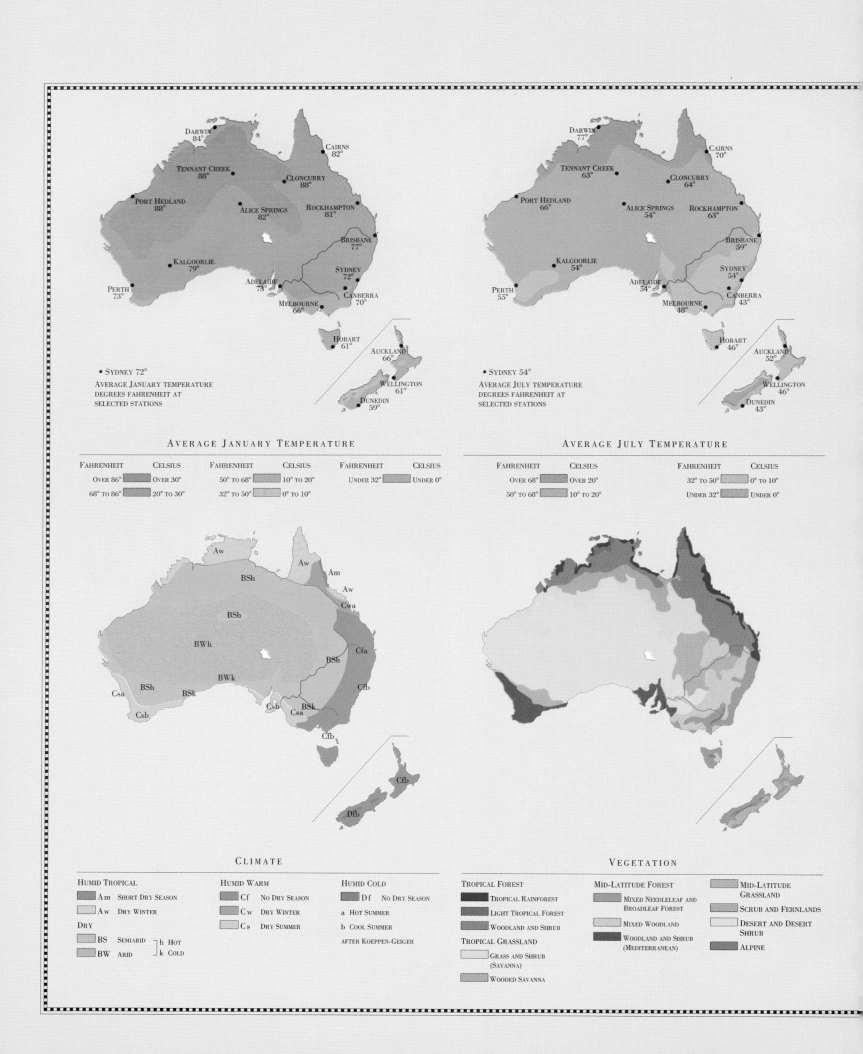

DARWIN
84°

CAIRNS
82°

TENNANT CREEK
88°

CLONCURRY
88°

PORT HEDLAND
88°

ALICE SPRINGS
82°

ROCKHAMPTON
81°

BRISBANE
77°

KALGOORLIE
79°

SYDNEY
72°

ADELAIDE
73°

CANBERRA
70°

PERTH
73°

MELBOURNE
66°

HOBART
61°

AUCKLAND
66°

WELLINGTON
61°

DUNEDIN
59°

• SYDNEY 72°
AVERAGE JANUARY TEMPERATURE
DEGREES FAHRENHEIT AT
SELECTED STATIONS

AVERAGE JANUARY TEMPERATURE

FAHRENHEIT	CELSIUS	FAHRENHEIT	CELSIUS	FAHRENHEIT	CELSIUS
OVER 86°	OVER 30°	50° TO 68°	10° TO 20°	UNDER 32°	UNDER 0°
68° TO 86°	20° TO 30°	32° TO 50°	0° TO 10°		

DARWIN
77°

CAIRNS
70°

TENNANT CREEK
63°

CLONCURRY
64°

PORT HEDLAND
66°

ALICE SPRINGS
54°

ROCKHAMPTON
63°

BRISBANE
59°

KALGOORLIE
54°

SYDNEY
54°

ADELAIDE
54°

CANBERRA
43°

PERTH
55°

MELBOURNE
48°

HOBART
46°

AUCKLAND
52°

WELLINGTON
46°

DUNEDIN
43°

• SYDNEY 54°
AVERAGE JULY TEMPERATURE
DEGREES FAHRENHEIT AT
SELECTED STATIONS

AVERAGE JULY TEMPERATURE

FAHRENHEIT	CELSIUS	FAHRENHEIT	CELSIUS
OVER 68°	OVER 20°	32° TO 50°	0° TO 10°
50° TO 68°	10° TO 20°	UNDER 32°	UNDER 0°

Aw

Aw

Am

BSh

Aw

BSh

Cwa

BWh

Cfa

BSh

BWk

Cfb

Csa

BSh

BSk

Csb

Csb

BSk

Csa

Cfb

Cfb

Dfb

CLIMATE

HUMID TROPICAL
- Am SHORT DRY SEASON
- Aw DRY WINTER

DRY
- BS SEMIARID — h HOT
- BW ARID — k COLD

HUMID WARM
- Cf NO DRY SEASON
- Cw DRY WINTER
- Cs DRY SUMMER

HUMID COLD
- Df NO DRY SEASON
- a HOT SUMMER
- b COOL SUMMER

AFTER KOEPPEN-GEIGER

VEGETATION

TROPICAL FOREST
- TROPICAL RAINFOREST
- LIGHT TROPICAL FOREST
- WOODLAND AND SHRUB

TROPICAL GRASSLAND
- GRASS AND SHRUB (SAVANNA)
- WOODED SAVANNA

MID-LATITUDE FOREST
- MIXED NEEDLELEAF AND BROADLEAF FOREST
- MIXED WOODLAND
- WOODLAND AND SHRUB (MEDITERRANEAN)

- MID-LATITUDE GRASSLAND
- SCRUB AND FERNLANDS
- DESERT AND DESERT SHRUB
- ALPINE

Australia, New Zealand - Comparisons

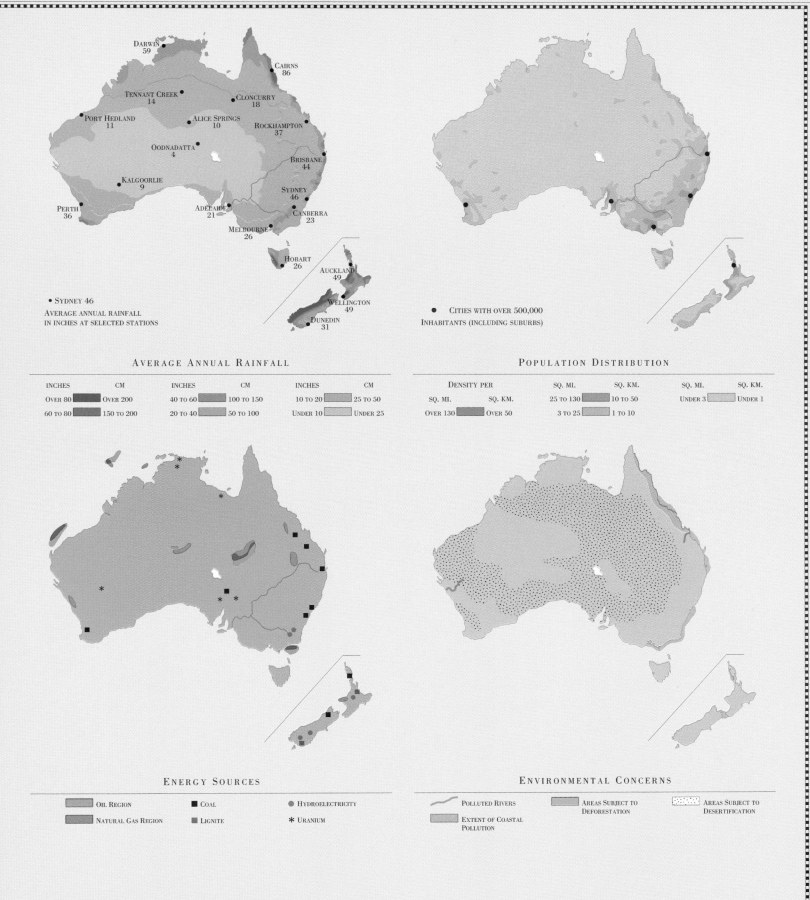

DARWIN 59
CAIRNS 86
TENNANT CREEK 14
CLONCURRY 18
PORT HEDLAND 11
ALICE SPRINGS 10
ROCKHAMPTON 37
OODNADATTA 4
BRISBANE 44
KALGOORLIE 9
SYDNEY 46
PERTH 36
ADELAIDE 21
CANBERRA 23
MELBOURNE 26
HOBART 26
AUCKLAND 49
WELLINGTON 49
DUNEDIN 31

• SYDNEY 46
AVERAGE ANNUAL RAINFALL
IN INCHES AT SELECTED STATIONS

• CITIES WITH OVER 500,000
INHABITANTS (INCLUDING SUBURBS)

AVERAGE ANNUAL RAINFALL

INCHES	CM	INCHES	CM	INCHES	CM
OVER 80	OVER 200	40 TO 60	100 TO 150	10 TO 20	25 TO 50
60 TO 80	150 TO 200	20 TO 40	50 TO 100	UNDER 10	UNDER 25

POPULATION DISTRIBUTION

DENSITY PER		SQ. MI.	SQ. KM.	SQ. MI.	SQ. KM.
SQ. MI.	SQ. KM.	25 TO 130	10 TO 50	UNDER 3	UNDER 1
OVER 130	OVER 50	3 TO 25	1 TO 10		

ENERGY SOURCES

OIL REGION   ■ COAL   ● HYDROELECTRICITY

NATURAL GAS REGION   ■ LIGNITE   * URANIUM

ENVIRONMENTAL CONCERNS

POLLUTED RIVERS   AREAS SUBJECT TO DEFORESTATION   AREAS SUBJECT TO DESERTIFICATION

EXTENT OF COASTAL POLLUTION

CHINA

Xiangtan
Changsha
Hengyang
Zhuzhou
Ji'an
Huaihua Shan
Daiyun Shan
1,649 m
Tongiu Zhang
1,526 m
Guilin
Guangzhou
Macau
MACAU
(PORT.)
Xiamen
Chaozhou
Shantou
Kaohsiung
HONG KONG
(CHINA)

Jingdezhen
Nanchang
Kincang Shan
4,375 m
Wenzhou
Fuzhou
Taipei
Taichung
Tainan

TAIWAN

Ningbo
Nanchang

EAST CHINA SEA

RYUKYU IS.

JAPAN

Kyūshū
Tokara Is.
Ōsumi Is.
Amami Is.
Nazei
Okinawa Is.
Naha
Ishigaki
Sakishima Is.
Daito Is.

Mukoshima Is.
Chichishima Is.
Hahashima Is.
BONIN IS.
(JAPAN)
Ogasawara

Ritaiō
VOLCANO IS.
(JAPAN)
Iwo Jima
Minamiō

Tori-Shima
(JAPAN)

Tropic of Cancer

Minami-Tori-Shima
(JAPAN)

Wake I.
(U.S.)

Kure I.
Midway
Island
(U.S.)

International Date Line

NORTH PA

SOUTH CHINA SEA

Laoag
Vigan
Dagupan
Baguio
Luzon
Cabanatuan
Mt. Pinatubo
1,759 m
Manila
Quezon City
Batangas
Lucena
Naga
Leqaspi
Mindoro
Masbate
Catanduanes

Atbayat I.
Batan Is.
Calayan I.
Babuyan Is.

Luzon Strait

Bashi Channel

PHILIPPINE SEA

PHILIPPINES

Palawan
Panay
Iloilo
Negros
Bacolod
Cebu
Cebu
Bohol
Samar
Leyte
Tacloban

Quezon
Kudat
Zamboanga
Basilan
Sandakan
MALAYSIA
Sabah
Tawau
Sulu Archipelago
Sulu Sea

Mindanao
Cagayan
de Oro
Davao
General Santos
Butuan

Farallon de Pajaros
Maug Is.
Asuncion
Agrihan
Pagan
Alamagan
Guguan
Sarigan
Anathan
Farallon de Medinilla
Saipan
Aguijan
Tinian
Rota
Agaña
Guam
(U.S.)

Okino-Tori-Shima
(JAPAN)

NORTHERN

MARIANAS

(U.S.)

Ulithi
Colonia
Yap Is.
Ngulu

Kavangel
Is.
Babelthuap
Koror
PALAU
Sonsorol Is.

Gaferut
Faraulep
West
Fayu
Sorol
Woleai
Olimarao
Ifalik
Eauripik

Namonuito
Pikelot
Lamotrek
Edao
Elato
CAROLINE ISLANDS

Moen
Truk Is.
Puluwat
Pulap

Oroluk
Ant
Satawan
Nukuoro
Ngatik
Pohnpei
Lukunor
Etal

Mi
c
r
o
n
e
s
i
a

Enewetak
Bikini
Rongelap
Rongerik
Ujelang
Wotho
Kwajalein
Erikub
Ujae
Lae
Namu
Ailinglapalap
Namorik
Jaluit
Ebon

Bikar
Utirik
Ailuk
Wotje
Maloelap
Aur
Arno
Mili
Majuro
Lelu
Kosrae
Pingelap

MARSHALL
ISLANDS

RATAK CHAIN
RALIK CHAIN

Kapingamarangi

FEDERATED STATES OF MICRONESIA

Makin
Butaritari
Abaiang
Bikenibeu
Tarawa
Maiana
Kuria
Abemama
Aranuka
Nonouti
Beru
Utiroa
Tabiteuea
Onotoa
Nikunau
Tamana
Arorae

GILBERT
ISLANDS

Banaba
Tabiang

NAURU

Mi
c
r
o
n
e
s
i
a

INDONESIA

Samarinda
Pare
Borneo
Tarakan

Manado
Gorontalo
Ternate
Gulf of Tomini

Morotai
Halmahera
Waigeo
Obi
Sula Is.
Ceram
Ambon
Celebes
Kendari
Butung
Muna
Salayar
Kabaena

Sorong
Manokwari
Schouten Is.
Yapen
Fakfak
Puncak Jaya
5,030 m
Maoke Mts.
Mt. Hagen
New Guinea
Kolepom
Merauke

Ninigo Is.
Admiralty
Islands
Manus
New
Hanover
Vanimo
Aitape
Wewak
Madang
Mt. Wilhelm
4,509 m
Kundiawa
Goroka
Lae
Bulolo
Wau

Mussau
St. Matthias Group
Kavieng
New Ireland
Namatanai

BISMARCK ARCHIPELAGO

Karkar I.
Umboi
Kimbe
New
Britain
Rabaul
Buka
Bougainville
Arawa
Kieta

Lyra Reef
Nuguria Is.
Tauu Is.
Nissan I.
Tulin Is.
Ontong Java
Nukumanu
Atoll

Mi
c
r
o
n
e
s
i
a

Lolua
Nanumea
Niutao
Nanumanga
Nui
Nukufetau
Vaitupu
Funafuti
Nukulaelae
Niulakita

TUVALU

INDONESIA

Jayapura
New Guinea

PAPUA
NEW GUINEA

Gulf of
Papua
Daru
Port Moresby

Popondetta
Buso
Samarai
Rossel I.
Louisiade
Arch.

Trobriand Is.
D'Entrecasteaux Is.
Woodlark I.
Normanby
Milne Bay
Esa'ala
Alotau
Tagula I.
Pocklington
Reef

Choiseul
Shortland Is.
Kia
Santa Isabel
Buala
New
Georgia
Gizo
Honiara
Guadalcanal
San
Cristobal
Aola

Auki
Malaita
Kirakira
Ndende
Utupua
Vanikoro

Reef Is.
Duff Is.
Lata
SANTA CRUZ IS.

Solomon Sea

SOLOMON
ISLANDS

M
e
l
a
n
e
s
i
a

P
o
l
y
n
e
s
i
a

Flores
Sumbawa
Ruteng
Leti Is.
Alor
Babar
Timor
Sumba
Kupang
Sawu Sea
Savu Sea
Dili
Tanimbar Is.
Kai Is.
Aru Is.
Wetar

BANDA SEA
FLORES SEA

CELEBES
SEA

Ujung
Pandang

Makassar Strait

Celebes

Gulf of Bone

Rotuma
(FR.)
Ahau
WALLIS &
FUTUNA
(FR.)
Futuna

Torres Is.
Banks Is.

ARAFURA SEA

Melville
I.
Darwin
Bathurst I.

Cape
York
Coen
Cooktown
Cairns

C. York
Torres Strait

Pine Creek
Katherine

INDIAN
OCEAN

Kimberley
Plateau
Wyndham
Halls Creek

Bonaparte Arch.
Broome

Great Sandy
Desert

Port Hedland
Roebourne
Marble Bar
Onslow
Mt. Bruce
1,235 m
Exmouth
Carnarvon

Gulf
of
Carpentaria

York
Peninsula

Daly Waters

Tennant Creek

Normanton
Hughenden
Cloncurry
Camooweal

AUSTRALIA

Alice Springs
Uluru (Ayers Rock)
867 m
Musgrave Ranges
Gibson Desert

Meekatharra
Wiluna

Great Victoria Desert

Laverton
Leonora

Geraldton
Northampton
Mullewa

Kalgoorlie-Boulder

Perth
Northam

Nullarbor Plain

Norseman
Merredin
Streaky Bay

Great
Australian
Bight

Port Augusta
Whyalla
Port Pirie
Port Lincoln
Adelaide
Murray Bridge

Great Dividing
Range

Townsville
Bowen
Mackay

Clermont
Emerald
Rockhampton
Bundaberg

Barcaldine
Longreach
Boulia
Birdsville

Charleville
Roma
Gympie

Charters
Toowoomba
Brisbane
Gold Coast

Great
Barrier
Reef

Great Dividing Range

CORAL
SEA

Chesterfield
Is.
Bellona
Reefs
New
Caledonia
Koumac
Hienghene
Mont Panié 1,628 m
New Kone
Bourail
Humboldt
1,618 m
Noumea
Ile des Pins

VANUATU

Espiritu Santo
Tabwemasana 1,879 m
Luganville
Norsup
Malekula
Port-Vila

NEW
CALEDONIA
(FR.)

Aoba
Maewo
Pentecost
Ambrym
Epi
Shepherd
Efate
Erromango
Tanna
Aneityum

NEW HEBRIDES

Thio
We
LOYALTY IS.

FIJI

Yasawa
Group
Lautoka
Viti Levu
Nadi
Suva
Vunisea
Kadavu

Vanua
Levu
Lambasa
Savusavu

Lau
Gro
Moala
Group

M
e
l
a
n
e
s
i
a

SOUTH

Cobar
Bourke
Moree
Saint
George
Cunnamulla

Armidale
Tamworth
Grafton
Lismore

Port Macquarie
Newcastle

Lord Howe I.
(AUSTL.)

Norfolk I.
(AUSTL.)
Kingston

Raoul I.
Macauley I.

KERMADEC IS.
(N.Z.)

Woomera
Broken Hill
Whyalla
Orange
Dubbo
Lithgow
Sydney
Wollongong
Mildura
Wagga Wagga
Canberra
Mt. Kosciusko
2,229 m
Albury
Cootamundra

Three
Kings Is.
North Cape

Whangarei
Auckland
Manukau

NEW
ZEALAND

Tauranga
Hamilton
Rotorua
North I.

TASMAN SEA

Murray Bridge

P
o
l
y
n
e
s
i
a

Below Sea 200 500 1,000 1,500 2,000 4,000 6,000 m.
Sea Lev. Level 700 1,600 3,300 5,000 6,500 13,000 19,700 ft.

Pacific Ocean

Africa - Physical

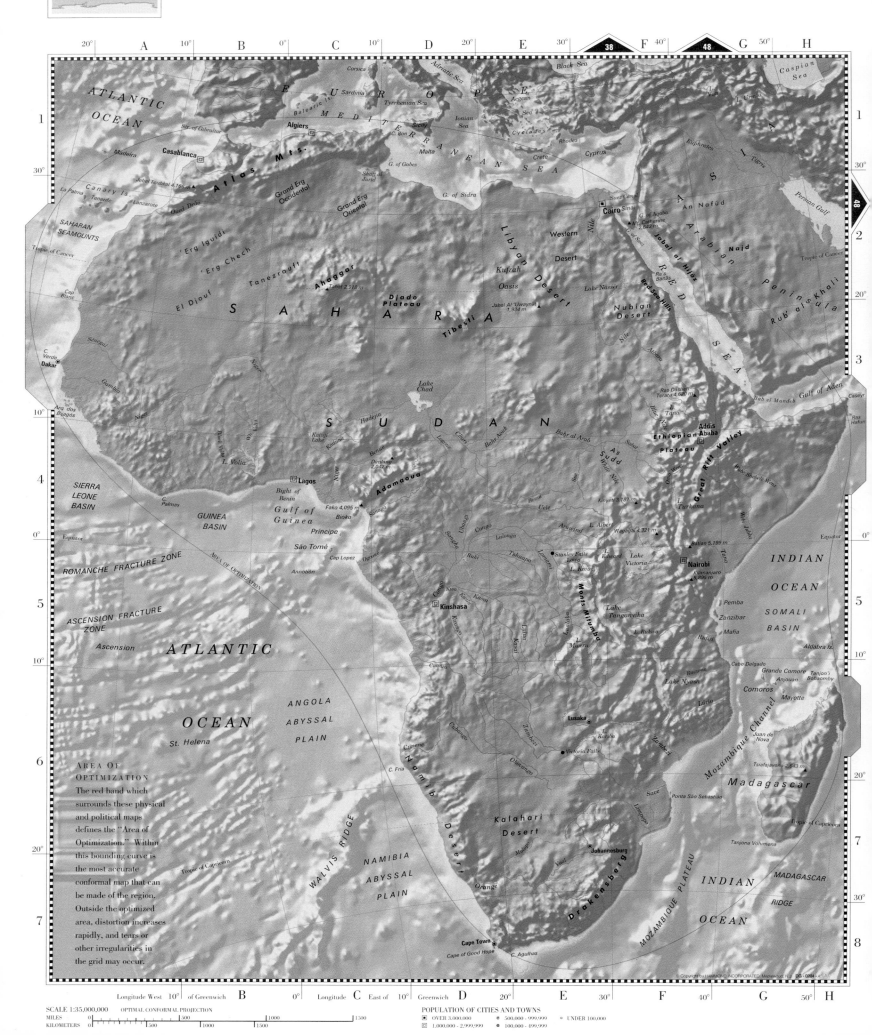

AREA OF OPTIMIZATION
The red band which surrounds these physical and political maps defines the "Area of Optimization." Within this bounding curve is the most accurate conformal map that can be made of the region. Outside the optimized area, distortion increases rapidly, and tears or other irregularities in the grid may occur.

SCALE 1:35,000,000   OPTIMAL CONFORMAL PROJECTION

POPULATION OF CITIES AND TOWNS
OVER 3,000,000   500,000 - 999,999   UNDER 100,000
1,000,000 - 2,999,999   100,000 - 499,999

Africa - Political

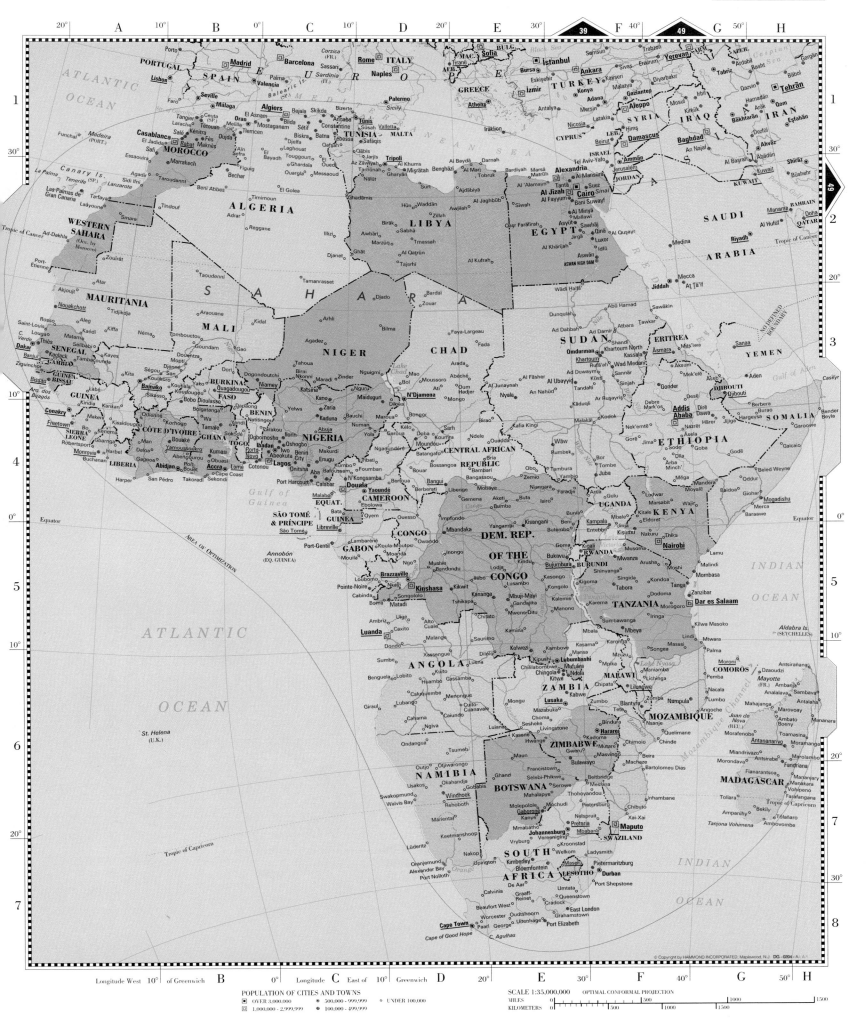

POPULATION OF CITIES AND TOWNS

□ OVER 3,000,000   ● 500,000 - 999,999   ○ UNDER 100,000
▣ 1,000,000 - 2,999,999   ● 100,000 - 499,999

SCALE 1:35,000,000   OPTIMAL CONFORMAL PROJECTION
MILES
KILOMETERS

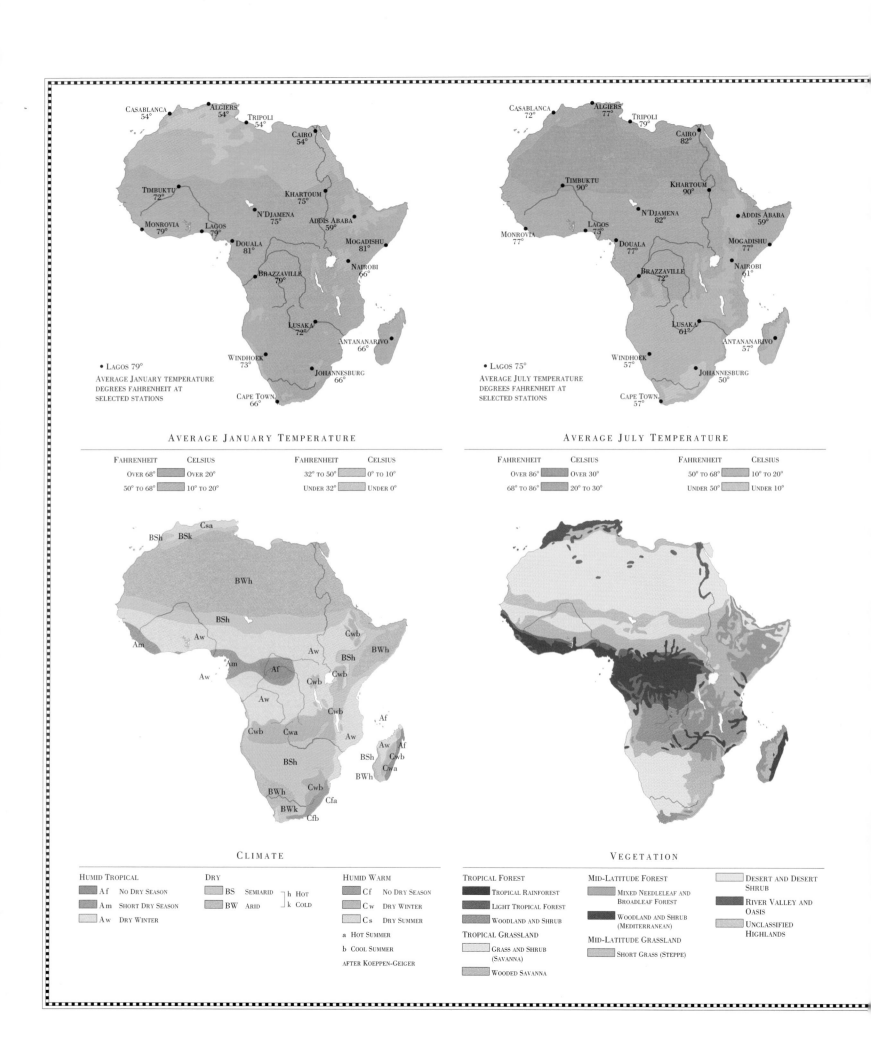

AVERAGE JANUARY TEMPERATURE

- Lagos 79°
AVERAGE JANUARY TEMPERATURE
DEGREES FAHRENHEIT AT
SELECTED STATIONS

FAHRENHEIT	CELSIUS		FAHRENHEIT	CELSIUS
OVER 68°	OVER 20°		32° TO 50°	0° TO 10°
50° TO 68°	10° TO 20°		UNDER 32°	UNDER 0°

AVERAGE JULY TEMPERATURE

- Lagos 75°
AVERAGE JULY TEMPERATURE
DEGREES FAHRENHEIT AT
SELECTED STATIONS

FAHRENHEIT	CELSIUS		FAHRENHEIT	CELSIUS
OVER 86°	OVER 30°		50° TO 68°	10° TO 20°
68° TO 86°	20° TO 30°		UNDER 50°	UNDER 10°

CLIMATE

HUMID TROPICAL
- Af NO DRY SEASON
- Am SHORT DRY SEASON
- Aw DRY WINTER

DRY
- BS SEMIARID
- BW ARID
- h HOT
- k COLD

HUMID WARM
- Cf NO DRY SEASON
- Cw DRY WINTER
- Cs DRY SUMMER
- a HOT SUMMER
- b COOL SUMMER

AFTER KOEPPEN-GEIGER

VEGETATION

TROPICAL FOREST
- TROPICAL RAINFOREST
- LIGHT TROPICAL FOREST
- WOODLAND AND SHRUB

TROPICAL GRASSLAND
- GRASS AND SHRUB (SAVANNA)
- WOODED SAVANNA

MID-LATITUDE FOREST
- MIXED NEEDLELEAF AND BROADLEAF FOREST
- WOODLAND AND SHRUB (MEDITERRANEAN)

MID-LATITUDE GRASSLAND
- SHORT GRASS (STEPPE)

- DESERT AND DESERT SHRUB
- RIVER VALLEY AND OASIS
- UNCLASSIFIED HIGHLANDS

Africa - Comparisons

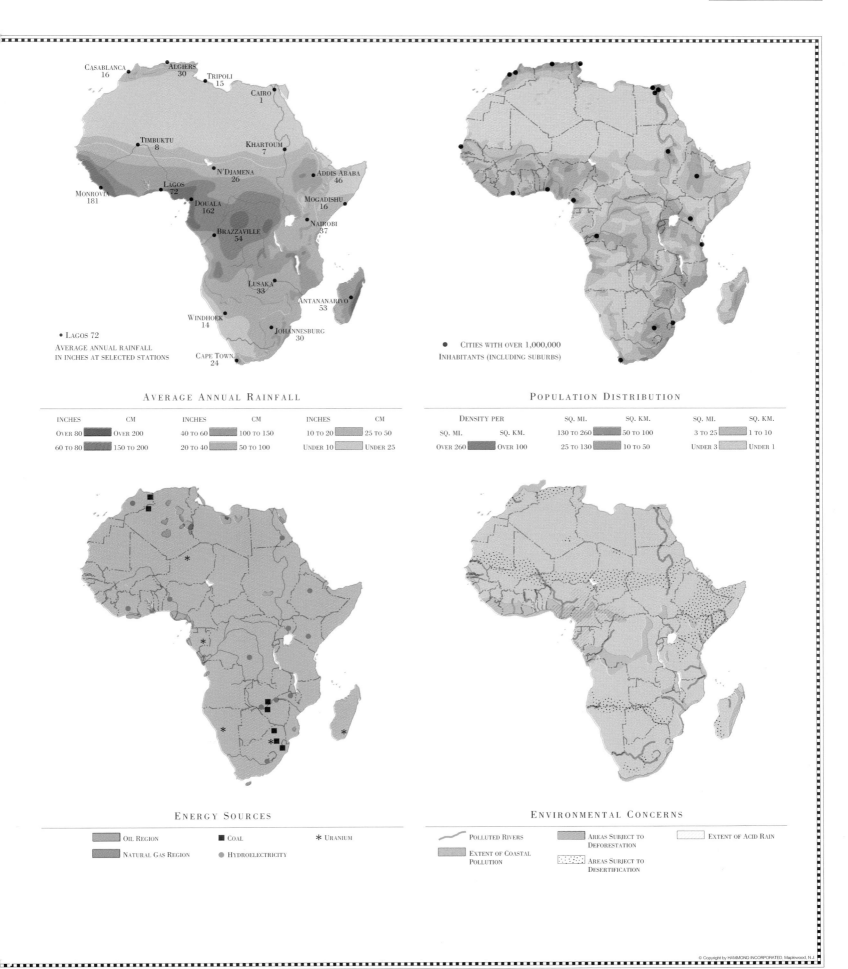

CASABLANCA 16
ALGIERS 30
TRIPOLI 15
CAIRO 1
TIMBUKTU 8
KHARTOUM 7
N'DJAMENA 26
ADDIS ABABA 46
LAGOS 72
MONROVIA 181
DOUALA 162
MOGADISHU 16
NAIROBI 37
BRAZZAVILLE 54
LUSAKA 33
ANTANANARIVO 53
WINDHOEK 14
JOHANNESBURG 30
CAPE TOWN 24

• LAGOS 72
AVERAGE ANNUAL RAINFALL
IN INCHES AT SELECTED STATIONS

AVERAGE ANNUAL RAINFALL

INCHES	CM	INCHES	CM	INCHES	CM
OVER 80	OVER 200	40 TO 60	100 TO 150	10 TO 20	25 TO 50
60 TO 80	150 TO 200	20 TO 40	50 TO 100	UNDER 10	UNDER 25

• CITIES WITH OVER 1,000,000
INHABITANTS (INCLUDING SUBURBS)

POPULATION DISTRIBUTION

DENSITY PER		SQ. MI.	SQ. KM.	SQ. MI.	SQ. KM.
SQ. MI.	SQ. KM.	130 TO 260	50 TO 100	3 TO 25	1 TO 10
OVER 260	OVER 100	25 TO 130	10 TO 50	UNDER 3	UNDER 1

ENERGY SOURCES

	OIL REGION	■ COAL	✳ URANIUM
	NATURAL GAS REGION	● HYDROELECTRICITY	

ENVIRONMENTAL CONCERNS

	POLLUTED RIVERS		AREAS SUBJECT TO DEFORESTATION		EXTENT OF ACID RAIN
	EXTENT OF COASTAL POLLUTION		AREAS SUBJECT TO DESERTIFICATION		

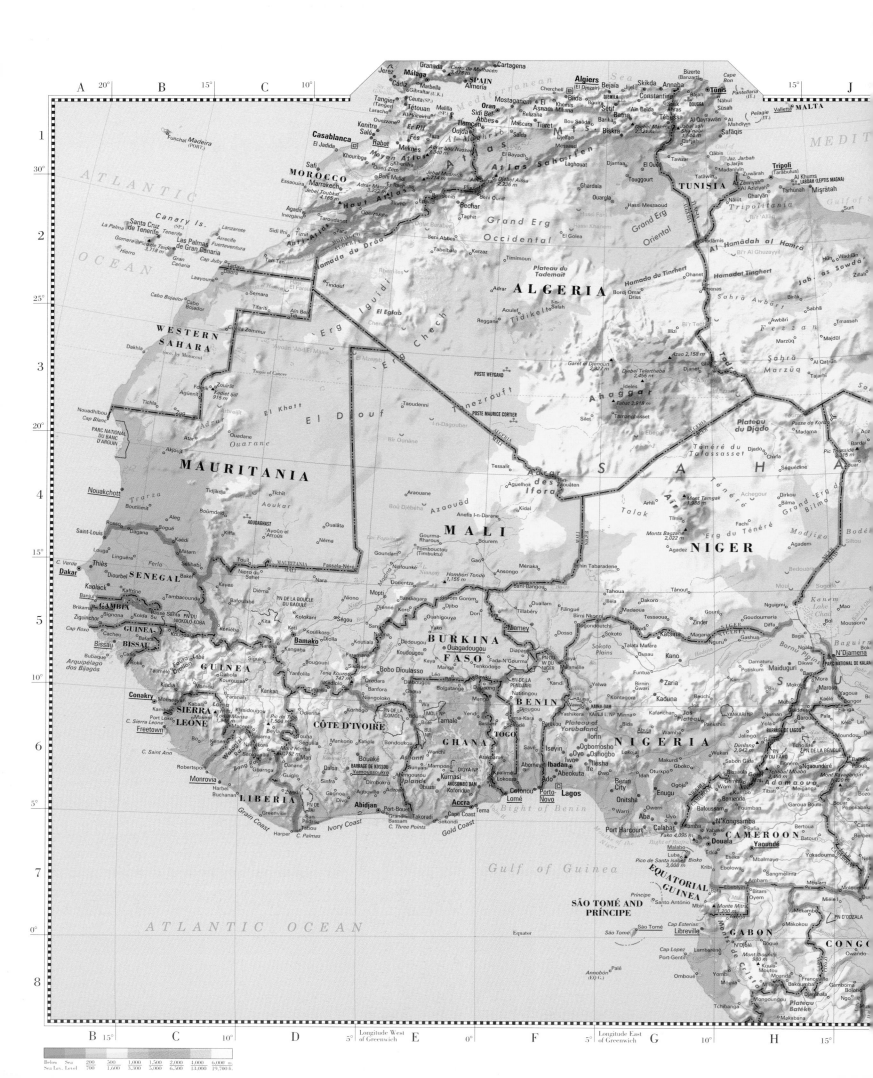

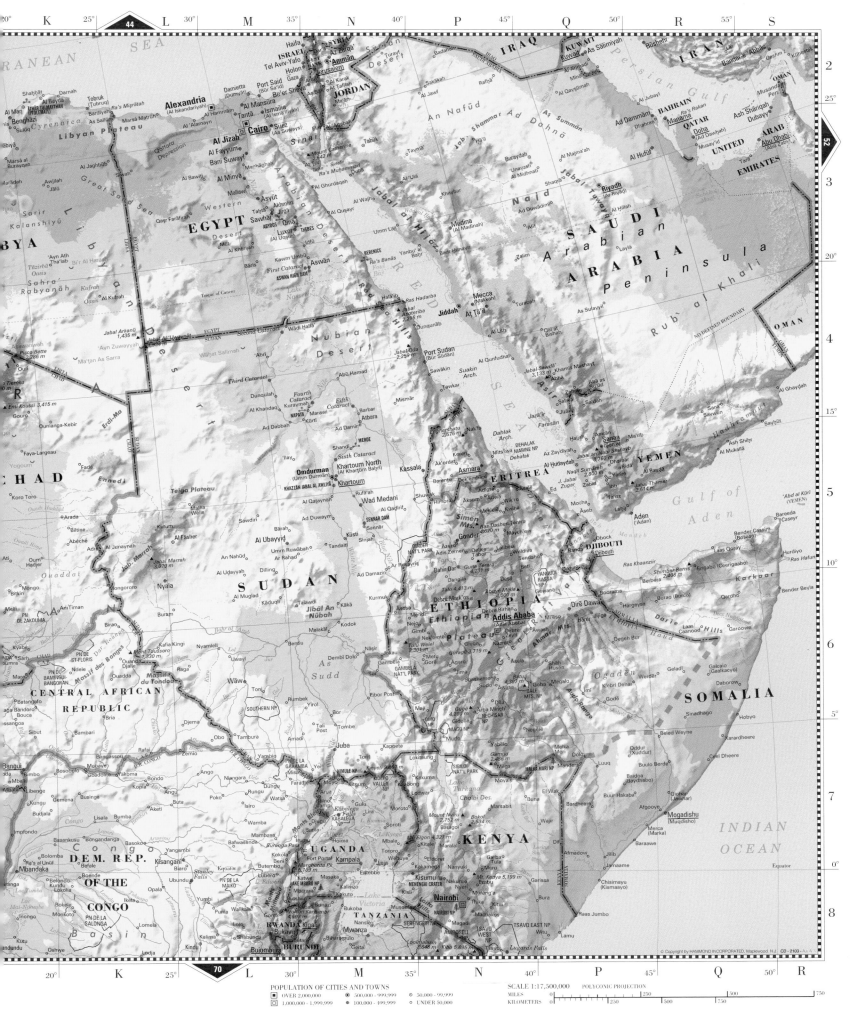

POPULATION OF CITIES AND TOWNS

■ OVER 2,000,000   ● 500,000 - 999,999   ● 50,000 - 99,999
□ 1,000,000 - 1,999,999   ● 100,000 - 499,999   ○ UNDER 50,000

SCALE 1:17,500,000   POLYCONIC PROJECTION

MILES   0   250   500   750

KILOMETERS   0   250   500   750

Southern Africa

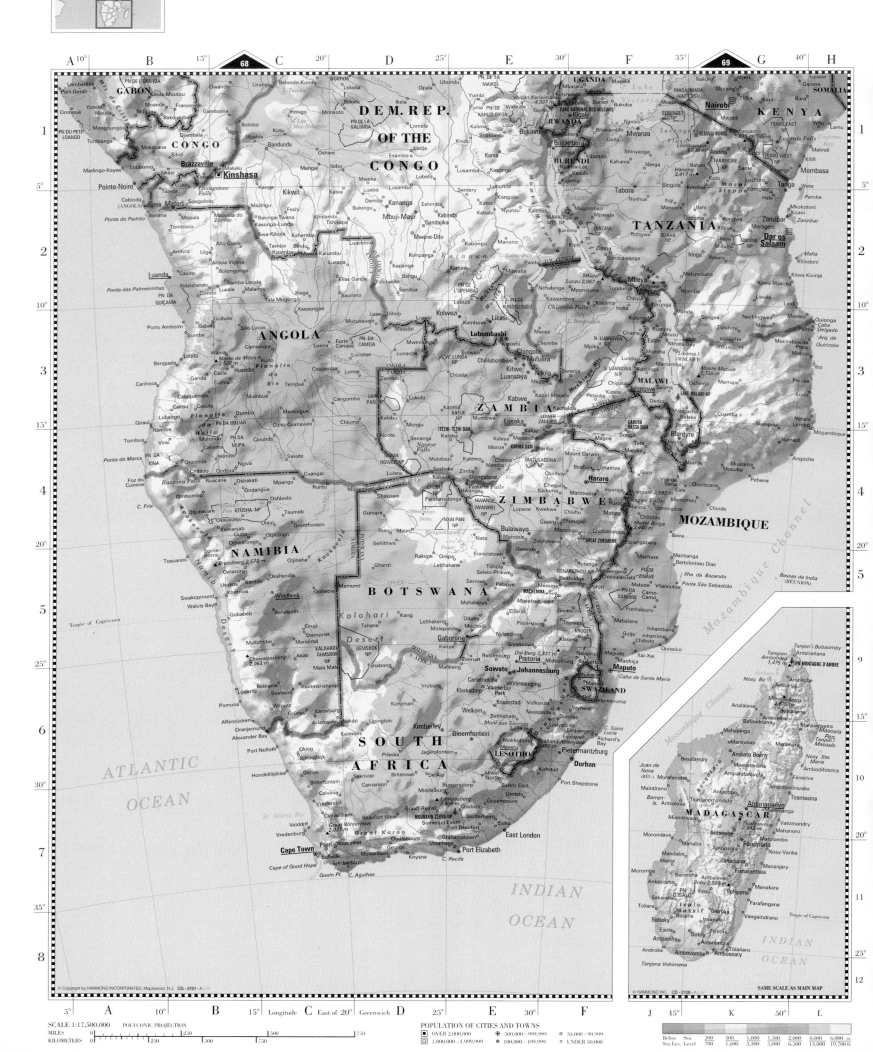

SCALE 1:17,500,000   POLYCONIC PROJECTION

MILES

KILOMETERS

POPULATION OF CITIES AND TOWNS

■ OVER 2,000,000   ● 500,000 – 999,999   ◉ 50,000 – 99,999
☐ 1,000,000 – 1,999,999   ◎ 100,000 – 499,999   ○ UNDER 50,000

© HAMMOND INC.   CD-2108-A

SAME SCALE AS MAIN MAP

Below Sea   200   500   1,000   1,500   2,000   4,000   6,000 m.
Sea Lev. Level   700   1,600   3,300   6,500   13,000   19,700 m.

Arctic Regions, Antarctica

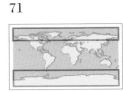

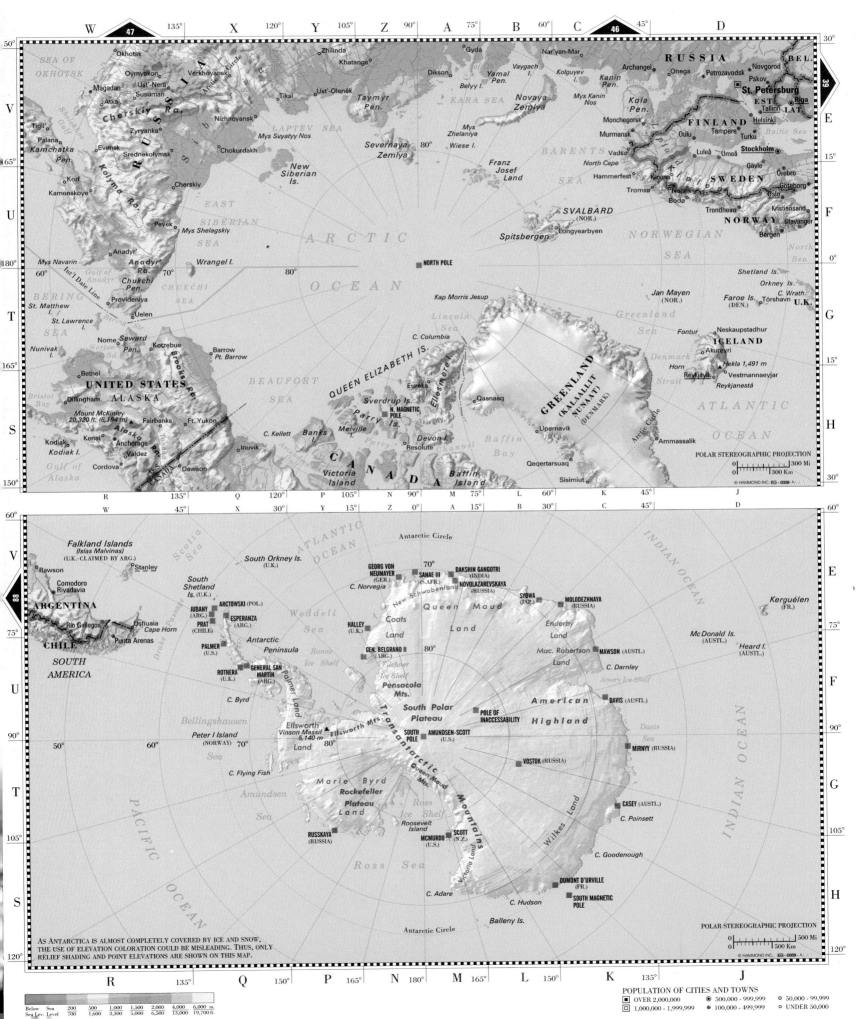

POLAR STEREOGRAPHIC PROJECTION

0   300 Mi
0   300 Km

© HAMMOND INC. EG - 0006-A

As Antarctica is almost completely covered by ice and snow,
the use of elevation coloration could be misleading. Thus, only
relief shading and point elevations are shown on this map.

POLAR STEREOGRAPHIC PROJECTION

0   500 Mi
0   500 Km

© HAMMOND INC.   EG - 0009 - A

POPULATION OF CITIES AND TOWNS
- ■ OVER 2,000,000
- □ 1,000,000 - 1,999,999
- ■ 500,000 - 999,999
- ◻ 100,000 - 499,999
- ○ 50,000 - 99,999
- ○ UNDER 50,000

Below Sea   200   500   1,000 1,500 2,000 4,000 6,000 m.
Sea Lev. Level 700 1,600 3,300 5,000 6,500 13,000 19,700 ft.

North America - Physical

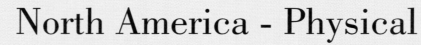

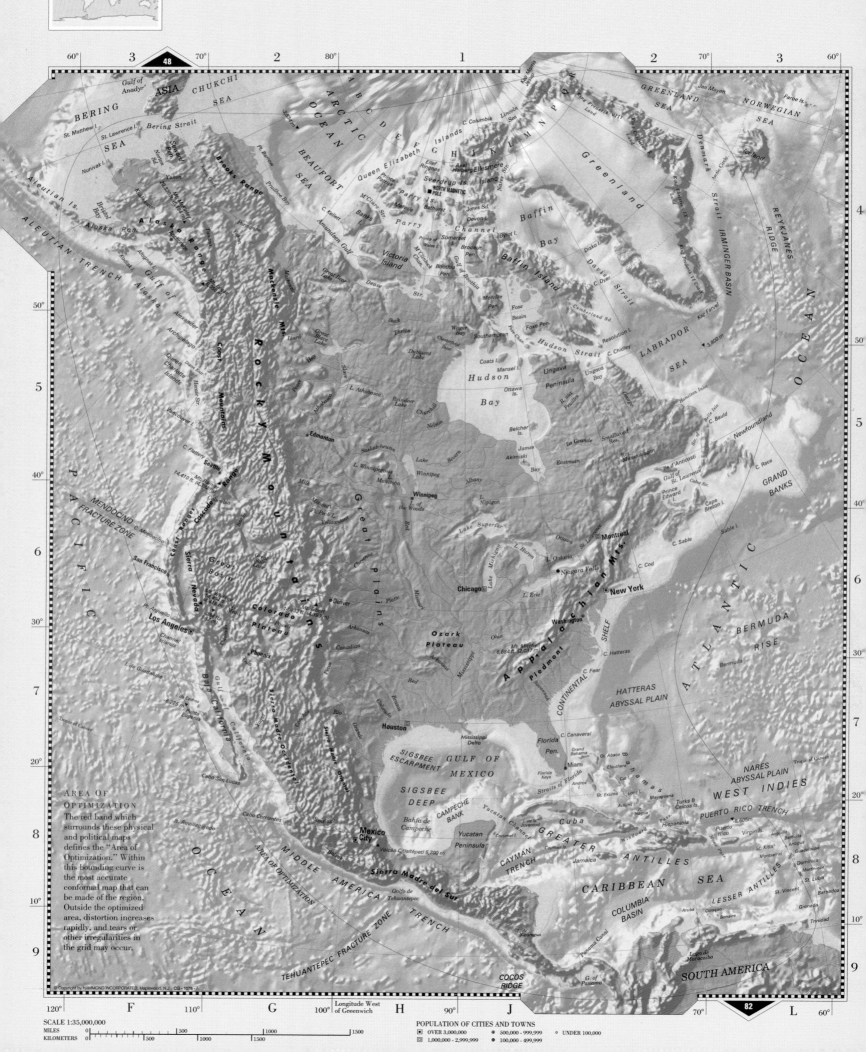

AREA OF OPTIMIZATION
The red band which surrounds these physical and political maps defines the "Area of Optimization." Within this bounding curve is the most accurate conformal map that can be made of the region. Outside the optimized area, distortion increases rapidly, and tears or other irregularities in the grid may occur.

SCALE 1:35,000,000

MILES   0   500   1000   1500
KILOMETERS 0   500   1000   1500

POPULATION OF CITIES AND TOWNS
◼ OVER 3,000,000   ◼ 500,000 - 999,999   ○ UNDER 100,000
◼ 1,000,000 - 2,999,999   ◼ 100,000 - 499,999

North America - Political

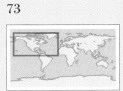

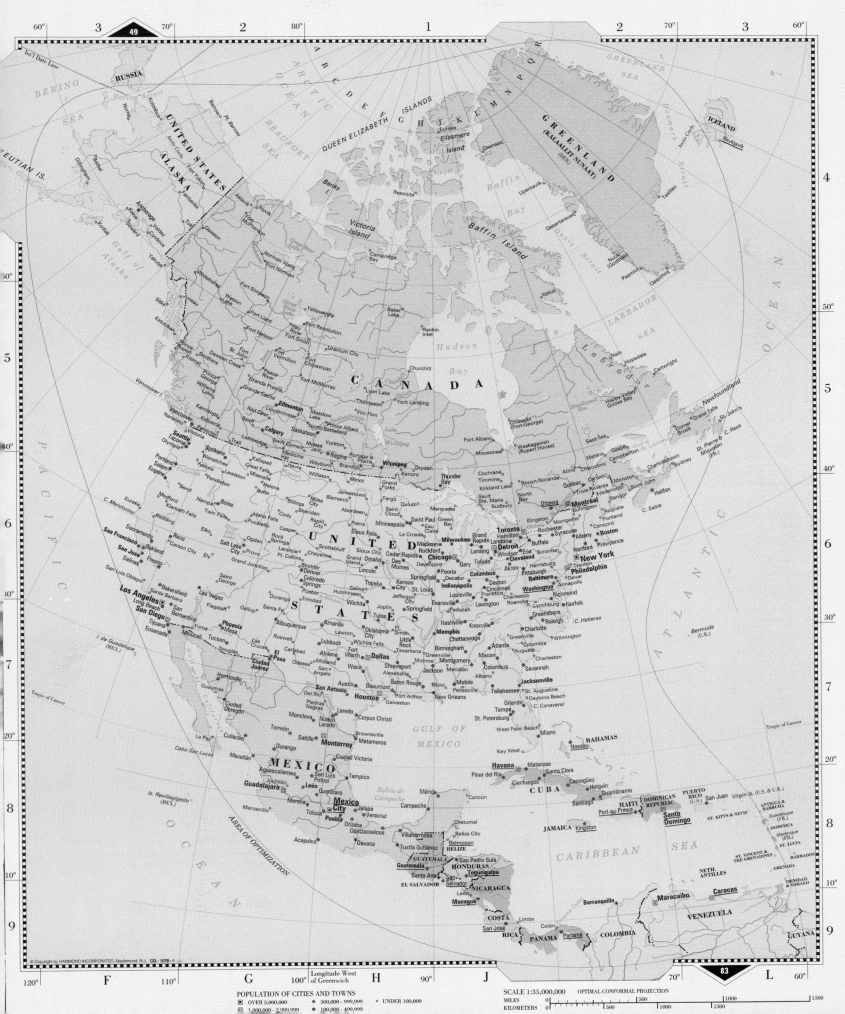

SCALE 1:35,000,000 OPTIMAL CONFORMAL PROJECTION

POPULATION OF CITIES AND TOWNS

■ OVER 3,000,000 ◩ 500,000 - 999,999 ● 100,000 - 499,999 ○ UNDER 100,000
◉ 1,000,000 - 2,999,999

MILES 0 500 1000 1500
KILOMETERS 0 500 1000 1500

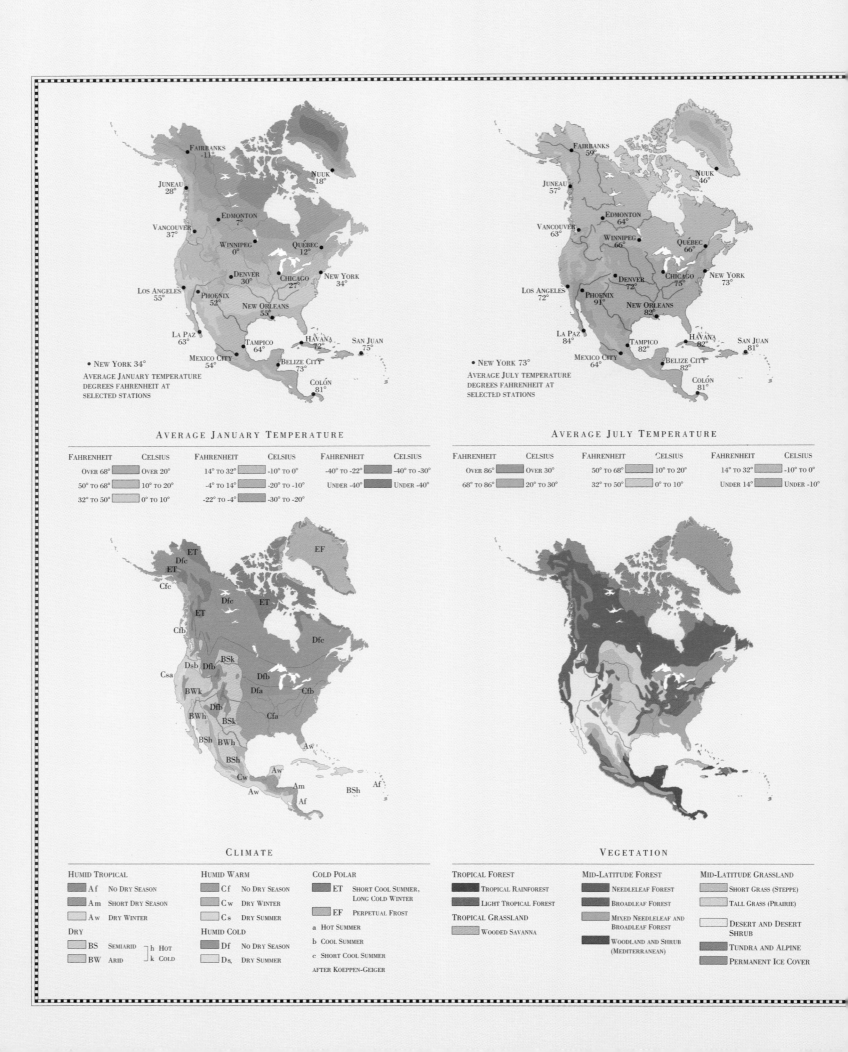

AVERAGE JANUARY TEMPERATURE

FAIRBANKS -11°
JUNEAU 28°
NUUK 18°
EDMONTON 7°
VANCOUVER 37°
WINNIPEG 0°
QUÉBEC 12°
DENVER 30°
CHICAGO 27°
NEW YORK 34°
LOS ANGELES 55°
PHOENIX 52°
NEW ORLEANS 55°
LA PAZ 63°
TAMPICO 64°
HAVANA 72°
SAN JUAN 75°
MEXICO CITY 54°
BELIZE CITY 73°
COLÓN 81°

● NEW YORK 34°
AVERAGE JANUARY TEMPERATURE
DEGREES FAHRENHEIT AT
SELECTED STATIONS

FAHRENHEIT	CELSIUS	FAHRENHEIT	CELSIUS	FAHRENHEIT	CELSIUS
OVER 68°	OVER 20°	14° TO 32°	-10° TO 0°	-40° TO -22°	-40° TO -30°
50° TO 68°	10° TO 20°	-4° TO 14°	-20° TO -10°	UNDER -40°	UNDER -40°
32° TO 50°	0° TO 10°	-22° TO -4°	-30° TO -20°		

AVERAGE JULY TEMPERATURE

FAIRBANKS 59°
JUNEAU 57°
NUUK 46°
EDMONTON 64°
VANCOUVER 63°
WINNIPEG 66°
QUÉBEC 66°
DENVER 72°
CHICAGO 75°
NEW YORK 73°
LOS ANGELES 72°
PHOENIX 91°
NEW ORLEANS 82°
LA PAZ 84°
TAMPICO 82°
HAVANA 82°
SAN JUAN 81°
MEXICO CITY 64°
BELIZE CITY 82°
COLÓN 81°

● NEW YORK 73°
AVERAGE JULY TEMPERATURE
DEGREES FAHRENHEIT AT
SELECTED STATIONS

FAHRENHEIT	CELSIUS	FAHRENHEIT	CELSIUS	FAHRENHEIT	CELSIUS
OVER 86°	OVER 30°	50° TO 68°	10° TO 20°	14° TO 32°	-10° TO 0°
68° TO 86°	20° TO 30°	32° TO 50°	0° TO 10°	UNDER 14°	UNDER -10°

CLIMATE

ET
Dfc
ET
Cfc
Dfc
ET
EF
ET
Cfb
Dfc
Dsb
Dfb
BSk
Csa
Dfb
BWk
Dfa
Cfb
BWh
Dfb
BSk
Cfa
BSh
BWh
BSh
Aw
Cw
Am
Aw
Af
Aw
BSh
Af

HUMID TROPICAL		
Af	NO DRY SEASON	
Am	SHORT DRY SEASON	
Aw	DRY WINTER	
DRY		
BS	SEMIARID	⎤ h HOT
BW	ARID	⎦ k COLD

HUMID WARM	
Cf	NO DRY SEASON
Cw	DRY WINTER
Cs	DRY SUMMER
HUMID COLD	
Df	NO DRY SEASON
Ds	DRY SUMMER

COLD POLAR	
ET	SHORT COOL SUMMER, LONG COLD WINTER
EF	PERPETUAL FROST
a	HOT SUMMER
b	COOL SUMMER
c	SHORT COOL SUMMER

AFTER KOEPPEN-GEIGER

VEGETATION

TROPICAL FOREST	
	TROPICAL RAINFOREST
	LIGHT TROPICAL FOREST
TROPICAL GRASSLAND	
	WOODED SAVANNA

MID-LATITUDE FOREST	
	NEEDLELEAF FOREST
	BROADLEAF FOREST
	MIXED NEEDLELEAF AND BROADLEAF FOREST
	WOODLAND AND SHRUB (MEDITERRANEAN)

MID-LATITUDE GRASSLAND	
	SHORT GRASS (STEPPE)
	TALL GRASS (PRAIRIE)
	DESERT AND DESERT SHRUB
	TUNDRA AND ALPINE
	PERMANENT ICE COVER

North America - Comparisons

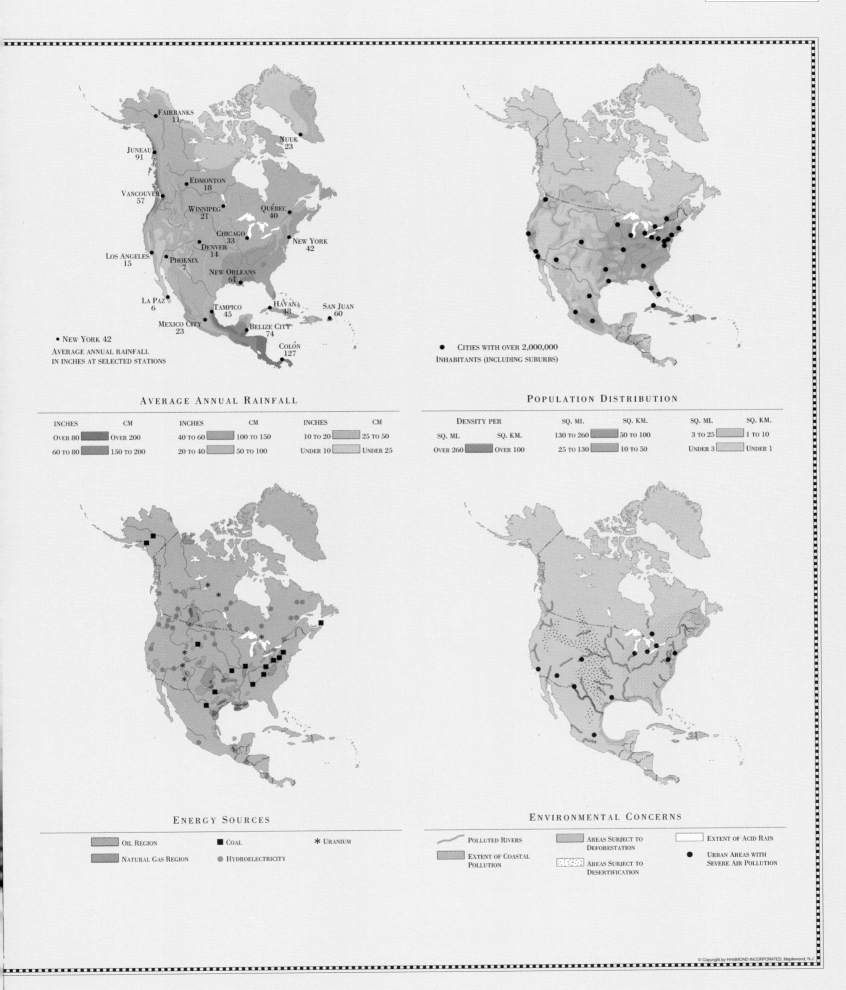

AVERAGE ANNUAL RAINFALL

FAIRBANKS 11
NUUK 23
JUNEAU 91
EDMONTON 18
VANCOUVER 57
WINNIPEG 21
QUÉBEC 40
CHICAGO 33
NEW YORK 42
DENVER 14
LOS ANGELES 15
PHOENIX 7
NEW ORLEANS 61
LA PAZ 6
TAMPICO 45
HAVANA 48
SAN JUAN 60
MEXICO CITY 23
BELIZE CITY 74
COLÓN 127

● NEW YORK 42
AVERAGE ANNUAL RAINFALL
IN INCHES AT SELECTED STATIONS

INCHES	CM	INCHES	CM	INCHES	CM
OVER 80	OVER 200	40 TO 60	100 TO 150	10 TO 20	25 TO 50
60 TO 80	150 TO 200	20 TO 40	50 TO 100	UNDER 10	UNDER 25

POPULATION DISTRIBUTION

● CITIES WITH OVER 2,000,000
INHABITANTS (INCLUDING SUBURBS)

DENSITY PER		SQ. MI.	SQ. KM.	SQ. MI.	SQ. KM.
SQ. MI.	SQ. KM.	130 TO 260	50 TO 100	3 TO 25	1 TO 10
OVER 260	OVER 100	25 TO 130	10 TO 50	UNDER 3	UNDER 1

ENERGY SOURCES

OIL REGION	■ COAL	✳ URANIUM
NATURAL GAS REGION	● HYDROELECTRICITY	

ENVIRONMENTAL CONCERNS

POLLUTED RIVERS	AREAS SUBJECT TO DEFORESTATION	EXTENT OF ACID RAIN
EXTENT OF COASTAL POLLUTION	AREAS SUBJECT TO DESERTIFICATION	● URBAN AREAS WITH SEVERE AIR POLLUTION

United States

Eastern United States, Southeastern Canada

SCALE 1:10,500,000 LAMBERT CONFORMAL CONIC PROJECTION

MILES

KILOMETERS

POPULATION OF CITIES AND TOWNS

□ OVER 2,000,000 ■ 500,000 - 999,999 ● 100,000 - 249,999 ● 10,000 - 29,999
■ 1,000,000 - 1,999,999 ● 250,000 - 499,999 ● 30,000 - 99,999 ● UNDER 10,000

Below Sea 200 500 1,000 1,500 2,000 4,000 6,000 m.
Sea Lev. Level 700 1,600 3,300 5,000 6,500 13,000 19,700 ft.

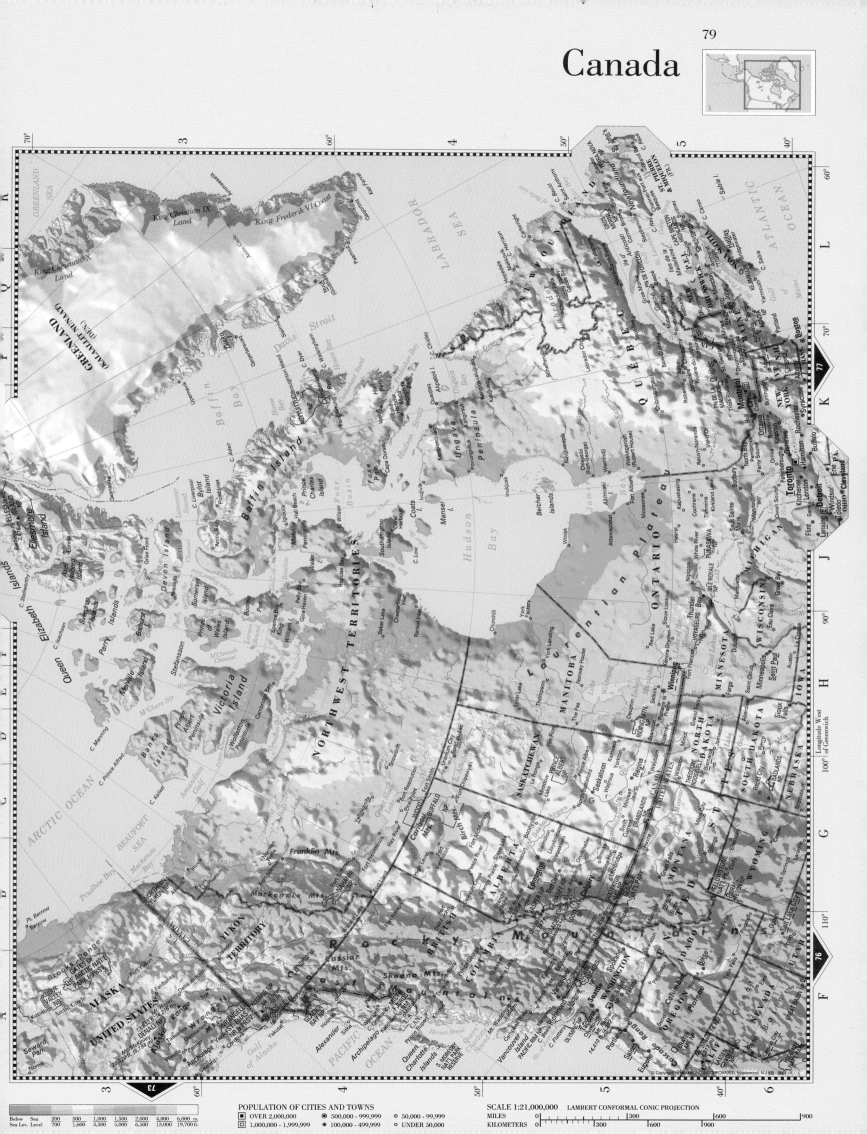

Canada

Mexico, Central America and West Indies

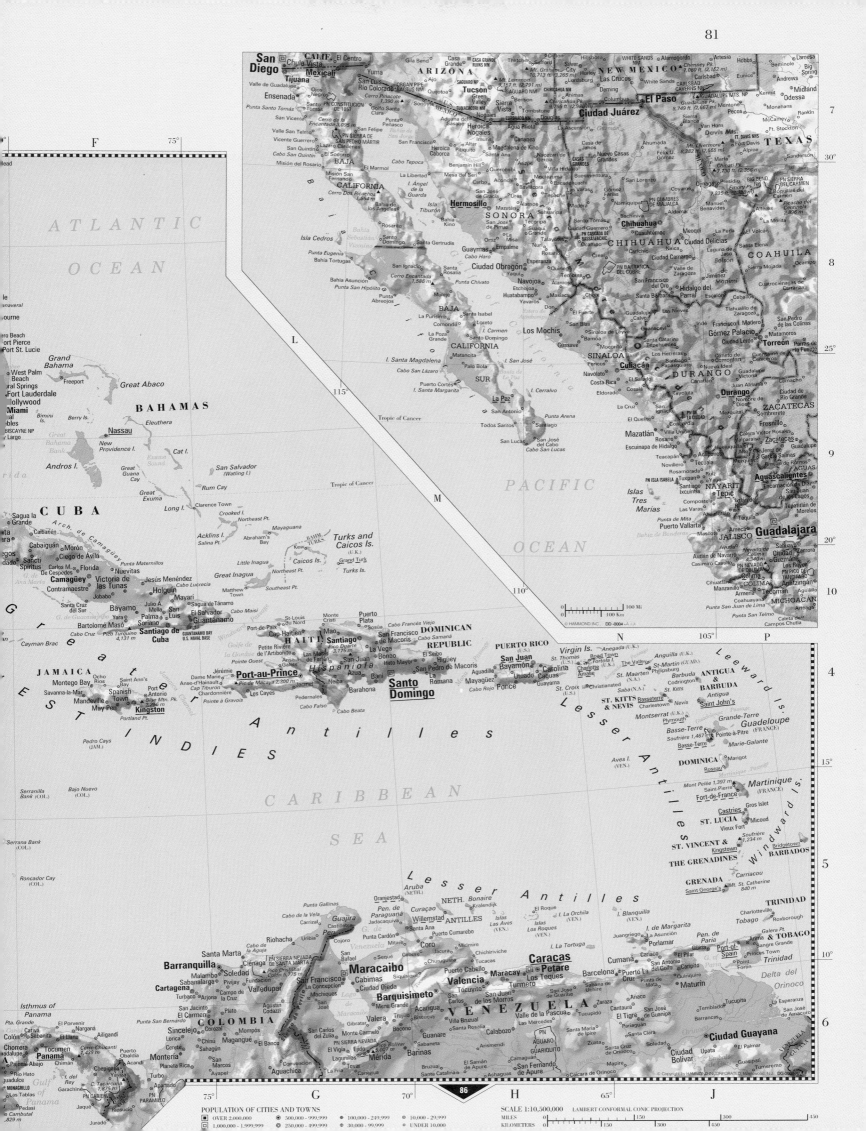

South America - Physical

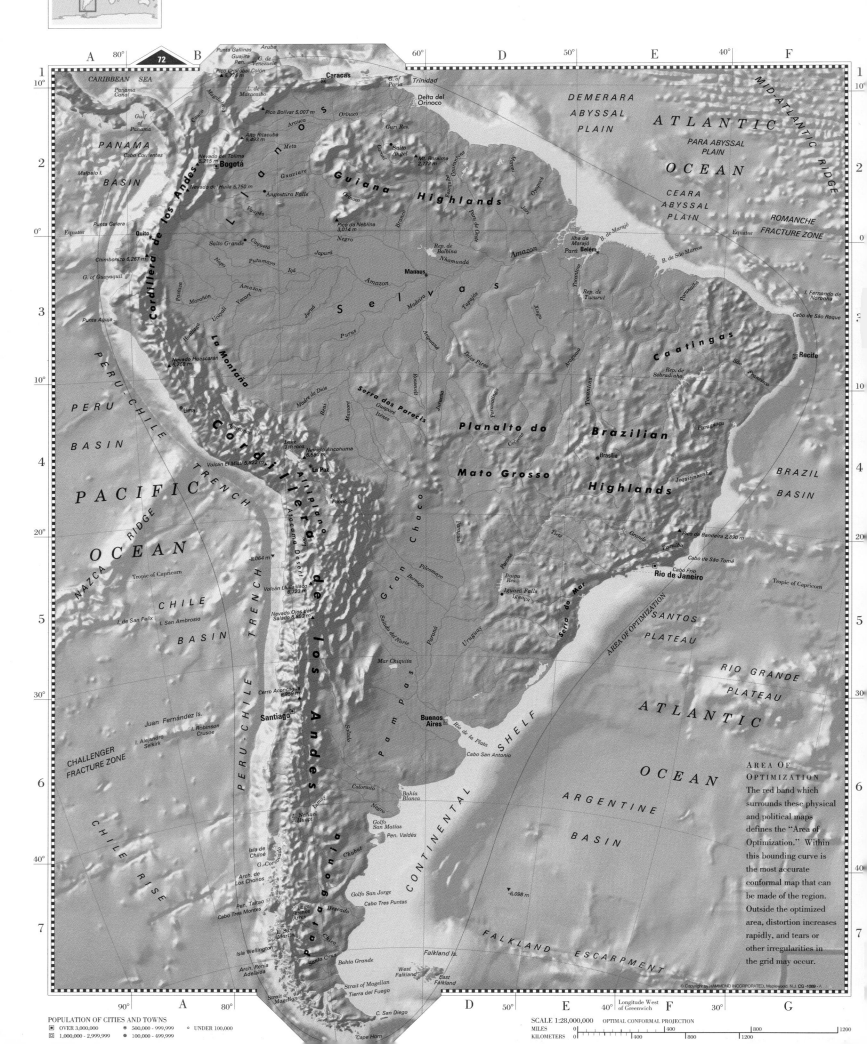

AREA OF OPTIMIZATION
The red band which surrounds these physical and political maps defines the "Area of Optimization." Within this bounding curve is the most accurate conformal map that can be made of the region. Outside the optimized area, distortion increases rapidly, and tears or other irregularities in the grid may occur.

Copyright by HAMMOND INCORPORATED, Maplewood, N.J. CG-1069-A

POPULATION OF CITIES AND TOWNS
■ OVER 3,000,000   ● 500,000 - 999,999   ○ UNDER 100,000
□ 1,000,000 - 2,999,999   ● 100,000 - 499,999

SCALE 1:28,000,000   OPTIMAL CONFORMAL PROJECTION
MILES
KILOMETERS

South America - Political

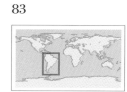

POPULATION OF CITIES AND TOWNS

- ◙ OVER 3,000,000
- ▣ 1,000,000-2,999,999
- ◘ 500,000-999,999
- ● 100,000-499,999
- ○ UNDER 100,000

SCALE 1:28,000,000   OPTIMAL CONFORMAL PROJECTION

MILES   0   400   800   1200
KILOMETERS 0   400   800   1200

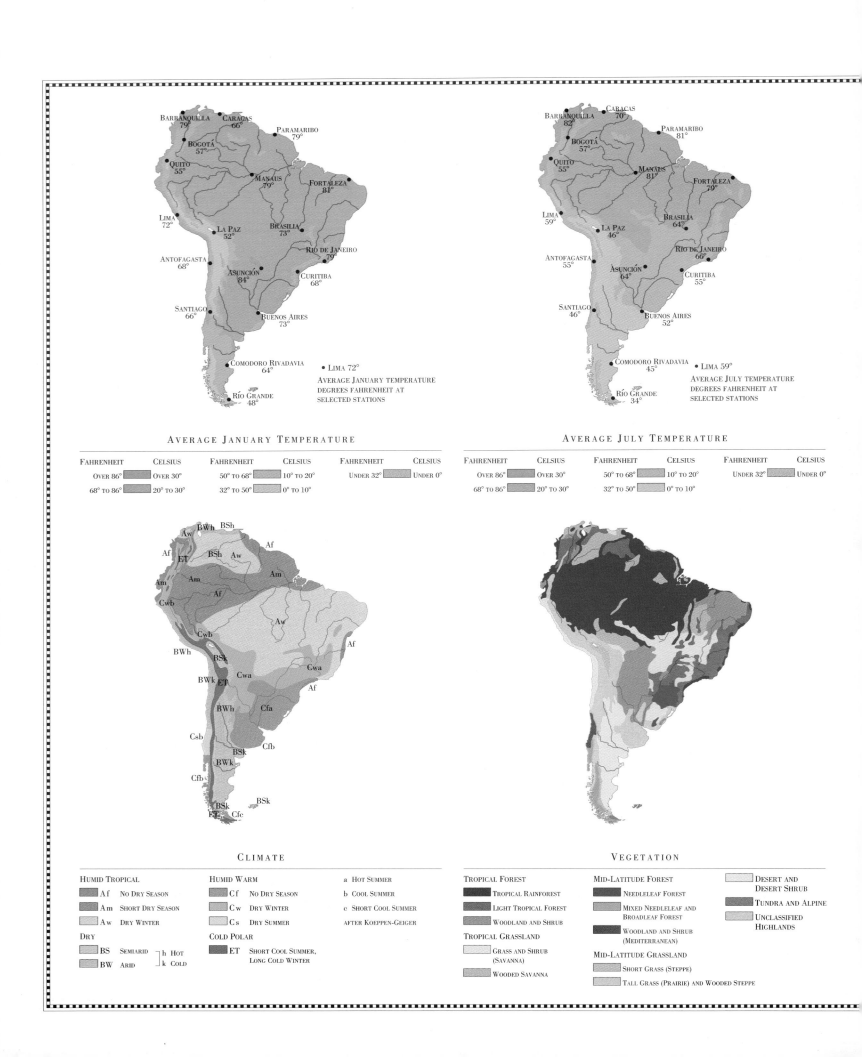

BARRANQUILLA
79°
CARACAS
66°
PARAMARIBO
79°
BOGOTÁ
57°
QUITO
55°
MANAUS
79°
FORTALEZA
81°
LIMA
72°
LA PAZ
52°
BRASILIA
73°
RÍO DE JANEIRO
79°
ANTOFAGASTA
68°
ASUNCIÓN
84°
CURITIBA
68°
SANTIAGO
66°
BUENOS AIRES
73°
COMODORO RIVADAVIA
64°
• LIMA 72°
AVERAGE JANUARY TEMPERATURE
DEGREES FAHRENHEIT AT
SELECTED STATIONS
RÍO GRANDE
48°

AVERAGE JANUARY TEMPERATURE

FAHRENHEIT	CELSIUS	FAHRENHEIT	CELSIUS	FAHRENHEIT	CELSIUS
OVER 86°	OVER 30°	50° TO 68°	10° TO 20°	UNDER 32°	UNDER 0°
68° TO 86°	20° TO 30°	32° TO 50°	0° TO 10°		

BARRANQUILLA
82°
CARACAS
70°
PARAMARIBO
81°
BOGOTÁ
57°
QUITO
55°
MANAUS
81°
FORTALEZA
79°
LIMA
59°
LA PAZ
46°
BRASILIA
64°
RÍO DE JANEIRO
66°
ANTOFAGASTA
55°
ASUNCIÓN
64°
CURITIBA
55°
SANTIAGO
46°
BUENOS AIRES
52°
COMODORO RIVADAVIA
45°
• LIMA 59°
AVERAGE JULY TEMPERATURE
DEGREES FAHRENHEIT AT
SELECTED STATIONS
RÍO GRANDE
34°

AVERAGE JULY TEMPERATURE

FAHRENHEIT	CELSIUS	FAHRENHEIT	CELSIUS	FAHRENHEIT	CELSIUS
OVER 86°	OVER 30°	50° TO 68°	10° TO 20°	UNDER 32°	UNDER 0°
68° TO 86°	20° TO 30°	32° TO 50°	0° TO 10°		

CLIMATE

HUMID TROPICAL
Af   NO DRY SEASON
Am   SHORT DRY SEASON
Aw   DRY WINTER

DRY
BS   SEMIARID   ⎫ h HOT
BW   ARID   ⎭ k COLD

HUMID WARM
Cf   NO DRY SEASON
Cw   DRY WINTER
Cs   DRY SUMMER

COLD POLAR
ET   SHORT COOL SUMMER,
     LONG COLD WINTER

a HOT SUMMER
b COOL SUMMER
c SHORT COOL SUMMER

AFTER KOEPPEN-GEIGER

VEGETATION

TROPICAL FOREST
TROPICAL RAINFOREST
LIGHT TROPICAL FOREST
WOODLAND AND SHRUB

TROPICAL GRASSLAND
GRASS AND SHRUB
(SAVANNA)
WOODED SAVANNA

MID-LATITUDE FOREST
NEEDLELEAF FOREST
MIXED NEEDLELEAF AND
BROADLEAF FOREST
WOODLAND AND SHRUB
(MEDITERRANEAN)

MID-LATITUDE GRASSLAND
SHORT GRASS (STEPPE)
TALL GRASS (PRAIRIE) AND WOODED STEPPE

DESERT AND
DESERT SHRUB
TUNDRA AND ALPINE
UNCLASSIFIED
HIGHLANDS

South America - Comparisons

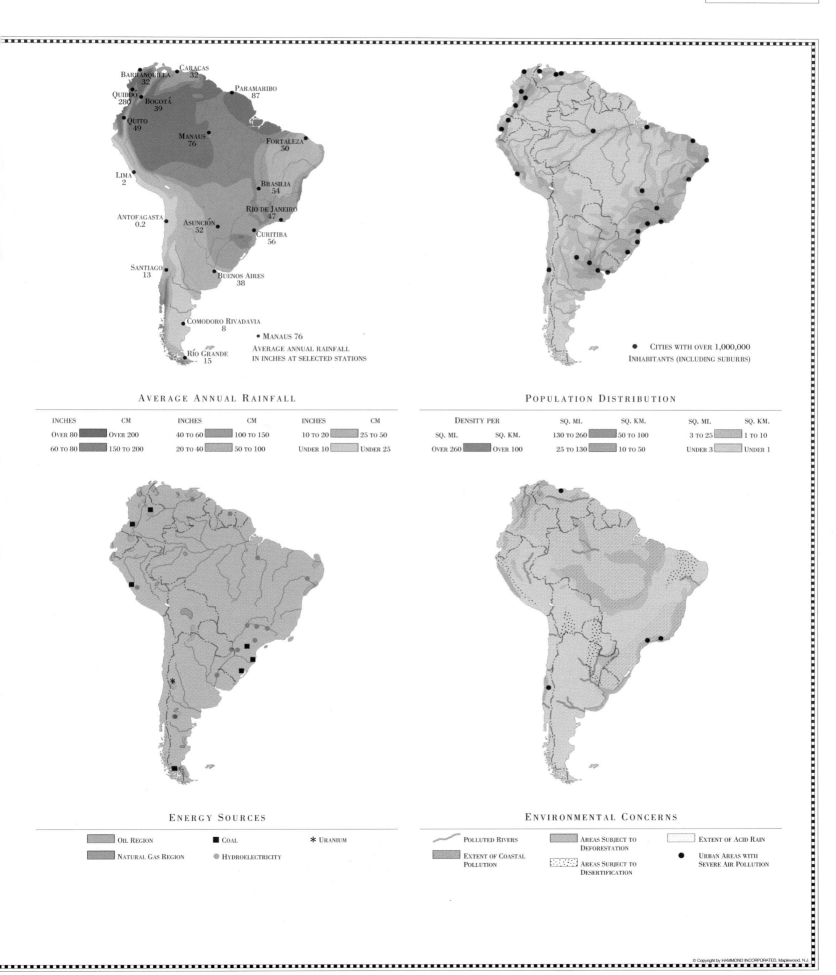

AVERAGE ANNUAL RAINFALL

BARRANQUILLA 32
CARACAS 32
PARAMARIBO 87
QUIBDÓ 280
BOGOTÁ 39
QUITO 49
MANAUS 76
FORTALEZA 50
LIMA 2
BRASILIA 54
ANTOFAGASTA 0.2
ASUNCIÓN 52
RIO DE JANEIRO 47
CURITIBA 56
SANTIAGO 13
BUENOS AIRES 38
COMODORO RIVADAVIA 8
RÍO GRANDE 15

● MANAUS 76
AVERAGE ANNUAL RAINFALL
IN INCHES AT SELECTED STATIONS

INCHES	CM	INCHES	CM	INCHES	CM
OVER 80	OVER 200	40 TO 60	100 TO 150	10 TO 20	25 TO 50
60 TO 80	150 TO 200	20 TO 40	50 TO 100	UNDER 10	UNDER 25

POPULATION DISTRIBUTION

● CITIES WITH OVER 1,000,000
INHABITANTS (INCLUDING SUBURBS)

DENSITY PER		SQ. MI.	SQ. KM.	SQ. MI.	SQ. KM.
SQ. MI.	SQ. KM.	130 TO 260	50 TO 100	3 TO 25	1 TO 10
OVER 260	OVER 100	25 TO 130	10 TO 50	UNDER 3	UNDER 1

ENERGY SOURCES

	OIL REGION	■ COAL	✳ URANIUM
	NATURAL GAS REGION	● HYDROELECTRICITY	

ENVIRONMENTAL CONCERNS

	POLLUTED RIVERS		AREAS SUBJECT TO DEFORESTATION		EXTENT OF ACID RAIN
	EXTENT OF COASTAL POLLUTION		AREAS SUBJECT TO DESERTIFICATION	●	URBAN AREAS WITH SEVERE AIR POLLUTION

ATLANTIC

OCEAN

St. Peter and
St. Paul Rocks
(BRAZIL)

Equator

Fernando de Noronha
(BRAZIL)

Rocas

SURINAME   FRENCH
GUIANA

Juliana Top
1,230 m

Tumac-Humac Mts.

PN DO
CABO ORANGE

Macapá

Ilha Grande
de Gurupá

Ilha de
Marajó

Belém

São Luís

PN DES LENÇÓIS
MARANHENSES

Fortaleza

PN DE SETE CIDADES

Teresina

Mossoró

Natal

Cabo de São Roque

João Pessoa

Campina
Grande

Recife

Olinda

Salvador

Planalto
do
Mato Grosso

ATLANTIC

OCEAN

Trinidade
(BRAZIL)

Martin Vaz
(BRAZIL)

Brasília

Goiânia

Planalto
Central

Belo Horizonte

Vitória

Campo Grande

Rio de Janeiro

São Paulo
Santo André

POPULATION OF CITIES AND TOWNS

■ OVER 2,000,000   ● 500,000 - 999,999   ○ 50,000 - 99,999
▣ 1,000,000 - 1,999,999   ● 100,000 - 499,999   ○ UNDER 50,000

SCALE 1:15,000,000   LAMBERT CONFORMAL CONIC PROJECTION

MILES   0   200   400   600
KILOMETERS   0   200   400   600

© Copyright by HAMMOND INCORPORATED, Maplewood, N.J. CG - 2107 - A A A

Southern South America

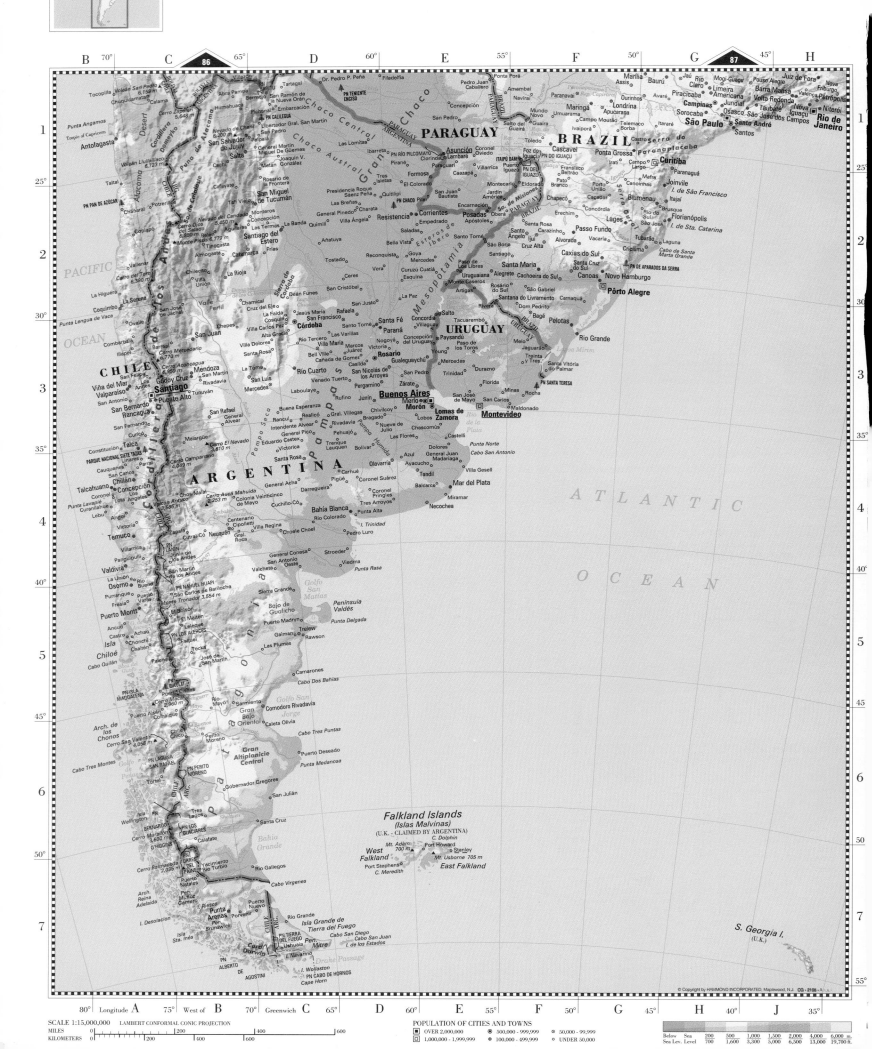

Population of Major World Cities

The following pages include population figures, given in thousands, for major cities in each country, and for all national capitals, regardless of size. Two dependencies, Macau and Puerto Rico, follow the country listings. National capitals are indicated with an asterisk (*).

Country / City	Population in thousands
A Afghanistan	
Kābul*	1,424
Qandahar	226
Albania	
Tiranë*	239
Algeria	
Algiers*	1,688
Annaba	228
Constantine	450
Oran	599
Andorra	
Andorra la Vella*	12
Angola	
Luanda*	1,530
Antigua and Barbuda	
Saint John's*	36
Argentina	
Avellaneda	347
Bahía Blanca	240
Buenos Aires*	2,961
Córdoba	1,148
General San Martin	408
Lanús	467
La Plata	520
Lomas de Zamora	573
Mar del Plata	512
Morón	642
Qilmes	509
Rosario	895
San Miguel de Tucumán	471
Santa Fé	343
Armenia	
Yerevan*	1,199
Australia	
Adelaide	957
Brisbane	1,146
Canberra*	276
Hobart	127
Melbourne	2,762
Newcastle	262
Perth	1,019
Sydney	3,098
Austria	
Graz	238
Vienna*	1,540
Azerbaijan	
Baku*	1,150
B Bahamas	
Nassau*	172
Bahrain	
Manama*	143
Bangladesh	
Chittagong	1,388
Dhaka*	3,638
Khulna	623
Barbados	
Bridgetown*	7
Belarus	
Homyel'	500
Minsk*	1,589
Mahilyow	356
Vitsyebsk	350
Belgium	
Antwerp	468
Brussels*	954
Ghent	230
Liège	195
Belize	
Belmopan*	4
Benin	
Cotonou	383
Porto-Novo*	144
Bhutan	
Thimphu*	12
Bolivia	
Cochabamba	404
La Paz*	977
Santa Cruz	529
Sucre*	106
Bosnia & Herzegovina	
Banja Luka	142
Sarajevo*	416
Botswana	
Gaborone*	129

Country / City	Population in thousands
Brazil	
Aracaju	401
Belém	765
Belo Horizonte	2,206
Brasília*	1,493
Campinas	748
Campo Grande	516
Cuiabá	253
Curitiba	842
Florianópolis	192
Fortaleza	1,027
Goiânia	912
João Pessoa	497
Juiz de Fora	378
Maceió	555
Manaus	1,006
Natal	460
Niterói	401
Nova Iguaçu	562
Osasco	567
Porto Alegre	1,237
Recife	1,297
Ribeirão Preto	416
Rio de Janeiro	5,474
Salvador	2,070
Santo André	518
Santos	416
São Bernardo do Campo	550
São Luís	164
São Paulo	9,394
Teresina	556
Vitória	184
Brunei	
Bandar Seri Begawan*	64
Bulgaria	
Plovdiv	374
Sofia*	1,142
Varna	311
Burkina Faso	
Ouagadougou*	442
Burundi	
Bujumbura*	215
C Cambodia	
Phnom Penh*	300
Cameroon	
Douala	1,030
Yaoundé*	654
Canada	
Calgary	711
Edmonton	617
Halifax	114
Hamilton	318
Laval	314
London	269
Mississauga	463
Montréal	1,018
Ottawa*	314
Québec	168
Regina	175
Saskatoon	201
Toronto	2,276
Vancouver	472
Windsor	193
Winnipeg	617
Cape Verde	
Praia*	57
Central African Republic	
Bangui*	474
Chad	
N'Djamena*	594
Chile	
Antofagasta	227
Concepción	327
Santiago*	4,298
Talcahuano	246
Valparaíso	282
Viña del Mar	306
China	
Anshan	1,215
Baotou	980
Beijing*	5,715
Benxi	767
Changchun	1,698
Changsha	1,077
Chengdu	1,719
Chongqing	2,265

Country / City	Population in thousands
Dalian	1,632
Dandong	525
Daqing	676
Datong	779
Fengcheng	996
Fushun	1,210
Fuxin	623
Fuzhou	890
Guangzhou	2,892
Guiyang	1,009
Handan	798
Hangzhou	1,119
Harbin	2,468
Hefei	733
Hegang	507
Hohhot	654
Huainan	674
Jilin	1,038
Jinan	1,361
Jinzhou	573
Jixi	638
Kaifeng	503
Kunming	1,108
Lanzhou	1,205
Lhasa	343
Liuzhou	602
Luoyang	730
Mudanjiang	562
Nanchang	1,026
Nanjing	2,114
Nanning	723
Ningbo	548
Qingdao	1,317
Qiqihar	1,066
Shanghai	7,551
Shantou	558
Shenyang	3,588
Shijiazhuang	1,065
Suzhou	697
Taiyuan	1,514
Tangshan	1,042
Tianjin	4,521
Ürümqi	1,071
Wuhan	3,177
Wuxi	806
Xi'an	1,954
Xining	559
Xuzhou	795
Yichun	787
Yinchuan	350
Zhangjiakou	525
Zhengzhou	1,139
Zibo	864
Colombia	
Barranquilla	1,000
Bogotá*	5,699
Bucaramanga	403
Cali	1,625
Cartagena	576
Cúcuta	462
Ibagué	336
Manizales	341
Medellín	1,485
Pereira	329
Comoros	
Moroni*	20
Congo, Dem. Rep. of the	
Kananga	291
Kinshasa*	2,654
Lubumbashi	543
Mbuji-Mayi	423
Congo, Rep. of the	
Brazzaville*	596
Pointe-Noire	298
Costa Rica	
San José*	241
Côte d'Ivoire	
Abidjan	1,929
Yamoussoukro*	107
Croatia	
Rijeka	168
Split	189
Zagreb*	704
Cuba	
Camagüey	279
Guantánamo	198
Havana*	2,078
Holguin	223

Country / City	Population in thousands
Santiago de Cuba	397
Cyprus	
Nicosia*	167
Czech Republic	
Brno	388
Ostrava	328
Prague*	1,212
D Denmark	
Århus	182
Copenhagen*	618
Djibouti	
Djibouti*	200
Dominica	
Roseau*	6
Dominican Republic	
Santiago de los Caballeros	279
Santo Domingo*	1,313
E Ecuador	
Guayaquil	1,513
Quito*	1,113
Egypt	
Alexandria	3,295
Al Jīzah	2,096
Asyūt	313
Cairo*	6,663
Port Said	449
Shubrā al Khaymah	812
Tantā	285
El Salvador	
San Salvador*	498
Equatorial Guinea	
Malabo*	37
Eritrea	
Asmara*	344
Estonia	
Tallinn*	482
Ethiopia	
Addis Ababa*	1,739
F Fiji	
Suva*	70
Finland	
Helsinki*	492
Tampere	172
France	
Bordeaux	213
Le Havre	197
Lille	178
Lyon	422
Marseille	808
Montpellier	211
Nantes	252
Nice	346
Paris*	2,175
Rennes	204
Saint-Étienne	202
Strasbourg	256
Toulouse	366
G Gabon	
Libreville*	352
Gambia	
Banjul*	44
Georgia	
Tbilisi*	1,260
Germany	
Berlin*	3,434
Bochum	396
Bonn	292
Bremen	551
Chemnitz	294
Cologne	954
Dortmund	599
Dresden	491
Duisburg	535
Düsseldorf	576
Essen	627
Frankfurt am Main	645
Hamburg	1,652
Hannover	513
Kiel	246
Leipzig	511
Magdeburg	279

Country / City	Population in thousands
Mannheim	310
Munich	1,229
Münster	259
Nürnberg	494
Rostock	249
Saarbrücken	192
Stuttgart	563
Wiesbaden	254
Ghana	
Accra*	860
Kumasi	349
Greece	
Athens*	748
Piraiévs	170
Thessaloníki	406
Grenada	
Saint George's*	5
Guatemala	
Guatemala*	1,676
Guinea	
Conakry*	526
Guinea-Bissau	
Bissau*	109
Guyana	
Georgetown*	72
H Haiti	
Port-au-Prince*	690
Honduras	
San Pedro Sula	287
Tegucigalpa*	577
Hungary	
Budapest*	2,017
Debrecen	212
Miskolc	196
Szeged	175
I Iceland	
Reykjavík*	96
India	
Āgra	892
Ahmadābād	2,877
Allahābād	793
Amritsar	709
Aurangābād	573
Bangalore	2,660
Bareilly	587
Baroda	1,031
Bhopāl	1,063
Bombay	9,926
Calcutta	4,400
Chandigarh	504
Cochin	565
Coimbatore	816
Cuttack	403
Delhi	7,207
Farīdābād	618
Gwalior	691
Howrah	950
Hubli-Dhārwār	648
Hyderābād	3,044
Indore	1,092
Jabalpur	742
Jaipur	1,458
Jammu	206
Jamshedpur	461
Jodhpur	666
Jullundur	510
Kalyān	1,015
Kānpur	1,874
Kota	537
Kozhikode	420
Lucknow	1,619
Ludhiāna	1,043
Madras	3,841
Madurai	940
Meerut	754
Mysore	481
Nāgpur	1,625
Nāsik	657
New Delhi*	301
Patna	917
Poona	1,567
Rānchī	599
Sholāpur	604
Srīnagar	606
Surat	1,499

Country / City	Population in thousands
Thāna	803
Tiruchchirāppalli	387
Trivandrum	524
Vāranāsi	929
Vijayawada	702
Visākhapatnam	752
Indonesia	
Bandung	2,027
Banjarmasin	381
Jakarta*	8,259
Malang	512
Medan	1,379
Padang	481
Palembang	787
Pontianak	305
Semarang	1,027
Surabaya	2,421
Surakarta	470
Ujung Pandang	709
Yogyakarta	399
Iran	
Ābādān	296
Ahvāz	580
Bākhtarān	561
Eşfahān	987
Mashhad	1,464
Qom	543
Rasht	291
Shīrāz	848
Tabrīz	971
Tehrān*	6,043
Zāhedān	282
Iraq	
Al Başrah	334
Baghdad*	1,984
Mosul	310
Ireland	
Cork	127
Dublin*	478
Israel	
Jerusalem*	499
Tel Aviv-Yafo	320
Italy	
Bari	353
Bologna	411
Catania	364
Florence	408
Genoa	701
Messina	275
Milan	1,432
Naples	1,206
Palermo	734
Rome*	2,693
Taranto	244
Trieste	231
Turin	992
Venice	110
Verona	259
J Jamaica	
Kingston*	104
Japan	
Amagasaki	499
Chiba	829
Fukuoka	1,237
Funabashi	533
Hamakita	811
Hamamatsu	535
Higashi-Ōsaka	518
Hiroshima	1,086
Kagoshima	536
Kawasaki	1,157
Kitakyūshū	1,034
Kōbe	1,477
Kumamoto	575
Kyōto	1,471
Nagoya	2,155
Niigata	485
Okayama	591
Osaka	2,624
Sakai	814
Sapporo	1,672
Sendai	910
Shizuoka	473
Tōkyō*	8,164
Toyonaka	414
Utsunomiya	423
Wakayama	399

Country / City	Population in thousands
Yokohama	3,220
Yokosuka	434
Jordan	
'Ammān*	936
K Kazakhstan	
Almaty	1,128
Aqmola*	277
Öskemen	324
Pavlodar	331
Qaraghandy	614
Semey	334
Shymkent	393
Zhambyl	307
Kenya	
Mombasa	442
Nairobi*	1,162
Kiribati	
Tarawa*	18
Korea, North	
Ch'ŏngjin	306
Hamhŭng	484
P'yŏngyang*	1,250
Wŏnsan	275
Korea, South	
Chŏnju	426
Inch'ŏn	1,387
Kwangju	906
Pusan	3,798
Seoul*	10,613
Taegu	2,229
Taejŏn	886
Kuwait	
Kuwait*	182
Kyrgyzstan	
Bishkek*	616
L Laos	
Vientiane*	377
Latvia	
Riga*	915
Lebanon	
Beirut*	475
Lesotho	
Maseru*	13
Liberia	
Monrovia*	421
Libya	
Benghāzī	287
Tripoli*	550
Liechtenstein	
Vaduz*	5
Lithuania	
Kaunas	423
Vilnius*	582
Luxembourg	
Luxembourg*	75
M Macedonia	
Skopje*	563
Madagascar	
Antananarivo*	452
Malawi	
Blantyre	332
Lilongwe*	234
Malaysia	
Ipoh	383
Kuala Lumpur*	1,145
Maldives	
Male*	55
Mali	
Bamako*	658
Malta	
Valletta*	9
Marshall Islands	
Majuro*	9
Mauritania	
Nouakchott*	135
Mauritius	
Port Louis*	134
Mexico	
Acapulco de Juárez	515
Aguascalientes	440
Chihuahua	516
Ciudad Juárez	790
Culiacán	415
Ecatepec de Morelos	1,218
Guadalajara	1,650
Guadalupe	535
Hermosillo	406
León	758
Mérida	529
Mexicali	439
Mexico City*	8,237
Monterrey	1,069
Morelia	429
Netzahualcóyotl	1,255
Puebla de Zaragoza	1,007
Saltillo	421
San Luis Potosí	489
Tijuana	699
Tlalnepantla de Galeana	702
Torreón	439
Veracruz Llave	439
Zapopan	668
Micronesia, Federated States of	
Palikir*	6
Moldova	
Chişinău*	665
Monaco	
Monaco*	27
Mongolia	
Ulaanbaatar*	515
Morocco	
Casablanca	2,263
Fès	449
Marrakech	440
Rabat*	368
Mozambique	
Maputo*	1,007
Myanmar (Burma)	
Mandalay	533
Moulmein	220
Yangon* (Rangoon)	2,513
N Namibia	
Windhoek*	115
Nepal	
Kāthmāndu*	423
Netherlands	
Amsterdam*	714
Eindhoven	194
Groningen	169
Rotterdam	590
The Hague*	445
Utrecht	233
New Zealand	
Auckland	316
Christchurch	293
Wellington*	150
Nicaragua	
Managua*	608
Niger	
Niamey*	225
Nigeria	
Abeokuta	308
Abuja*	306
Ibadan	1,060
Ilorin	282
Kano	399
Lagos	1,097
Ogbomosho	432
Oshogbo	345
Port Harcourt	242
Zaria	224
Norway	
Bergen	218
Oslo*	457
O Oman	
Muscat*	67
P Pakistan	
Faisalabad	1,104
Gujrānwāla	659
Hyderābād	752
Islāmābād*	204
Karāchi	5,076
Lahore	2,953
Multān	732
Peshāwar	566
Quetta	286
Rāwalpindi	795
Sargodha	291
Siālkot	302
Palau	
Koror*	9
Panama	
Panamá*	389
Papua New Guinea	
Port Moresby*	124
Paraguay	
Asunción*	502
Peru	
Callao	515
Chiclayo	280
Comas	287
Lima*	376
Trujillo	355
Philippines	
Caloocan	616
Cebu	627
Davao	844
Makati	409
Manila*	1,876
Quezon	1,587
Zamboanga	443
Poland	
Białystok	268
Bydgoszcz	380
Gdańsk	462
Gdynia	251
Katowice	366
Kraków	746
Łódź	849
Lublin	349
Poznań	587
Szczecin	411
Warsaw*	1,651
Wrocław	641
Portugal	
Lisbon*	678
Porto	311
Q Qatar	
Doha*	217
R Romania	
Braşov	324
Bucharest*	2,068
Cluj-Napoca	329
Constanţa	351
Iaşi	344
Ploieşti	253
Timişoara	334
Russia	
Archangel	416
Astrakhan'	509
Barnaul	602
Bryansk	452
Cheboksary	420
Chelyabinsk	1,143
Groznyy	401
Irkutsk	626
Ivanovo	481
Izhevsk	635
Kazan'	1,094
Kemerovo	520
Khabarovsk	601
Krasnodar	620
Krasnoyarsk	912
Kursk	424
Lipetsk	450
Magnitogorsk	440
Moscow*	8,769
Murmansk	468
Naberezhnye Chelny	501
Nizhniy Novgorod	1,438
Nizhniy Tagil	440
Novokuznetsk	600
Novosibirsk	1,436
Omsk	1,148
Orenburg	547
Penza	483
Perm'	1,091
Rostov	1,020
Ryazan'	515
Saint Petersburg	4,456
Samara	1,257
Saratov	905
Simbirsk	625
Tol'yatti	630
Tomsk	502
Tula	540
T'ver	451
Tyumen'	477
Ufa	1,083
Vladivostok	648
Volgograd	999
Voronezh	887
Vyatka	441
Yaroslavl'	633
Yekaterinburg	1,367
Rwanda	
Kigali*	118
S Saint Kitts and Nevis	
Basseterre*	14
Saint Lucia	
Castries*	56
Saint Vincent and the Grenadines	
Kingstown*	17
Samoa	
Apia*	32
San Marino	
San Marino*	4
Sao Tome and Principe	
São Tomé*	8
Saudi Arabia	
Jiddah	561
Mecca	367
Riyadh*	667
Senegal	
Dakar*	799
Seychelles	
Victoria*	16
Sierra Leone	
Freetown*	470
Singapore	
Singapore*	2,704
Slovak Republic	
Bratislava*	442
Košice	235
Slovenia	
Ljubljana*	287
Solomon Islands	
Honiara*	30
Somalia	
Mogadishu*	500
South Africa	
Cape Town*	855
Durban	716
Johannesburg	714
Port Elizabeth	303
Pretoria*	526
Soweto	597
Spain	
Alicante	266
Barcelona	1,668
Bilbao	351
Córdoba	305
Granada	262
Las Palmas de Gran Canaria	354
Madrid*	2,991
Málaga	605
Murcia	315
Palma	297
Saragossa	574
Seville	654
Valencia	719
Valladolid	332
Vigo	262
Sri Lanka	
Colombo*	609
Sudan	
Khartoum*	474
Omdurman	526
Suriname	
Paramaribo*	68
Swaziland	
Mbabane*	38
Sweden	
Göteborg	431
Malmö	232
Stockholm*	669
Switzerland	
Bern*	136
Zürich	365
Syria	
Aleppo	1,355
Damascus*	1,378
Ḩimş	481
T Taiwan	
Kaohsiung	1,227
Keelung	348
Taichung	607
Tainan	582
Taipei*	2,268
Tajikistan	
Dushanbe*	595
Tanzania	
Dar es Salaam*	1,096
Thailand	
Bangkok*	5,876
Thon Buri	628
Togo	
Lomé*	370
Tonga	
Nuku'alofa*	21
Trinidad and Tobago	
Port-of-Spain*	51
Tunisia	
Tūnis*	597
Turkey	
Adana	916
Ankara*	2,559
Antalya	378
Bursa	835
Diyarbakır	381
Eskişehir	413
Gaziantep	603
İstanbul	6,620
İzmir	1,757
Kayseri	421
Konya	513
Malatya	281
Mersin	422
Turkmenistan	
Ashgabat*	398
Tuvalu	
Funafuti*	2
U Uganda	
Kampala*	458
Ukraine	
Chernihiv	296
Dniprodzerzhyns'k	282
Dnipropetrovs'k	1,179
Donets'k	1,110
Horlivka	337
Kharkiv	1,611
Kherson	355
Kiev*	2,587
Kryvyy Rih	713
Luhans'k	497
L'viv	790
Makiyivka	430
Mariupol'	517
Mykolayiv	503
Odesa	1,115
Poltava	315
Sevastopol'	356
Simferopol'	344
Sumy	291
Vinnytsya	374
Zaporizhzhya	884
Zhytomyr	292
United Arab Emirates	
Abu Dhabi*	243
Dubayy	266
United Kingdom	
Belfast	295
Birmingham	1,014
Bradford	293
Bristol	414
Cardiff	262
Coventry	319
Edinburgh	420
Glasgow	765
Hull	322
Leeds	452
Leicester	324
Liverpool	539
London*	6,680
Manchester	449
Nottingham	273
Plymouth	239
Sheffield	471
Stoke-on-Trent	272
Wolverhampton	264
United States	
Albuquerque	385
Atlanta	394
Austin	466
Baltimore	736
Boston	574
Buffalo	328
Charlotte	396
Chicago	2,784
Cincinnati	364
Cleveland	506
Columbus (Ohio)	633
Dallas	1,007
Denver	468
Detroit	1,028
El Paso	515
Fort Worth	448
Fresno	354
Honolulu	365
Houston	1,631
Indianapolis	742
Jacksonville	635
Kansas City (Mo.)	435
Long Beach	429
Los Angeles	3,485
Memphis	610
Miami	359
Milwaukee	628
Minneapolis	368
Nashville	488
New Orleans	497
New York	7,323
Oakland	372
Oklahoma City	445
Omaha	336
Philadelphia	1,586
Phoenix	983
Pittsburgh	370
Portland	437
Sacramento	369
Saint Louis	397
San Antonio	936
San Diego	1,111
San Francisco	724
San Jose	782
Seattle	516
Toledo	333
Tucson	405
Tulsa	367
Virginia Beach	393
Washington, D.C.*	607
Wichita	304
Uruguay	
Montevideo*	1,252
Uzbekistan	
Andijon	293
Namangan	308
Samarqand	366
Tashkent*	2,073
V Vanuatu	
Port-Vila*	19
Venezuela	
Barquisimeto	625
Caracas*	1,822
Ciudad Guayana	453
Maracaibo	1,124
Maracay	354
Petare	338
Valencia	903
Vietnam	
Đà Nang	319
Haiphong	1,279
Hanoi*	2,571
Ho Chi Minh City	3,420
Y Yemen	
Aden	272
Sanaa*	140
Yugoslavia	
Belgrade*	1,555
Niš	176
Novi Sad	179
Z Zambia	
Kitwe	472
Lusaka*	870
Ndola	443
Zimbabwe	
Bulawayo	414
Harare*	656
Dependency	
Macau (Port.)	
Macau	342
Puerto Rico (U.S.)	
San Juan	427

Index of the World

This alphabetical list gives countries, cities, regions, political divisions, and physical features for the world. Latitude/longitude coordinates are given for each entry, where possible, followed by the page number for the map on which the entry appears to the best advantage. The entry may be located on other maps as well by the use of the coordinates given. Capitals are designated by asterisks (*).

Index Abbreviations

Afghan.	Afghanistan	Eng.	England	Mor.	Morocco	Okla.	Oklahoma	Sp.	Spain, Spanish
Ala.	Alabama	Eq. Guin.	Equatorial Guinea	Moz.	Mozambique	Ont.	Ontario	St. Ste.	Saint, Sainte
Alg.	Algeria	Falk. Is.	Falkland Islands	mt., mts.	mountain, mountains	Ore.	Oregon	Switz.	Switzerland
Alta.	Alberta	Fla.	Florida	N,. No.	North, Northern	Pa.	Pennsylvania	Tanz.	Tanzania
Amer.	America	Fr.	France, French	Nat'l Pk	National Park	Pak.	Pakistan	Tas.	Tasmania
arch.	archipelago	Ga.	Georgia	N.B.	New Brunswick	Para.	Paraguay	Tenn.	Tennessee
Arg.	Argentina	Ger.	Germany	N.C.	North Carolina	P.E.I.	Prince Edward Island	Terr.	Territory
Ariz.	Arizona	Guat.	Guatemala	N.D.	North Dakota	pen.	peninsula	Thai.	Thailand
Ark.	Arkansas	Ill.	Illinois	Neb.	Nebraska	plat.	plateau	U.K.	United Kingdom
Austl.	Australia	Ind.	Indiana	Neth.	Netherlands	P.N.G.	Papua New Guinea	Un.	United
Belg.	Belgium	Indon.	Indonesia	Neth. Ant.	Netherlands Antilles	Port.	Portugal, Portuguese	U.S.	United States
Br. Col.	British Columbia	isl., isls.	island, islands	Nev.	Nevada	P.R.	Puerto Rico	Va.	Virginia
Calif.	California	Kans.	Kansas	New Cal.	New Caledonia	prom.	promontory	Ven.	Venezuela
Can.	Canada	Kazak.	Kazakhstan	Newf.	Newfoundland	prov.	province, provincial	Vt.	Vermont
CAfr.	Central African Republic	Ky.	Kentucky	N.H.	New Hampshire	Qué.	Québec	W.	West, Western
chan.	channel	La.	Louisiana	Nic.	Nicaragua	Queens.	Queensland	Wash.	Washington
Col.	Colombia	Lux.	Luxembourg	N.J.	New Jersey	Rep.	Republic	Wis.	Wisconsin
Colo.	Colorado	Man.	Manitoba	N. Korea	North Korea	res.	reservoir	W. Va.	West Virginia
Conn.	Connecticut	Mart.	Martinique	N.M.	New Mexico	R.I.	Rhode Island	Wyo.	Wyoming
C.R.	Costa Rica	Mass.	Massachusetts	No. Ire.	Northern Ireland	Rom.	Romania	Yugo.	Yugoslavia
Czech Rep.	Czech Republic	Md.	Maryland	No. Terr.	Northern Territory	S., So.	South, Southern	Zim.	Zimbabwe
D.C.	District of Columbia	Mex.	Mexico	N.S.	Nova Scotia	S. Afr.	South Africa		
Del.	Delaware	Mich.	Michigan	N.S.W.	New South Wales	Sask.	Saskatchewan		
Den.	Denmark	Minn.	Minnesota	N.W. Terrs.	Northwest Territories (Canada)	S.C.	South Carolina		
Dom. Rep.	Dominican Republic	Miss.	Mississippi			Scot.	Scotland		
E.	East, Eastern	Mo.	Missouri	N.Y.	New York	S. D.	South Dakota		
El Sal.	El Salvador	Mont.	Montana	N.Z.	New Zealand	Sol. Is.	Solomon Islands		

A

NAME	LATITUDE	LONGITUDE	PAGE
Aberdeen, Scot.	57° 09′ N	02° 06′ W	42
Abidjan, Côte d'Ivoire	05 20 N	04 01 W	68
Abilene, Texas	32 28 N	99 43 W	76
Abu Dhabi,* United Arab Emirates	24 28 N	54 22 E	52
Abuja,* Nigeria	67 20 N	09 05 E	68
Acapulco, Mex.	16 51 N	99 55 W	80
Accra,* Ghana	05 33 N	00 12 W	68
Aconcagua (mt.)	32 45 S	70 14 W	88
Adana, Turkey	37 00 N	35 15 E	44
Ad Dahna' (desert)	27 30 N	45 00 E	52
Addis Ababa,* Ethiopia	09 01 N	38 45 E	69
Adelaide, Austl.	34 55 S	138 37 E	59
Aden, Yemen	12 45 N	45 05 E	52
Adirondack (mts.)	44 00 N	74 00 W	78
Adrar de Iforas (plat.)	20 00 N	02 00 E	68
Adriatic (sea)	42 50 N	15 40 E	44
Aegean (sea)	40 23 N	25 00 E	44
Afghanistan	34 00 N	65 00 E	49
Agaña,* Guam	13 29 N	144 47 E	62
Agra, India	27 10 N	78 08 E	53
Aguascalientes, Mex,	21 53 N	102 18 W	80
Agulhas (cape)	34 51 S	19 59 E	70
Ahaggar (mts.)	23 00 N	05 00 E	68
Ahmadabad, India	23 00 N	72 44 E	53
Ahvāz, Iran	31 19 N	48 42 E	52
Aklavik, N.W. Terrs.	68 12 N	135 00 W	79
Akron, Ohio	41 05 N	81 31 W	78
Alabama (state), U.S.	33 00 N	87 00 W	78
Åland (isls.)	60 15 N	20 00 E	43
Alaska (gulf)	59 00 N	145 00 W	76
Alaska (pen.)	57 00 N	158 00 W	76
Alaska (range)	63 00 N	151 00 W	76
Alaska (state), U.S.	65 00 N	154 00 W	76
Albania	41 00 N	20 00 E	44
Albany (river)	52 16 N	81 30 W	79
Albany,* N.Y.	42 39 N	73 45 W	78
Albert (lake)	01 45 N	31 00 E	69
Alberta (prov.), Canada	54 00 N	115 00 W	79
Albuquerque, N.M.	35 05 N	106 39 W	76
Aleppo, Syria	36 12 N	37 10 E	52
Aleutian (isls.)	52 00 N	175 00 W	76
Alexandria, Egypt	31 12 N	29 55 E	69
Alexandria, La.	31 18 N	92 27 W	77
Algeria	30 00 N	04 00 E	68
Algiers,* Alg.	36 45 N	03 04 E	68
Alicante, Spain	38 21 N	00 29 W	42
Al Jīsah, Egypt	30 01 N	31 13 E	69
Allahabad, India	25 30 N	81 58 E	69
Allentown, Pa.	40 37 N	75 29 W	77
Almaty, Kazak.	43 15 N	76 57 E	54
Alps (mts.)	46 40 N	10 00 E	42
Alsace (region)	48 30 N	07 35 E	42
Altai (mts.)	47 00 N	92 00 E	54
Altun (mts.)	37 30 N	88 00 E	54
Amarillo, Texas	35 13 N	101 50 W	76
Amazon (river)	00 00	49 00 W	87
American Highland (upland)	72 30 S	78 00 E	71
American Samoa	14 20 S	170 00 W	63
Amherst, N.S.	45 50 N	64 12 W	79
Amman,* Jordan	31 57 N	35 56 E	52
Amritsar, India	31 45 N	74 58 E	53
Amsterdam,* Neth.	52 20 N	04 50 E	42
Amudar'ya (river)	43 40 N	59 01 E	46
Amundsen (sea)	72 00 S	109 00 W	71
Amur (river)	52 56 N	141 10 E	55
Anadyr' (mts.)	67 00 N	176 00 E	47
Anatolia (region)	39 00 N	30 00 E	44
Anchorage, Alaska	61 10 N	149 55 W	76
Andaman (isls.)	12 00 N	92 45 E	53
Andes (mts.)	27 00 S	69 00 W	82
Andorra	42 34 N	01 35 E	42
Angara (river)	56 05 N	101 48 E	47
Angola	12 00 S	17 00 E	70
Ankara,* Turkey	39 55 N	32 52 E	44
Annapolis,* Md.	38 58 N	76 30 W	78
Ann Arbor, Mich.	42 17 N	83 45 W	78
Anshan, China	41 08 N	122 59 E	55
Antananarivo,* Madagascar	18 54 S	47 30 E	70
Antarctic (pen.)	69 30 S	65 00 W	71
Anticosti (isl.)	49 30 N	63 00 W	79
Antigua and Barbuda	17 05 N	61 48 W	81
Antwerp, Belg.	51 20 N	04 25 E	42
Apennines (mts.)	43 00 N	13 00 E	44
Apia,* Samoa	13 56 S	171 45 W	63
Appalachian (mts.)	40 00 N	78 00 W	78
Appleton, Wis.	44 16 N	88 25 W	78
Aqaba (gulf)	29 30 N	35 05 E	52
Aqmola,* Kazakhstan	51 10 N	71 30 E	62
Aqtōbe, Kazakhstan	50 17 N	57 10 E	45
Arafura (sea)	09 00 S	134 00 E	57
Arakan (mts.)	19 00 N	94 00 E	53
Aral (sea)	44 46 N	60 00 E	45
Ararat (mt.)	39 42 N	44 18 E	45
Aras (river)	39 56 N	48 20 E	45
Archangel, Russia	64 34 N	40 32 E	43
Ardennes (region)	50 10 N	05 30 E	42
Arequipa, Peru	16 24 S	71 33 W	86
Argentina	35 00 S	65 00 W	88
Århus, Den.	56 11 N	10 15 E	43
Arizona (state), U.S.	34 00 N	112 00 W	76
Arkansas (river)	33 48 N	91 07 W	77
Arkansas (state), U.S.	34 45 N	92 30 W	77
Armenia	40 15 N	45 00 E	45
Aruba (isl.) Neth.	12 30 N	69 58 W	81
Ascension (isl.)	07 57 S	14 22 W	12
Asheville, N.C.	35 35 N	82 33 W	77
Ashgabat,* Turkmenistan	37 57 N	58 23 E	45
Asir (region)	18 00 N	42 00 E	52
Asmara,* Eritrea	15 20 N	38 57 E	69
Astrakhan', Russia	46 21 N	48 03 E	69
Asunción,* Para.	25 16 S	57 40 W	88
Atacama (desert)	24 00 S	70 00 W	88
Atatürk (res.)	37 30 N	38 30 E	44
Athabasca (lake)	59 20 N	109 00 W	79
Athabasca (river)	58 30 N	111 00 W	79
Athens, Ga.	33 57 N	83 23 W	78
Athens,* Greece	37 59 N	23 44 E	44
Atlanta,* Georgia	33 45 N	84 24 W	78
Atlantic City, N.J.	39 21 N	74 27 W	78
Atlas (mts.)	34 00 N	00 01 W	68
Attu (isl.)	52 55 N	172 55 E	76
Auckland, N.Z.	36 53 S	174 45 E	61
Augsburg, Germany	48 20 N	10 53 E	42
Augusta, Ga.	33 28 N	81 58 W	78
Augusta,* Maine	44 19 N	69 46 W	78
Austin,* Texas	30 16 N	97 45 W	77
Australia	25 00 S	135 00 E	59
Australian Capital Terr.	35 18 S	149 07 E	59
Austria	47 15 N	14 00 E	42
Axel Heiberg (isl.)	79 00 N	90 00 W	79
Azerbaijan	40 30 N	48 00 E	45
Azores (isls.)	38 30 N	28 00 W	12
Azov (sea)	46 00 N	37 00 E	44

B

NAME	LATITUDE	LONGITUDE	PAGE
Baffin (bay)	74° 00′ N	68° 00′ W	79
Baffin (isl.)	68 30 N	70 00 W	79
Baghdad,* Iraq	33 21 N	44 24 E	52
Bahamas	24 00 N	76 00 W	81
Bahrain	26 00 N	50 40 E	52
Baja, California (pen.)	28 00 N	114 00 W	81
Bakersfield, Calif.	35 22 N	119 01 W	76
Bākhtarān, Iran	34 19 N	47 04 E	52
Baku,* Azerbaijan	40 23 N	49 51 E	45
Balaton (lake)	46 50 N	17 50 E	44
Balearic (isls.)	39 30 N	03 00 E	42
Bali (isl.)	08 30 S	115 30 E	56
Balkan (mts.)	43 15 N	23 00 E	44
Balkhash (lake)	46 00 N	74 00 E	54
Baltic (sea)	56 30 N	19 00 E	43
Baltimore, Md.	39 17 N	76 37 W	78
Bamako,* Mali	12 38 N	07 59 W	68
Banaba (isl.)	00 52 S	169 35 E	62
Banda (sea)	06 00 S	128 00 E	57
Bandar Seri Begawan,* Brunei	04 55 N	114 55 E	56
Bandung, Indon.	06 56 S	107 36 E	56
Bangalore, India	12 59 N	77 28 E	53
Bangka (isl.)	02 22 S	106 08 E	56
Bangkok,* Thai.	13 45 N	100 30 E	56
Bangladesh	23 30 N	90 00 E	53
Bangor, Maine	44 48 N	68 46 W	78
Bangui,* CAfr.	04 22 N	18 36 E	69
Bangweulu (lake)	11 00 S	29 45 E	70
Banjul,* Gambia	13 28 N	16 35 W	68
Banks (isl.)	73 00 N	122 00 W	79
Baotou, China	40 40 N	109 59 E	55
Barbados	13 10 N	59 30 W	81
Barcelona, Spain	41 38 N	02 10 E	42
Barents (sea)	70 00 N	45 00 E	46
Bari, Italy	41 07 N	16 52 E	44
Barisan (mts.)	03 00 S	102 15 E	56
Barkly Tableland (plat.)	18 00 S	136 00 E	59
Baroda, India	22 18 N	73 12 E	53
Barquisimeto, Ven.	10 04 N	69 19 W	86
Barranquilla, Col.	10 59 N	74 50 W	86
Basel, Switz.	47 35 N	07 32 E	42
Bass (strait)	40 15 S	146 00 E	61
Bathurst, N.B.	47 36 N	65 39 W	79
Baton Rouge,* La.	30 27 N	91 11 W	78
Battle Creek, Mich.	42 19 N	85 11 W	78
Baykal (lake)	54 00 N	109 00 E	47
Beaufort (sea)	71 00 N	140 00 W	79
Beaumont, Texas	30 05 N	94 06 W	77
Beersheba, Israel	31 14 N	34 47 E	52
Beijing (Peking),* China	39 56 N	116 24 E	55
Beira, Moz.	19 50 S	34 50 E	70
Beirut,* Lebanon	33 55 N	35 30 E	52
Belarus	53 00 N	28 00 E	43
Belém, Brazil	01 28 S	48 27 W	87
Belfast,* No. Ire.	54 35 N	05 55 W	42
Belgium	50 45 N	04 30 E	42
Belgrade,* Yugo.	44 48 N	20 29 E	44
Belitung (isl.)	02 54 S	107 58 E	56
Belize	17 00 N	88 45 W	80
Belle Isle (strait)	51 30 N	56 30 W	79
Bellingshausen (sea)	69 00 S	81 00 E	71
Belmopan,* Belize	17 15 N	88 47 W	80
Belo Horizonte, Brazil	19 56 S	43 57 W	87
Bengal (bay)	18 00 N	90 00 E	53
Benghazi, Libya	32 07 N	20 03 E	69
Benin	09 00 N	02 00 E	68
Benin, Bight of (bay)	05 00 N	04 00 E	68
Ben Nevis (mt.)	56 48 N	04 59 W	42
Bergen, Norway	60 25 N	05 20 E	43
Bering (sea)	55 00 N	180 00	47
Bering (strait)	67 00 N	170 00 W	76
Berkeley, Calif.	37 52 N	122 16 W	76
Berlin,* Germany	52 30 N	13 20 E	42
Bermuda	32 20 N	64 40 W	73
Bern,* Switz.	47 00 N	07 30 E	42
Bhopāl, India	23 16 N	77 24 E	53
Bhutan	27 15 N	90 00 E	53
Bialystok, Poland	53 09 N	23 09 E	44
Bikini (isl.)	11 37 N	165 33 E	62
Bilbao, Spain	43 16 N	03 05 W	42
Biloxi, Miss.	30 24 N	88 53 W	78
Binghamton, N.Y.	42 06 N	75 55 W	78
Birmingham, Ala.	33 31 N	86 49 W	78
Birmingham, Eng.	52 30 N	01 55 W	42
Biscay (bay)	45 00 N	05 00 W	42
Bishkek,* Kyrgyzstan	42 54 N	74 36 E	54
Bismarck (arch.)	04 00 S	150 00 E	62
Bismarck,* N.D.	46 48 N	100 47 W	76
Bissau,* Guinea-Bissau	11 51 N	15 35 W	68
Bitterroot (mts.)	46 30 N	114 25 W	76
Black (sea)	42 30 N	35 00 E	44
Black Hills (mts.)	44 00 N	103 30 W	76

NAME	LATITUDE	LONGITUDE	PAGE
Blanc (mt.)	45 50 N	06 51 E	42
Blantyre, Malawi	15 49 S	35 00 E	70
Bloemfontein, S. Afr.	29 07 S	26 14 E	70
Bloomington, Ill.	40 29 N	88 59 W	78
Bloomington, Ind.	39 10 N	86 32 W	78
Blue Nile (river)	15 37 N	32 31 E	69
Bogotá,* Col.	04 36 N	74 05 W	86
Boise,* Idaho	43 37 N	116 12 W	76
Bolivia	16 00 S	64 00 W	86
Bologna, Italy	44 30 N	11 20 E	42
Bombay, India	19 00 N	72 48 E	53
Bonaire (isl.), Neth. Ant.	12 12 N	68 15 W	81
Bonifacio (strait)	41 18 N	09 15 E	42
Bonn, Germany	50 44 N	07 06 E	42
Boothia (pen.)	70 00 N	95 00 W	79
Bordeaux, France	44 50 N	00 35 W	42
Borneo (isl.)	00 00	113 00 E	56
Bornholm (isl.)	55 10 N	15 00 E	43
Bosnia and Herzegovina	44 00 N	18 00 E	44
Bosporus (strait)	41 15 N	29 10 E	44
Boston,* Mass.	42 21 N	71 03 W	78
Bothnia (gulf)	62 00 N	20 00 E	43
Botou, China	38 05 N	116 30 E	55
Botswana	22 00 S	24 00 E	70
Bougainville (isl.)	06 10 S	155 15 E	62
Bouvet (isl.)	54 26 S	03 24 E	12
Bozeman, Mont.	45 41 N	111 02 W	76
Bradford, Eng.	53 47 N	01 45 W	42
Brahmaputra (river)	29 30 N	95 00 E	53
Brăila, Rom.	45 15 N	27 58 E	44
Brandon, Man.	49 50 N	99 57 W	79
Brasília,* Brazil	15 47 S	47 55 W	87
Braşov, Romania	45 39 N	25 37 E	44
Bratislava,* Slovakia	48 09 N	17 07 E	44
Braunschweig, Germany	52 22 N	10 42 E	42
Brazil	14 00 S	50 00 W	83
Brazos (river)	28 57 N	95 18 W	77
Brazzaville,* Congo	04 17 S	15 14 E	70
Bremen, Germany	53 10 N	08 40 E	42
Brescia, Italy	45 30 N	10 15 E	42
Bridgeport, Conn.	41 11 N	73 12 W	78
Bridgetown,* Barbados	13 06 N	59 37 W	81
Brisbane, Austl.	27 25 S	153 05 E	59
Bristol (bay)	57 45 N	160 00 W	76
Bristol, Eng.	51 28 N	02 35 W	42
Britanny (region)	48 00 N	03 00 W	42
British Columbia (prov.), Canada	55 00 N	125 00 W	79
British Indian Ocean Terr.	06 00 S	72 00 E	13
Brno, Czech Rep.	49 10 N	16 30 E	42
Brooks (mts.)	68 30 N	153 00 W	76
Brownsville, Texas	25 54 N	97 30 W	77
Brunei	04 30 N	115 00 E	56
Brussels,* Belg.	50 50 N	04 22 E	42
Bryan, Texas	30 40 N	96 22 W	77
Bucharest,* Rom.	44 25 N	26 06 E	44
Budapest,* Hungary	47 30 N	19 10 E	44
Buenos Aires,* Arg.	34 36 S	58 26 W	88
Buffalo, N.Y.	42 53 N	78 52 W	78
Bujumbura,* Burundi	03 23 S	29 22 E	70
Bulgaria	42 30 N	25 30 E	44
Burgundy (region)	47 00 N	05 00 E	42
Burkina Faso	12 00 N	01 30 W	68
Burlington, Vt.	44 28 N	73 12 W	78
Burma	20 00 N	96 00 E	49
Bursa, Turkey	40 11 N	29 04 E	44
Burundi	03 30 S	30 00 E	70
Bydgoszcz, Poland	53 50 N	27 35 E	42

C

NAME	LATITUDE	LONGITUDE	PAGE
Caatingas (region)	07° 00′ N	43° 00′ W	87
Cádiz, Spain	36 32 N	06 18 W	42
Cagliari, Italy	39 13 N	09 07 E	42
Cairo,* Egypt	30 03 N	31 15 E	69
Calcutta, India	22 30 N	88 30 E	53
Calgary, Alta.	51 01 N	114 05 W	79
Cali, Col.	03 28 N	76 30 W	86
California (gulf)	28 00 N	112 00 W	81
California (state), U.S.	37 00 N	120 00 W	76
Callao, Peru	12 03 S	77 10 W	86
Camagüey, Cuba	21 53 N	77 55 W	81
Cambodia	12 00 N	105 00 E	56
Cameroon	05 00 N	13 00 E	68
Campbellton, N.B.	48 00 N	66 40 W	79
Campeche (bay)	20 00 N	93 00 W	80
Canada	60 00 N	100 00 W	79
Canadian (river)	35 28 N	95 04 W	76
Canary (isls.)	28 00 N	16 00 W	68
Canaveral (cape)	28 27 N	80 32 W	77
Canberra,* Aust.	35 18 S	149 07 E	61
Cannes, France	43 33 N	07 01 E	42
Cantabrica (mts.)	43 15 N	05 00 W	42
Canton (Guangzhou), China	23 07 N	113 15 E	55
Canton, Ohio	40 48 N	81 23 W	78
Cape Town,* S. Afr.	33 57 S	18 28 E	70
Cape Verde	16 00 N	24 00 W	12
Cape York (pen.)	13 00 S	142 30 E	59
Caprivi Strip (region)	18 00 S	23 00 E	70
Caracas,* Ven.	10 30 N	66 55 W	86
Cardiff,* Wales	51 30 N	03 12 W	42
Caribbean (sea)	15 00 N	75 00 W	81
Caroline (isls.)	08 00 N	150 00 E	62
Carpathian (mts.)	48 00 N	23 00 E	44
Carpentaria (gulf)	15 00 S	139 00 E	59
Carson City,* Nev.	39 10 N	119 45 W	76
Cartegena, Spain	37 36 N	00 59 W	42
Casablanca, Mor.	33 36 N	07 38 W	68
Cascades (mts.)	45 00 N	122 00 W	76
Casper, Wyo.	42 51 N	106 19 W	76
Caspian (sea)	42 00 N	50 00 E	44
Catalonia (region)	41 15 N	02 00 E	42
Caucasus (mts.)	42 30 N	45 00 E	45
Cayenne,* Fr. Guiana	04 56 N	52 20 W	87
Cayman (isls.)	19 30 N	80 40 W	80
Cebu, Philippines	10 18 N	123 54 E	57
Cebu (isl.)	10 18 N	123 54 E	57
Cedar Rapids, Iowa	42 00 N	91 41 W	78
Celebes (isl.)	02 00 S	121 00 E	57
Central African Republic	06 00 N	20 00 E	69
Ceuta, Spain	35 52 N	05 20 W	68
Ceylon (Sri Lanka)	07 00 N	81 00 E	53
Chad	15 00 N	18 00 E	69
Chad (lake)	13 15 N	14 30 E	68
Champaign, Ill.	40 07 N	88 14 W	78
Champlain (lake)	44 30 N	73 20 W	78
Changchun, China	43 53 N	125 18 E	55
Chang (Yangtze) (river)	31 48 N	121 10 E	55
Changsha, China	28 12 N	112 59 E	55
Channel (isls.)	49 30 N	02 30 W	42
Chaozhou, China	23 40 N	116 38 E	55
Charleston, S.C.	32 47 N	79 56 W	78
Charleston,* W. Va.	38 21 N	81 38 W	78
Charlotte, N.C.	35 14 N	80 51 W	78
Charlottesville, Va.	38 02 N	78 30 W	78
Charlottetown,* P.E.I.	46 14 N	63 08 W	79
Chattanooga, Tenn.	35 03 N	85 19 W	78
Chelyabinsk, Russia	55 10 N	61 24 E	45
Chelyuskin (cape)	77 45 N	104 30 E	47
Chemnitz, Germany	50 40 N	12 55 E	42
Chengdu, China	30 40 N	104 04 E	54
Chesapeake (bay)	38 35 N	76 25 W	78
Cheshskaya (bay)	67 30 N	47 00 E	43
Chesterfield Inlet, N.W. Terrs.	63 40 N	91 45 W	79
Cheyenne,* Wyo.	41 08 N	104 49 W	76
Chibougamau, Qué.	49 55 N	74 22 W	79
Chicago, Ill.	41 52 N	87 38 W	78
Chicoutimi, Qué.	48 30 N	71 00 W	79
Chidley (cape)	60 23 N	64 26 W	79
Chihuahua, Mex.	28 38 N	106 05 W	81
Chile	32 00 S	71 00 W	83
Chilliwack, Br. Col.	49 10 N	121 57 W	76
Chiloé (isl.)	42 00 S	74 00 W	88
Chimborazo (mt.)	01 28 S	78 48 W	86
China	35 00 N	105 00 E	54
Chişinău,* Moldova	47 00 N	28 50 E	44
Chittagong, Bangladesh	22 15 N	91 55 E	53
Chongqing, China	29 34 N	106 35 E	54
Chonos (arch.)	45 00 S	74 00 W	88
Christchurch, N. Z.	43 32 S	172 39 E	59
Christmas (isl.)	10 30 S	105 40 E	13
Chuckchi (pen.)	66 00 N	175 00 W	47
Churchill (river)	58 47 N	94 11 W	79
Churchill, Man.	58 46 N	94 10 W	79
Cimarron (river)	36 07 N	96 30 W	76
Cincinnati, Ohio	39 06 N	84 31 W	78
Ciudad Guayana, Ven.	08 22 N	62 40 W	86
Ciudad Juárez, Mex.	31 44 N	106 29 W	81
Cleveland, Ohio	41 30 N	81 42 W	78
Clipperton (isl.)	10 13 N	109 10 W	12
Cluj-Napoca, Romania	46 45 N	23 36 E	44
Coast Ranges (mts.)	42 00 N	123 15 W	76
Cocos (isls.)	05 31 N	87 00 W	13
Cod (cape)	42 04 N	70 10 W	78
Cologne, Germany	51 00 N	07 00 E	42
Colombia	05 00 N	74 00 W	86
Colombo,* Sri Lanka	06 55 N	79 50 E	53
Colorado (river), Arg.	39 51 S	62 08 W	88
Colorado (river), U.S., Mexico	31 49 N	114 45 W	76
Colorado (river), U.S., Texas	28 52 N	96 02 W	76
Colorado (state), U.S.	39 00 N	105 30 W	76
Colorado Springs, Colo.	38 50 N	104 49 W	76
Columbia (river)	46 15 N	123 40 W	76
Columbia, Mo.	38 57 N	92 20 W	78
Columbia,* S.C.	34 00 N	81 02 W	78
Columbus, Ga.	32 28 N	84 59 W	78
Columbus,* Ohio	39 58 N	83 00 W	78
Comorin (cape)	07 37 N	77 28 E	53
Comoros	12 00 S	44 00 E	65
Conakry,* Guinea	09 31 N	13 42 W	68
Concepción, Chile	36 50 S	73 01 W	88
Concord,* N.H.	43 12 N	71 32 W	78
Congo	00 00	15 00 E	65
Congo (basin)	00 00	22 00 E	69
Congo, Dem. Rep. of the	02 00 S	24 00 E	65
Congo (river)	06 05 S	12 20 E	70
Connecticut (state), U.S.	41 38 N	72 45 W	78
Constantine, Alg.	36 23 N	06 38 E	68
Cook (isls.)	20 00 S	158 00 W	63
Cook (mt.)	43 36 S	170 08 E	59
Cook (strait)	41 15 S	174 30 E	59
Copenhagen,* Denmark	55 40 N	12 35 E	43
Coppermine, N.W. Terrs.	67 50 N	115 05 W	79
Coral (sea)	14 00 S	156 00 E	59
Córdoba, Arg.	31 25 S	64 10 W	88
Córdoba, Spain	37 54 N	04 46 W	42
Corfu (isl.)	39 38 N	19 56 E	44
Corinth (gulf)	38 19 N	22 04 E	44
Cork, Ireland	51 55 N	08 30 W	42
Corner Brook, Newf.	48 57 N	57 56 W	79
Cornwall, Ont.	45 01 N	74 44 W	79
Coromandel Coast	13 00 N	80 15 E	53
Corpus Christi, Texas	27 48 N	97 24 W	77
Corsica (isl.)	42 00 N	09 00 E	42
Corvallis, Ore.	44 34 N	123 16 W	76
Costa del Sol (coast)	36 30 N	04 00 W	42
Costa Rica	10 00 N	84 00 W	80
Côte d'Ivoire	07 00 N	05 00 W	68
Coventry, Eng.	52 25 N	01 33 W	42
Cranbrook, Br. Col.	49 31 N	115 46 W	79
Crete (isl.)	35 15 N	25 00 E	44
Crimea (pen.)	45 00 N	34 00 E	44
Croatia	45 30 N	16 00 E	44
Cuba	22 00 N	80 00 W	81
Curaçao (isl.), Neth. Ant.	12 11 N	69 00 W	81
Curitiba, Brazil	25 25 S	49 15 W	88
Cyclades (isls.)	37 00 N	75 00 E	44
Cyprus	35 00 N	33 00 E	52
Czech Republic	49 00 N	17 00 E	44
Czectochowa, Poland	50 49 N	19 06 E	44

D

NAME	LATITUDE	LONGITUDE	PAGE
Da Hinggang (mts.)	48° 30′ N	120° 00′ E	55
Dakar,* Senegal	14 40 N	17 28 W	68
Dalian, China	38 55 N	121 39 E	55
Dallas, Texas	32 47 N	96 48 W	77
Damascus,* Syria	33 35 N	36 28 E	52
Damavand (mt.)	35 57 N	52 08 E	52
Da Nang, Vietnam	16 04 N	108 13 E	56
Danube (river)	45 20 N	29 40 E	44
Dardanelles (strait)	40 07 N	26 23 E	44
Dar es Salaam,* Tanzania	06 48 S	39 17 E	70
Darling (river)	32 00 S	142 57 E	59
Darwin, Austl.	12 27 S	130 50 E	59
Davao, Philippines	07 18 N	125 25 E	57
Davenport, Iowa	41 31 N	90 34 W	78
Davis (strait)	66 30 N	58 00 W	79
Dawson, Yukon Terr.	64 04 N	139 25 W	79
Dayton, Ohio	39 46 N	84 12 W	78
Daytona Beach, Fla.	29 13 N	81 01 W	78
Dead (sea)	31 30 N	35 30 E	52
Death Valley Nat'l Park, U.S.	37 00 N	117 07 W	76
Debrecen, Hungary	47 32 N	21 38 E	44
Deccan (plat.)	17 00 N	78 00 E	53
Delaware (state), U.S.	39 00 N	75 30 W	78
Delgado (cape)	10 41 S	40 38 E	70
Delhi, India	28 29 N	77 15 E	53
Denmark	56 00 N	10 30 E	43
Denver,* Colo.	39 45 N	104 59 W	76
Des Moines,* Iowa	41 35 N	93 37 W	78
Detroit, Mich.	42 20 N	83 03 W	78
Devon (isl.)	75 00 N	86 00 W	79
Dezhneva (cape)	66 05 N	169 40 W	47
Dhaka,* Bangladesh	23 45 N	90 25 E	53
Diego Garcia (isl.)	07 36 S	72 28 E	13
Dinaric Alps (mts.)	43 30 N	17 00 E	44
District of Columbia, U.S.	38 54 N	77 01 W	78
Diyarbakir, Turkey	37 55 N	40 14 E	44
Djibouti	12 00 N	43 00 E	69
Djibouti,* Djibouti	11 35 N	43 09 E	69
Dnepr (river)	46 30 N	32 36 E	44
Dnestr (river)	46 20 N	30 18 E	44
Dnipropetrovs'k, Ukraine	48 27 N	35 01 E	44
Doğukaradeniz (mts.)	40 30 N	39 00 E	44
Doha,* Qatar	25 17 N	51 32 E	52
Dominica	15 25 N	61 20 W	81
Dominican Republic	19 00 N	70 00 W	81
Don (river)	47 04 N	39 18 E	44
Donets (river)	47 36 N	40 54 E	44
Donets'k, Ukraine	48 00 N	37 48 E	44
Dortmund, Germany	51 30 N	07 30 E	42
Douala, Cameroon	04 03 N	09 37 E	68
Douro (river)	41 09 N	08 39 W	42
Dover (strait)	51 00 N	01 30 E	42
Dover,* Del.	39 09 N	75 32 W	78
Drake (passage)	60 00 S	67 00 W	88
Dresden, Germany	51 10 N	13 45 E	42
Dublin,* Ire.	53 20 N	06 10 W	42
Dubrovnik, Croatia	42 38 N	18 07 E	44
Duluth, Minn.	46 47 N	92 06 W	78
Dundee, Scot.	56 30 N	02 58 W	42
Durango, Mex.	24 02 N	104 40 W	81
Durban, S. Afr.	29 51 S	31 00 E	70
Durham, N.C.	35 59 N	78 54 W	78
Dushanbe,* Tajikistan	38 33 N	68 48 E	46
Düsseldorf, Germany	51 20 N	06 40 E	42
Dvina, Northern (river)	64 32 N	40 37 E	46

E

NAME	LATITUDE	LONGITUDE	PAGE
East China (sea)	30° 00′ N	125° 00′ E	55
Easter (isl.)	27 08 S	109 25 W	63
Eastern Ghats (mts.)	17 30 N	83 00 E	53
East London, S. Afr.	33 01 S	27 55 E	70
Eau Claire, Wis.	44 49 N	91 30 W	78
Ebro (river)	40 43 N	00 54 E	42
Ecatepec, Mex.	19 35 N	99 04 W	80
Ecuador	01 00 S	79 00 W	86
Edinburgh,* Scot.	55 55 N	03 10 W	42
Edmonton,* Alta.	53 32 N	113 30 W	79
Edmundston, N.B.	47 22 N	68 20 W	79
Edward (lake)	00 20 S	29 35 E	69
Edwards (plat.)	30 30 N	101 00 W	76
Efate (isl.)	17 40 S	168 23 E	62
Egypt	27 00 N	30 00 E	69
Elbe (river)	53 30 N	09 45 E	42
Elbert (mt.)	39 07 N	106 26 W	76
El'brus (mt.)	43 21 N	42 26 E	45
Elburz (mts.)	36 00 N	52 00 E	52
Ellesmere (isl.)	79 00 N	82 00 W	79
El Paso, Texas	31 45 N	106 29 W	76
El Salvador	13 30 N	89 00 W	80
Enewetak (isl.)	11 11 N	162 21 E	62
England, U.K.	53 00 N	01 00 W	42
English (chan.)	50 00 N	02 30 W	42
Equatorial Guinea	01 30 N	10 00 E	68
Erie (lake)	42 20 N	81 00 W	78
Erie, Pa.	42 07 N	80 05 W	78
Eritrea	15 00 N	40 00 E	69
Erzgebirge ,(mts.)	50 30 N	13 00 E	42
Esfahān, Iran	32 40 N	51 38 E	52
Espíritu Santo (isl.)	15 15 S	166 55 E	62
Essen, Germany	51 30 N	07 00 E	42
Estonia	59 00 N	26 00 E	43
Ethiopia	10 00 N	40 00 E	69
Eugene, Ore.	44 03 N	123 06 W	76
Euphrates (river)	38 00 N	39 05 E	52
Evansville, Ind.	37 58 N	87 34 W	78
Everest (mt.)	27 58 N	87 05 E	53
Everglades Nat'l Park, U.S.	25 15 N	81 00 W	77
Eyre (lake)	28 30 S	137 15 E	59

F

NAME	LATITUDE	LONGITUDE	PAGE
Fairbanks, Alaska	64° 51′ N	147° 43′ W	76
Faisalabad, Pak.	31 25 N	73 05 E	53
Falkland (isls.)	52 00 S	59 00 W	88
Fall River, Mass.	41 42 N	71 09 W	78
Fargo, N.D.	46 52 N	96 48 W	77
Faroe (isls.)	62 00 N	07 00 W	39
Fayetteville, Ark.	36 04 N	94 09 W	77
Fayetteville, N.C.	35 03 N	78 52 W	78
Ferrara, Italy	44 50 N	11 40 E	42
Fezzan (region)	27 00 N	14 00 E	68
Fiji	17 00 S	179 00 E	62
Finisterre (cape)	42 53 N	09 16 W	42
Finland	64 00 N	26 00 E	43
Finland (gulf)	60 00 N	27 00 E	43
Flin Flon, Man.-Sask.	54 46 N	101 53 W	79
Flint, Mich.	43 01 N	83 42 W	78
Florence, Italy	43 46 N	11 13 E	42
Flores (isl.)	08 30 S	121 00 E	57
Flores (sea)	05 39 S	119 54 E	56
Florida (keys)	24 44 N	81 00 W	78
Florida (state), U.S.	28 00 N	82 00 W	78
Fortaleza, Brazil	03 41 S	38 33 W	87

NAME	LATITUDE	LONGITUDE	PAGE
Fort Collins, Colo.	40 35 N	105 05 W	76
Fort-de-France,* Mart.	14 36 N	61 05 W	81
Fort Frances, Ont.	48 37 N	93 25 W	79
Fort McMurray, Alta.	56 44 N	111 23 W	79
Fort Myers, Fla.	26 38 N	81 52 W	78
Fort Nelson, Br. Col.	58 49 N	122 36 W	79
Fort Smith, Ark.	35 23 N	94 26 W	77
Fort Smith, N.W. Terrs.	60 00 N	112 00 W	79
Fort Wayne, Ind.	41 04 N	85 08 W	78
Fort Worth, Texas	32 45 N	97 20 W	77
Foxe (basin)	68 00 N	78 00 W	79
France	47 00 N	02 00 E	42
Frankfort,* Ky.	38 12 N	84 53 W	78
Frankfurt, Germany	50 10 N	08 30 E	42
Franz Josef Land (isls.)	81 00 N	51 00 E	46
Fraser (river)	49 08 N	123 10 W	79
Fredericton,* N.B.	45 57 N	66 38 W	79
Freetown,* Sierra Leone	08 29 N	13 13 W	68
French Guiana	04 00 N	53 00 W	87
French Polynesia	15 00 S	140 00 W	63
Fresno, Calif.	36 44 N	119 47 W	76
Fukuoka, Japan	33 35 N	130 24 E	55
Funafuti (isl.)	08 31 S	179 08 E	62
Fundy (bay)	45 00 N	66 00 W	79
Fushun, China	41 52 N	123 53 E	55
Fuzhou, China	26 05 N	119 19 E	55

G

NAME	LATITUDE	LONGITUDE	PAGE
Gabon	00° 00′	12° 00′ E	68
Gaborone,* Botswana	24 40 S	25 54 E	70
Gainesville, Fla.	29 39 N	82 20 W	78
Galápagos (isls.)	00 15 S	90 00 W	12
Galaţi, Romania	45 26 N	28 03 E	44
Galveston, Texas	29 18 N	94 48 W	77
Gambia	13 30 N	15 30 W	68
Gäncä, Azerbaijan	40 40 N	46 22 E	45
Ganges (river)	26 00 N	80 15 E	53
Garonne (river)	45 01 N	00 36 W	42
Gary, Ind.	41 35 N	87 20 W	77
Gaspé (pen.)	48 30 N	65 00 W	79
Gaziantep, Turkey	37 05 N	37 22 E	44
Gdańsk, Poland	54 20 N	18 30 E	43
Gdynia, Poland	54 32 N	18 33 E	43
Geneva (lake)	46 25 N	06 25 E	42
Geneva, Switzerland	46 12 N	06 10 E	42
Genoa, Italy	44 25 N	08 55 E	42
Georgetown,* Guyana	06 49 N	58 10 W	68
Georgetown, Malaysia	05 25 N	100 19 E	56
Georgia	42 00 N	43 00 E	45
Georgia (state), U.S.	32 30 N	83 15 W	78
Georgian (bay)	45 15 N	80 45 W	79
Germany	51 00 N	10 00 E	42
Ghana	07 00 N	01 00 W	68
Ghent, Belgium	51 10 N	03 40 E	42
Gibraltar (strait)	35 55 N	05 35 W	42
Gibraltar	36 08 N	05 22 W	42
Gijón, Spain	43 32 N	05 40 W	42
Glacier Nat'l Park, U.S.	48 35 N	114 00 W	76
Glasgow, Scot.	55 50 N	04 10 W	42
Gobi (desert)	43 00 N	110 00 E	54
Godavari (river)	19 00 N	79 00 E	53
Godwin Austen (K2) (mt.)	35 53 N	76 30 E	53
Goiânia, Brazil	16 40 S	49 16 W	87
Good Hope (cape)	34 21 S	18 29 E	70
Göteborg, Sweden	57 43 N	11 58 E	43
Gotland (isl.)	57 45 N	18 45 E	43
Grampians (mts.)	56 45 N	04 30 W	42
Granada, Spain	37 11 N	03 36 W	42
Gran Chaco (region)	24 00 S	62 00 W	88
Grand Canyon Nat'l Park, U.S.	36 03 N	112 08 W	76
Grande Prairie, Alta.	55 10 N	118 48 W	79
Grand Falls, Newf.	48 56 N	55 40 W	79
Grand Forks, N.D.	47 52 N	97 03 W	77
Grand Rapids, Mich.	42 58 N	85 40 W	78
Graz, Austria	47 00 N	15 30 E	42
Great Australian Bight (bay)	33 00 S	130 00 E	59
Great Barrier (reef)	16 00 S	145 50 E	59
Great Bear (lake)	66 00 N	121 00 W	79
Great Britain (isl.)	54 00 N	02 00 W	42
Great Dividing Range (mts.)	35 00 S	149 35 E	59
Great Indian (desert)	28 00 N	73 00 E	53
Great Rift (valley)	09 00 N	41 00 E	69
Great Salt (lake)	41 05 N	112 30 W	76
Great Sandy (desert)	20 00 S	124 00 E	59
Great Slave (lake)	61 00 N	114 00 W	79
Great Victoria (desert)	27 00 S	130 00 E	59
Greater Antilles (isls.)	18 00 N	74 00 W	81
Greece	39 00 N	23 00 E	44
Greeley, Colo.	40 25 N	101 41 W	76
Green Bay, Wis.	44 31 N	88 00 W	78
Greenland (isl.)	70 00 N	40 00 W	73
Greensboro, N.C.	36 04 N	79 47 W	78
Greenland (sea)	75 00 N	15 00 W	71
Greenville, S.C.	34 51 N	82 24 W	78
Grenada	12 05 N	61 40 W	81
Grenoble, France	45 10 N	05 43 E	42
Guadalajara, Mex.	20 40 N	103 20 W	81
Guadalcanal (isl.)	09 40 S	160 15 E	62
Guadalupe (isl.)	29 11 N	118 17 W	73
Guadarrama (mts.)	41 00 N	03 30 W	42
Guadeloupe (isl.)	16 15 N	61 35 W	81
Guajira (pen.)	11 30 N	72 45 W	86
Guam (isl.)	13 30 N	144 47 E	62
Guangzhou, China	23 07 N	113 15 E	55
Guatemala	15 30 N	90 15 W	80
Guatemala,* Guat.	14 37 N	90 31 W	80
Guayaquil, Ecuador	02 12 S	79 53 W	86
Guernsey (isl.)	49 27 N	02 33 W	42
Guiana Highlands (plat.)	05 00 N	60 00 W	86
Guinea	10 00 N	11 00 W	68
Guinea (gulf)	03 00 N	04 00 E	68
Guinea-Bissau	11 50 N	15 00 W	68
Guwāhati, India	26 10 N	91 45 E	53
Guyana	05 00 N	59 00 W	86

H

NAME	LATITUDE	LONGITUDE	PAGE
Hadhramaut (region)	16° 00′ N	51° 00′ E	52
Hague, The,* Netherlands	52 05 N	04 20 E	42
Haifa, Israel	32 50 N	35 00 E	52
Hainan (isl.)	19 00 N	110 00 E	55
Haiphong, Vietnam	20 52 N	106 41 E	55
Haiti	19 00 N	72 30 W	81
Halifax,* N. S.	44 40 N	63 36 W	79
Halle, Germany	51 30 N	12 00 E	42
Halmahera (isl.)	01 30 N	128 00 E	57
Hamburg, Germany	53 30 N	10 00 E	42
Hamilton, Ohio	39 24 N	84 33 W	78
Hamilton, Ont.	43 12 N	79 50 W	79
Hangzhou, China	30 17 N	120 10 E	55
Hannover, Germany	52 20 N	09 30 E	42
Hanoi,* Vietnam	21 02 N	105 50 E	54
Happy Valley-Goose Bay, Newf.	53 18 N	60 23 W	79
Harare,* Zim.	17 50 S	31 03 E	70
Harbin, China	45 42 N	126 36 E	55
Harrisburg,* Pa.	40 16 N	76 53 W	78
Hartford,* Conn.	41 46 N	72 41 W	78
Hatteras (cape)	35 13 N	75 31 W	78
Havana,* Cuba	23 08 N	82 24 W	80
Hawaii (isl.)	19 30 N	155 30 W	76
Hawaii (state), U.S.	21 00 N	00 10 E	76
Hay River, N.W. Terrs.	60 51 N	115 42 W	79
Heard (isl.)	53 07 S	73 20 E	71
Hebrides (isls.)	57 20 N	07 00 W	42
Hecate (strait)	53 20 N	131 00 W	79
Helena,* Mont.	46 36 N	112 02 W	76
Helmand (river)	31 00 N	64 00 E	53
Helsingborg, Sweden	56 07 N	12 45 E	43
Helsinki,* Finland	60 12 N	25 00 E	43
Herāt, Afgh.	34 20 N	62 12 E	52
Hermosillo, Mex.	29 04 N	110 58 W	81
Hijāz (region)	24 30 N	39 00 E	52
Himalaya (mts.)	28 00 N	81 00 E	53
Hindu Kush (mts.)	35 45 N	70 30 E	53
Hiroshima, Japan	34 24 N	132 25 E	55
Hiva Oa (isl.)	09 46 S	139 00 W	63
Hobart, Austl.	42 52 S	147 18 E	59
Ho Chi Minh City, Vietnam	10 47 N	106 41 E	56
Hokkaido (isl.)	43 00 N	143 00 E	55
Homyel', Belarus	52 25 N	31 00 E	43
Honduras	15 00 N	87 00 W	80
Hong Kong	22 15 N	114 10 E	55
Honiara,* Sol. Is.	09 25 S	160 00 E	62
Honolulu,* Hawaii	21 18 N	157 51 W	76
Honshu (isl.)	36 00 N	137 00 E	55
Horn (cape)	55 59 S	67 16 W	88
Houston, Texas	29 45 N	95 22 W	77
Howrah, India	22 35 N	82 20 E	53
Hrodna, Belarus	53 41 N	23 50 E	44
Huang (river)	38 06 N	118 24 E	55
Hudson (bay)	59 00 N	86 00 W	79
Hudson (strait)	61 30 N	72 00 W	79
Hue, Vietnam	16 29 N	107 34 E	56
Hull, Eng.	53 45 N	00 20 W	42
Hull, Qué.	45 26 N	75 44 W	79
Hungary	47 00 N	19 00 E	44
Huntington, W. Va.	38 25 N	82 27 W	78
Huntsville, Ala.	34 44 N	86 35 W	78
Huron (lake)	44 30 N	82 30 W	78
Hyderabad, India	17 15 N	78 30 E	53
Hyderabad, Pak.	25 28 N	68 35 E	53

I

NAME	LATITUDE	LONGITUDE	PAGE
Ilbadan, Nigeria	07° 23′ N	03° 54′ E	68
Ibiza (isl.)	39 00 N	01 25 E	42
Iceland	65 00 N	19 00 W	39
Idaho (state), U.S.	44 00 N	114 00 W	76
Iliamna (lake)	59 30 N	155 00 W	76
Illinois (state), U.S.	40 00 N	89 15 W	78
Inch'on, S. Korea	36 51 N	127 26 E	55
India	23 00 N	80 00 E	53
Indiana (state), U.S.	40 00 N	86 00 W	78
Indianapolis,* Ind.	39 46 N	86 10 W	78
Indonesia	05 00 S	120 00 E	56
Indore, India	22 40 N	75 58 E	53
Indus (river)	33 00 N	71 30 E	53
Inner Mongolia (region)	42 00 N	110 00 E	55
Inuvik, N.W. Terrs.	68 21 N	133 43 W	79
Ionian (sea)	38 00 N	19 00 E	44
Iowa (state), U.S.	42 00 N	93 30 W	77
Iowa City, Iowa	41 40 N	91 32 W	78
Iqaluit, N.W. Terrs.	63 45 N	68 31 W	79
Iran	33 00 N	55 00 E	52
Iraq	33 00 N	44 00 E	52
Ireland	53 00 N	08 00 W	42
Irish (sea)	53 40 N	04 30 W	42
Irkutsk, Russia	52 16 N	104 20 E	47
Irrawaddy (river)	23 19 N	96 00 E	53
Irtysh (river)	61 02 N	68 47 E	46
Ishevsk, Russia	56 51 N	53 14 E	45
Islamabad,* Pakistan	33 42 N	73 10 E	53
Israel	32 00 N	35 00 E	52
Istanbul, Turkey	41 10 N	29 00 E	44
Itaipu (res.)	25 00 S	54 30 W	88
Italy	42 00 N	13 00 E	39
Ivanovo, Russia	57 00 N	40 59 E	43
Iwo Jima (isl.)	24 47 N	141 20 E	62
Izmir, Turkey	38 25 N	27 10 E	44

J

NAME	LATITUDE	LONGITUDE	PAGE
Jackson,* Miss.	32° 18′ N	90° 11′ W	78
Jacksonville, Fla.	30 20 N	81 40 W	78
Jaipur, India	26 55 N	75 49 E	53
Jakarta,* Indonesia	06 10 S	106 50 E	56
Jamaica	18 15 N	77 30 W	81
James (bay)	53 00 N	80 30 W	79
Jan Mayen (isl.)	71 00 N	08 30 W	39
Japan	38 00 N	138 00 E	55
Japan (sea)	40 00 N	135 00 E	55
Java (isl.)	07 00 S	110 00 E	56
Java (sea)	05 00 S	110 00 E	56
Jayapura, Indon.	02 32 S	140 42 E	57
Jefferson City,* Mo.	38 36 N	92 12 W	78
Jersey (isl.)	49 13 N	02 07 W	42
Jerusalem,* Israel	31 46 N	35 14 E	52
Jidda, Saudi Arabia	21 29 N	39 12 E	52
Jilin, China	43 51 N	126 33 E	55
Jinan, China	36 40 N	117 00 E	55
Johannesburg, S. Afr.	26 12 S	28 03 E	70
Johnston (isl.)	16 44 N	169 31 W	63
Jonquière, Qué.	48 25 N	71 15 W	79
Jordan	31 00 N	37 00 E	52
Joshua Tree Nat'l Park, U.S.	33 55 N	115 56 W	76
Juan de Fuca (strait)	49 15 N	123 30 W	79
Juan Fernández (isls.)	33 36 S	78 55 W	12
Juneau,* Alaska	58 18 N	134 25 W	76
Jura (mts.)	47 10 N	07 00 E	42
Jutland (pen.)	56 00 N	09 00 E	43
Juventud (isl.)	21 40 N	82 50 W	80

K

NAME	LATITUDE	LONGITUDE	PAGE
Kabul,* Afgh.	34° 31′ N	69° 00′ E	52
Kahoolawe (isl.)	20 33 N	156 37 W	76
Kaifeng, China	34 48 N	114 21 E	55
Kalaallit Nunaat (Greenland) (isl.)	70 00 N	40 00 W	73
Kalahari (desert)	23 00 S	22 00 E	70
Kalamazoo, Mich.	42 17 N	85 35 W	78
Kalimantan (region)	01 00 S	113 00 E	56
Kalyān, India	19 15 N	73 09 E	53
Kama (river)	55 10 N	49 20 E	45
Kamchatka (pen.)	56 00 N	160 00 E	47
Kamloops, Br. Col.	50 40 N	120 20 W	79
Kampala,* Uganda	00 19 N	32 35 E	69
Kampuchea (Cambodia)	12 00 N	105 00 E	56
Kananga, D.R. Congo	05 54 S	22 25 E	70
Kanazawa, Japan	36 34 N	136 39 E	55
Kanin (pen.)	67 30 N	45 00 E	43
Kano, Nigeria	12 00 N	08 31 E	68
Kanpur, India	26 28 N	80 21 E	53
Kansas (state), U.S.	38 30 N	98 30 W	76
Kansas City, Kans.	39 06 N	94 38 W	77
Kansas City, Mo.	39 05 N	94 35 W	77
Kaohsiung, China	22 38 N	120 17 E	55
Kara (sea)	72 00 N	62 00 E	46
Karachi, Pak.	24 55 N	67 00 E	53
Karaganda, Kazakhstan	49 50 N	73 10 E	47
Karakoram (mts.)	36 00 N	77 00 E	53
Karakumy (desert)	41 30 N	58 00 E	45
Karlsruhe, Germany	49 00 N	08 28 E	42
Kasai (river)	03 10 S	16 11 E	70
Kassel, Germany	51 20 N	09 15 E	42
Kathmandu,* Nepal	27 45 N	85 25 E	53
Katowice, Poland	50 16 N	19 00 E	44
Kattegat (strait)	57 00 N	11 30 E	43
Kauai (isl.)	22 05 N	159 30 W	76
Kaunas, Lithuania	54 54 N	23 54 E	43
Kavir, Dasht-e (desert)	35 00 N	55 00 E	52
Kawasaki, Japan	35 30 N	139 47 E	55
Kazakhstan	48 00 N	67 00 E	46
Kazan', Russia	55 45 N	49 08 E	45
Kelowna, Br. Col.	49 54 N	119 29 W	79
Kemerovo, Russia	55 20 N	86 05 E	47
Kenora, Ont.	49 46 N	94 28 W	79
Kentucky (lake)	37 00 N	88 16 W	78
Kentucky (state), U.S.	37 30 N	85 00 W	78
Kenya	00 00	38 00 E	69
Kenya (mt.)	00 08 S	37 18 E	69
Kerguélen (isls.)	49 00 S	69 00 E	13
Khabarovsk, Russia	48 30 N	135 06 E	55
Kharkiv, Ukraine	50 00 N	36 15 E	44
Khartoum,* Sudan	15 35 N	32 33 E	69
Khulna, Bangladesh	22 48 N	89 33 E	53
Kiel, Germany	54 20 N	10 10 E	42
Kiev,* Ukraine	50 27 N	30 32 E	44
Kigali,* Rwanda	01 57 S	30 04 E	70
Kilimanjaro (mt.)	03 04 S	37 21 E	70
Kimberley, S. Afr.	28 43 S	24 46 E	70
Kimberley (plat.)	16 00 S	127 00 E	59
Kingston,* Jamaica	18 00 N	76 48 W	81
Kingston, Ont.	44 10 N	76 44 W	79
Kinshasa,* D.R. Congo	04 19 S	15 23 E	70
Kirgiz Steppe (grassland)	49 30 N	57 00 E	45
Kiribati	00 00	175 00 E	62
Kitakyushu, Japan	33 53 N	130 50 E	55
Kjölen (mts.)	65 00 N	15 00 E	43
Knoxville, Tenn.	35 58 N	83 55 W	78
Kobe, Japan	34 41 N	135 10 E	55
Kodiak (isl.)	57 30 N	153 30 W	76
Kola (pen.)	67 20 N	37 00 E	43
Kolguyev (isl.)	68 30 N	49 00 E	43
Kolyma (mts.)	63 00 N	160 00 E	47
Kolyma (river)	69 30 N	161 12 E	47
Komandorskiye (isls.)	55 00 N	167 00 E	47
Konya, Turkey	37 52 N	32 31 E	44
Korea, North	40 00 N	127 00 E	55
Korea, South	37 30 N	128 00 E	55
Koror,* Palau	07 20 N	134 28 E	62
Kosciusko (mt.)	36 28 S	148 16 E	59
Kota Kinabalu, Malaysia	05 59 N	116 04 E	56
Kraków, Poland	50 05 N	19 55 E	44
Krasnodar, Russia	45 02 N	39 00 E	44
Krasnoyarsk, Russia	56 02 N	92 48 E	46
Krishna (river)	15 57 N	80 59 E	53
Krung Thep (Bangkok),* Thailand	13 45 N	100 30 E	56
Kryvyy Rih, Ukraine	47 55 N	33 21 E	44
Kuala Lumpur,* Malaysia	03 09 N	101 42 E	56
Kuching, Malaysia	01 34 N	111 22 E	56
Kumamoto, Japan	32 48 N	130 43 E	55
Kumasi, Ghana	06 41 N	01 37 W	68
Kunming, China	25 04 N	102 41 E	54
Kunlun (mts.)	36 00 N	90 00 E	54
Kura (river)	39 24 N	49 19 E	45
Kuril (isls.)	45 00 N	150 00 E	47
Kutch (Kachchh), Rann of (salt lake)	24 00 N	70 00 E	53
Kuwait	29 30 N	47 45 E	52
Kuwait,* Kuwait	29 20 N	48 02 E	52
Kwajalein (isl.)	08 43 N	167 44 E	62
Kyoto, Japan	34 58 N	135 45 E	55
Kyrgyzstan	41 00 N	75 00 E	46
Kyushu (isl.)	33 00 N	131 00 E	55

L

NAME	LATITUDE	LONGITUDE	PAGE
Labrador (region)	54° 00′ N	60° 00′ W	79
Laccadive, (sea)	11 00 N	73 00 E	53
Ladoga (lake)	61 00 N	31 00 E	43
Lafayette, Ind.	40 25 N	86 53 W	78

NAME	LATITUDE	LONGITUDE	PAGE
Skeena (mts.)	56 30 N	129 00 W	79
Skopje,* Macedonia	42 00 N	21 26 E	44
Slovakia	48 30 N	19 00 E	44
Slovenia	46 00 N	15 00 E	44
Snake (river)	46 12 N	119 02 W	76
Society (isls.)	17 00 S	152 00 W	63
Socotra (isl.)	12 30 N	54 00 E	52
Sofia,* Bulgaria	42 42 N	23 20 E	44
Solomon (sea)	08 00 S	152 00 E	62
Solomon Islands	09 00 S	160 00 E	62
Somalia	05 00 N	47 00 E	69
Somerset (isl.)	73 30 N	93 30 W	79
South (isl.), N.Z.	44 00 S	171 00 E	59
South Africa	30 00 S	25 00 E	70
Southampton (isl.)	64 45 N	84 30 W	79
Southampton, Eng.	50 55 N	01 28 W	42
South Australia, Austl.	31 00 S	136 00 E	59
South Bend, Ind.	41 40 N	86 15 W	78
South Carolina (state), U.S.	34 00 N	81 00 W	78
South China (sea)	15 00 N	115 00 E	56
South Dakota (state), U.S.	44 30 N	100 30 W	76
South Georgia (isl.)	54 20 S	36 40 W	88
South Orkney (isls.)	60 38 S	45 35 W	71
South Sandwich (isls.)	56 00 S	26 30 W	12
South Shetland (isls.)	62 00 S	58 00 W	71
Spain	40 00 N	04 00 W	42
Spokane, Wash.	47 40 N	117 26 W	76
Spratly (isls.)	08 00 N	113 00 E	56
Springfield,* Ill.	39 48 N	89 39 W	78
Springfield, Mass.	42 06 N	72 35 W	78
Springfield, Mo.	37 13 N	93 18 W	78
Springfield, Ohio	39 55 N	83 48 W	78
Sri Lanka	07 00 N	81 00 E	53
Srinagar, India	34 07 N	74 45 E	53
Stanley,* Falk. Is.	51 42 S	57 51 W	88
Stanovoy (mts.)	55 40 N	126 00 E	47
Stavanger, Norway	58 58 N	05 45 E	43
Stikine (river)	56 37 N	132 21 W	79
Stockholm,* Sweden	59 16 N	18 00 E	43
Stockton, Calif.	37 57 N	121 17 W	76
Strasbourg, France	48 35 N	07 45 E	42
Stuttgart, Germany	48 40 N	09 10 E	42
Subotica, Yugo.	46 06 N	19 40 E	44
Sucre,* Bolivia	19 03 S	65 18 W	86
Sudan	13 00 N	30 00 E	69
Sudan (region)	12 00 N	10 00 E	68
Sudbury, Ont.	46 32 N	81 15 W	79
Sudd (swamp)	08 00 N	30 00 E	69
Sudeten (mts.)	51 00 N	17 00 E	44
Suez (canal)	30 45 N	32 20 E	69
Sulu (arch.)	09 00 N	120 30 E	57
Sulu (sea)	09 08 N	120 00 E	57
Sumatra (isl.)	00 00	102 00 E	56
Sumba (isl.)	10 00 S	120 00 E	57
Sumbawa (isl.)	08 30 S	117 26 E	56
Sunda (isls.)	09 00 S	105 00 E	57
Sunda (strait)	06 28 S	105 24 E	56
Sundsvall, Sweden	62 23 N	17 19 E	43
Superior (lake)	87 00 N	48 00 W	77
Surabaya, Indon.	07 16 S	112 44 E	56
Surat, India	21 10 N	72 50 E	53
Suriname	04 00 N	56 00 W	87
Sutlej (river)	30 00 N	73 00 E	53
Suva,* Fiji	18 08 S	178 24 E	62
Svalbard (arch.)	79 00 N	19 00 E	71
Swansea, Wales	51 58 N	03 55 W	42
Swaziland	26 30 S	31 30 E	70
Sweden	62 00 N	16 00 E	43
Swift Current, Sask.	50 17 N	107 46 W	79
Switzerland	46 48 N	08 00 E	42
Sydney, Austl.	33 52 S	151 10 E	59
Sydney, N.S.	46 09 N	60 10 W	79
Syracuse, N.Y.	43 03 N	76 09 W	78
Syrdar'ya (river)	46 03 N	61 06 E	45
Syria	35 00 N	38 00 E	52
Szczecin, Poland	53 50 N	14 30 E	44

T

NAME	LATITUDE	LONGITUDE	PAGE
Tacoma, Wash.	47° 15' N	122° 26' W	76
Tagus (river)	38 45 N	09 00 W	42
Tahiti (isl.)	17 38 S	149 25 W	63
Tai'an, China	36 12 N	117 07 E	55
Taipei,* Taiwan, China	25 02 N	121 31 E	55
Taiwan	24 00 N	121 00 E	55
Taiyuan, China	37 52 N	112 35 E	55
Tajikistan	39 00 N	71 00 E	46
Takla Makan (desert)	39 20 N	83 00 E	54
Tallahassee,* Fla.	30 27 N	84 17 W	78
Tallinn,* Estonia	59 25 N	24 45 E	43
Tampa, Fla.	27 57 N	82 27 W	78
Tampere, Finland	61 30 N	23 45 E	43
Tampico, Mex.	22 13 N	97 51 W	80
Tana (lake)	12 00 N	37 20 E	69
Tanganyika (lake)	06 00 S	29 30 E	70
Tangier, Morocco	35 48 N	05 45 W	68
Tangshan, China	39 38 N	118 11 E	55
Tanzania	07 00 S	35 00 E	70
Tapajós (river)	02 24 S	54 47 W	87
Taranto (gulf)	40 15 N	17 15 E	44
Tarawa,* Kiribati	01 27 N	172 58 E	62
Tashkent,* Uzbekistan	41 20 N	69 18 E	46
Tasman (sea)	35 00 S	160 00 E	62
Tasmania, Austl.	42 00 S	147 00 E	59
Tatar (strait)	50 25 N	140 30 E	47
Taurus (mts.)	36 45 N	32 00 E	44
Taymyr (pen.)	76 00 N	104 00 E	46
Tbilisi,* Georgia	41 42 N	44 46 E	45
Tegucigalpa,* Honduras	14 06 N	87 13 W	80
Tehran,* Iran	35 41 N	51 26 E	52
Tehuantepec (isth.)	17 00 N	95 00 W	80
Tel Aviv-Jaffa, Israel	32 02 N	34 49 E	52
Tenerife (isl.)	28 15 N	16 35 W	68
Tennessee (river)	37 04 N	88 33 W	78
Tennessee (state), U.S.	36 00 N	86 00 W	78
Terre Haute, Ind.	39 28 N	87 24 W	78
Texas (state), U.S.	31 00 N	99 00 W	76
Thailand	14 00 N	101 00 E	56
Thailand (gulf)	10 00 N	102 30 E	56
The Hague,* Netherlands	52 05 N	04 20 E	42
The Pas, Man.	53 49 N	101 14 W	79
Thessaloniki, Greece	40 39 N	22 56 E	44
Thimphu,* Bhutan	27 29 N	89 37 E	53
Thompson, Man.	55 45 N	97 52 W	79

NAME	LATITUDE	LONGITUDE	PAGE
Thunder Bay, Ont.	48 24 N	89 19 W	79
Tianjin, China	38 59 N	117 24 E	55
Tian Shan (mts.)	42 12 N	78 13 E	54
Tiber (river)	41 44 N	12 14 E	42
Tibesti (mts.)	20 30 N	18 00 E	68
Tibet, China	30 00 N	90 00 E	54
Tierra del Fuego (isl.)	54 00 S	68 00 W	88
Tigris (river)	32 30 N	45 45 E	52
Tijuana, Mex.	32 32 N	117 01 W	81
Timişoara, Rom.	45 45 N	21 20 E	44
Timmins, Ont.	48 28 N	81 19 W	79
Timor (isl.)	09 30 S	125 00 E	57
Timor (sea)	11 00 S	125 00 E	59
Tinian (isl.)	15 01 N	145 38 E	62
Tiranë,* Albania	41 20 N	19 48 E	44
Tisza (river)	45 15 N	20 17 E	44
Titicaca (lake)	16 00 S	69 00 W	86
Tlalnepantla, Mex.	19 33 N	99 12 W	80
Tobago (isl.)	11 15 N	60 40 W	81
Tocantins (river)	01 50 S	49 10 W	87
Togo	08 00 N	01 00 E	68
Tokelau (isls.)	09 00 S	172 00 W	63
Tokyo,* Japan	35 42 N	139 46 E	55
Toledo, Ohio	41 39 N	83 33 W	78
Tol'yatti, Russia	53 31 N	49 26 E	45
Tomsk, Russia	56 30 N	84 58 E	46
Tonga	21 00 S	175 15 W	63
Tonkin (gulf)	19 40 N	107 30 E	56
Topeka,* Kans.	39 03 N	95 40 W	77
Toronto,* Ont.	43 38 N	79 27 W	79
Torrens (lake)	31 00 S	137 45 E	59
Torreón, Mex.	25 33 N	103 26 W	81
Torres (strait)	10 25 S	142 12 E	59
Toulon, France	43 08 N	05 56 E	42
Toulouse, France	43 36 N	01 27 E	42
Trail, Br. Col.	49 06 N	117 43 W	76
Transantarctic (mts.)	85 00 S	175 00 W	71
Transylvania (region)	47 00 N	23 30 E	44
Trenton,* N.J.	40 14 N	74 44 W	78
Trinidad and Tobago	10 30 N	61 15 W	81
Tripoli,* Libya	32 54 N	13 11 E	68
Tristan da Cunha (isl.)	37 00 S	12 30 W	12
Trivandrum, India	08 29 N	76 55 E	53
Trois-Rivières, Qué.	46 27 N	72 30 W	79
Tromsø, Norway	69 40 N	18 58 E	43
Trondheim, Norway	63 25 N	10 26 E	43
Troy, N.Y.	42 44 N	73 41 W	78
Truk (isls.)	07 25 N	151 45 E	62
Tuamotu (arch.)	17 00 S	142 00 W	63
Tucson, Ariz.	32 13 N	110 58 W	76
Tuktoyaktuk, N.W. Terrs.	69 27 N	133 03 W	79
Tula, Russia	54 12 N	37 36 E	43
Tulsa, Okla.	36 09 N	96 00 W	77
Tunis,* Tunisia	36 48 N	10 10 E	68
Tunisia	35 00 N	10 00 E	68
Turin, Italy	45 04 N	07 40 E	42
Turkana (lake)	03 30 N	36 00 E	69
Turkey	39 00 N	35 00 E	44
Turkmenistan	39 00 N	60 00 E	46
Turks and Caicos (isls.)	22 00 N	71 30 W	81
Tuscaloosa, Ala.	33 12 N	87 34 W	78
Tutuila (isl.)	14 17 S	170 40 W	63
Tuvalu	08 00 S	178 00 E	62
Tuz (lake)	38 00 N	33 30 E	44
Tuzla, Bosnia	44 32 N	18 41 E	44
T'ver, Russia	56 50 N	35 55 E	43
Tyrrhenian (sea)	39 00 N	13 00 E	42

U

NAME	LATITUDE	LONGITUDE	PAGE
Ucayali (river)	04° 30' S	73° 26' W	86
Ufa, Russia	54 43 N	55 55 E	45
Uganda	01 00 N	32 00 E	69
Ukraine	49 00 N	32 00 E	44
Ulaanbaatar,* Mongolia	45 55 N	106 53 E	54
United Arab Emirates	24 00 N	55 00 E	52
United Kingdom	55 00 N	02 00 W	42
United States	44 58 N	103 46 W	76-77
Ural (mts.)	56 00 N	60 00 E	46
Ural (river)	47 00 N	51 48 E	45
Uruguay	33 00 S	56 00 W	88
Uruguay (river)	34 05 S	58 20 W	88
Urmia (lake)	37 35 N	45 05 E	52
Urfa, Turkey	37 10 N	38 50 E	44
Ustyurt (plat.)	43 00 N	56 00 E	45
Utah (state), U.S.	39 30 N	111 30 W	76
Utica, N.Y.	43 06 N	75 13 W	78
Utrecht, Neth.	52 05 N	05 08 E	42
Uzbekistan	41 00 N	62 00 E	46

V

NAME	LATITUDE	LONGITUDE	PAGE
Vaal (river)	29° 04' S	23° 38' E	70
Vaduz,* Leichtenstein	47 08 N	9 31 E	42
Val-d'Or, Qué.	48 07 N	77 46 W	79
Valencia, Spain	39 29 N	00 23 W	42
Valencia, Ven.	10 11 N	68 00 W	86
Valladolid, Spain	41 39 N	04 43 W	42
Valletta,* Malta	35 53 N	14 30 E	44
Valparaiso, Chile	33 01 S	71 38 W	88
Van (lake)	38 36 N	42 49 E	45
Vancouver (isl.)	49 40 N	125 50 W	79
Vancouver, Br. Col.	49 15 N	123 08 W	79
Vänern (lake)	59 00 N	13 30 E	43
Vanua Levu (isl.)	16 30 S	179 15 E	62
Vanuatu	17 00 S	168 30 E	62
Vāranāsi, India	25 17 N	83 08 E	53
Varna, Bulgaria	43 13 N	27 55 E	44
Vatican City	41 54 N	12 30 E	42
Venezuela	08 00 N	66 00 W	86
Venice, Italy	45 26 N	12 20 E	42
Veracruz, Mex.	32 25 N	115 05 W	80
Verde (cape)	14 43 N	17 30 W	68
Verkhoyansk (mts.)	65 00 N	130 00 E	47
Vermont (state), U.S.	44 00 N	72 45 W	78
Vernon, Br. Col.	50 16 N	119 16 W	76
Verona, Italy	45 29 N	11 00 E	42
Victoria (falls)	17 57 S	25 52 E	70
Victoria (isl.)	71 00 N	110 00 W	79
Victoria (lake)	01 00 S	33 00 E	69
Victoria, Austl.	37 00 S	145 00 E	59

NAME	LATITUDE	LONGITUDE	PAGE
Victoria,* Br. Col.	48 27 N	123 25 W	79
Vienna,* Austria	48 20 N	16 30 E	44
Vientiane,* Laos.	17 58 N	102 37 E	56
Vietnam	16 00 N	108 00 E	49
Vilnius,* Lithuania	54 41 N	25 19 E	43
Virgin (isls.)	18 20 N	64 40 W	81
Virginia (state), U.S.	37 30 N	76 30 W	78
Visalia, Calif.	36 20 N	119 18 W	76
Vistula (river)	54 20 N	18 50 E	44
Viti Levu (isl.)	17 50 S	178 00 E	62
Vladivostok, Russia	43 06 N	131 50 E	55
Volcano (isls.)	24 43 N	141 20 E	62
Volga (river)	46 15 N	48 24 E	45
Volgograd, Russia	48 42 N	44 30 E	45
Volta (lake)	07 00 N	00 00	68
Volta (river)	05 45 N	00 41 E	68
Voronezh, Russia	51 40 N	39 00 E	45
Vyatka, Russia	58 33 N	49 42 E	45

W

NAME	LATITUDE	LONGITUDE	PAGE
Wabash (river)	37° 48' N	88° 01' W	78
Waco, Tex.	31 33 N	97 08 W	77
Wake (isl.)	19 18 N	166 38 E	62
Wales, U.K.	52 30 N	04 00 W	42
Wallis and Futuna (isls.)	13 18 S	176 10 W	62
Walvis Bay, S. Afr.	22 57 S	14 30 E	70
Warsaw,* Poland	52 10 N	21 00 E	44
Wasatch Range (mts.)	41 00 N	111 35 W	76
Washington, D.C.,* U.S.	38 54 N	77 01 W	78
Washington (state), U.S.	47 15 N	121 00 W	76
Waterloo, Iowa	42 30 N	92 20 W	78
Weddell (sea)	70 00 S	40 00 W	71
Wellington,* N.Z.	41 19 S	174 47 E	59
Weser (river)	53 30 N	08 34 E	42
Western Australia, Austl.	25 00 S	122 00 E	59
Western Ghats (mts.)	15 00 N	74 30 E	53
Western Sahara	25 00 N	14 00 W	68
West Palm Beach, Fla.	26 43 N	80 03 W	78
West Virginia (state), U.S.	38 30 N	81 00 W	78
Wheeling, W. Va.	40 04 N	80 43 W	78
White (sea)	65 30 N	38 00 E	43
Whitehorse,* Yukon Terr.	60 45 N	135 04 W	79
White Nile (river)	15 37 N	32 31 E	69
Whitney (mt.)	36 35 N	118 18 W	76
Wichita, Kans.	37 42 N	97 20 W	77
Wiesbaden, Germany	50 05 N	08 15 E	42
Wilkes-Barre, Pa.	41 15 N	75 53 W	78
Willemstad,* Neth. Ant.	12 07 N	68 57 W	81
Wilmington, Del.	39 45 N	75 33 W	78
Windhoek,* Namibia	22 34 S	17 06 E	70
Windsor, Ont.	42 19 N	83 02 W	79
Windward (isls.)	13 00 N	62 00 W	81
Windward (passage)	20 00 N	73 50 W	81
Winnipegosis (lake)	52 30 N	100 00 W	79
Winnipeg (lake)	49 50 N	97 00 W	79
Winnipeg,* Man.	49 53 N	97 10 W	79
Wisconsin (state), U.S.	44 30 N	90 00 W	78
Woods, Lake of the (lake)	49 30 N	94 30 W	79
Worcester, Mass.	42 16 N	71 48 W	78
Wrangel (isl.)	71 00 N	180 00	47
Wroclaw, Poland	51 10 N	17 02 E	44
Wuhan, China	30 35 N	114 16 E	55
Würzburg, Germany	49 48 N	09 58 E	42
Wyoming (state), U.S.	43 00 N	107 30 W	76

X

NAME	LATITUDE	LONGITUDE	PAGE
Xi'an, China	34° 16' N	108° 54' E	54
Xiantao, China	30 25 N	113 25 E	55
Xingu (river)	01 44 S	51 56 W	87

Y

NAME	LATITUDE	LONGITUDE	PAGE
Yablonovyy (mts.)	52° 30' N	113° 00' E	47
Yakima, Wash.	46 36 N	120 31 W	76
Yamoussoukro,* Côte d'Ivoire	06 49 N	05 17 W	68
Yamal (pen.)	70 00 N	70 00 E	46
Yangon (Rangoon)*, Myanmar	16 48 N	96 09 E	56
Yaoundé,* Cameroon	03 53 N	11 32 E	68
Yap (isl.)	09 30 N	138 10 E	62
Yarmouth, N.S.	43 50 N	66 07 W	79
Yaroslavl', Russia	57 35 N	39 50 E	45
Yekaterinburg, Russia	56 50 N	60 38 E	45
Yellow (sea)	37 00 N	123 00 E	55
Yellowknife,* N.W. Terrs.	62 27 N	114 21 W	79
Yellowstone (river)	48 00 N	104 00 W	79
Yellowstone Nat'l Park, U.S.	44 30 N	110 30 W	76
Yemen	15 00 N	44 00 E	52
Yenisey (river)	69 35 N	84 25 E	46
Yerevan,* Armenia	40 11 N	44 30 E	45
Yogyakarta, Indon.	07 48 S	110 22 E	56
Yokohama, Japan	35 25 N	139 31 E	55
York, Pa.	39 57 N	76 44 W	78
Yorkton, Sask.	51 13 N	102 28 W	79
Youngstown, Ohio	41 06 N	80 39 W	78
Yucatán (pen.)	20 00 N	89 00 W	80
Yugoslavia	44 00 N	21 00 E	44
Yukon (river)	62 36 N	164 46 W	79
Yukon Territory, Canada	65 00 N	137 00 W	79
Yuzhno-Sakhalinsk, Russia	46 58 N	142 42 E	47

Z

NAME	LATITUDE	LONGITUDE	PAGE
Zagreb,* Croatia	45° 48' N	16° 00' E	44
Zagros (mts.)	34 00 N	47 30 E	52
Zambezi (river)	18 50 S	36 15 E	70
Zambia	14 00 S	27 00 E	70
Zanzibar (isl.)	06 00 S	39 30 E	70
Zaozhuang, China	34 53 N	117 34 E	55
Zaporizhzhya, Ukraine	47 50 N	35 10 E	44
Zaragoza (Saragossa), Spain	41 39 N	00 51 W	42
Zhengzhou, China	34 48 N	113 39 E	55
Zhytomyr, Ukraine	50 16 N	28 40 E	44
Zibo, China	36 47 N	118 01 E	55
Zimbabwe	19 00 S	30 00 E	70
Zürich, Switz.	47 22 N	08 22 E	42